Theory-Based
DATA ANALYSIS
for the
SOCIAL SCIENCES

spuriousness - chpt 4
divorce 177

hH

THE PINE FORGE PRESS SERIES IN RESEARCH METHODS AND STATISTICS

Edited by Kathleen S. Crittenden

- *Multiple Regression: A Primer* by Paul Allison
- *Theory-Based Data Analysis for the Social Sciences* by Carol S. Aneshensel
- *A Guide to Field Research* by Carol A. Bailey
- *Designing Surveys: A Guide to Decisions and Procedures* by Ronald Czaja and Johnny Blair
- *Social Statistics for a Diverse Society, 3rd Edition* by Chava Frankfort-Nachmias and Anna Leon-Guerrero
- *Social Statistics for a Diverse Society, 3rd Edition with Student SPSS® v. 11.0* by Chava Frankfort-Nachmias and Anna Leon-Guerrero
- *Experimental Design and the Analysis of Variance* by Robert Leik
- *How Sampling Works* by Richard Maisel and Caroline Hodges Persell
- *Investigating the Social World: The Process and Practice of Research, 3rd Edition* by Russell K. Schutt
- *Investigating the Social World: The Process and Practice of Research, 3rd Edition with Student SPSS® v. 10.0* by Russell K. Schutt
- *The Practice of Research in Criminology and Criminal Justice* by Ronet Bachman and Russell K. Schutt
- *The Practice of Research in Criminology and Criminal Justice with Student SPSS® v. 10.0* by Ronet Bachman and Russell K. Schutt

Titles of Related Interest

- *Adventures in Social Research: Data Analysis Using SPSS v. 11.0 for Windows 95/98/2000* by Earl Babbie, Fred Halley and Jeanne Zaino
- *Sociology For A New Century* by York Bradshaw, Joseph F. Healey, and Rebecca Smith

Theory-Based
DATA ANALYSIS
for the
SOCIAL SCIENCES

focal relationship: single hypothesized relationship

CAROL S. ANESHENSEL

University of California at Los Angeles

PINE FORGE PRESS
An Imprint of Sage Publications, Inc.
Thousand Oaks • London • New Delhi

For information:

 Pine Forge Press
An imprint of Sage Publications, Inc.
2455 Teller Road
Thousand Oaks, California 91320
E-mail: order@pfp.sagepub.com

SAGE Publications Ltd
1 Oliver's Yard
55 City Road
London EC1Y 1SP

SAGE Publications India Pvt Ltd
B-42, Panchsheel Enclave
Post Box 4109
New Delhi 110 017

Printed in the United States of America

Library of Congress Cataloging-in-Publication Data
Aneshensel, Carol S.
  Theory-based data analysis for the social sciences / by Carol S. Aneshensel.
    p. cm. — (The Pine Forge series in research methods and statistics)
Includes bibliographical references and index.
  ISBN 0-7619-8736-3 (pbk. : alk. paper)
  1. Social sciences—Statistical methods. I. Title. II. Pine Forge Press series in research methods and statistics.
  HA29 .A665 2002
  001.4'22—dc21
                                        2001008018

This book is printed on acid-free paper.

05   06   7   6   5   4   3   2

Acquisition Editor: Jerry Westby
Editorial Assistant: Vonessa Vondera
Production Editor: Sanford Robinson
Typesetter: Technical Typesetting, Inc.
Cover Designer: Michelle Lee

About the Author

Carol S. Aneshensel, a sociologist (Ph.D., Cornell University, 1976), is Professor, School of Public Health, University of California, Los Angeles. She is internationally recognized for her research in social stress and mental health. Her other main areas of research include social stratification and health, informal caregiving, aging and the life course, and research methods. In addition to numerous research articles, she coauthored one previous book, *Profiles in Caregiving: The Unexpected Caregiver* (Academic Press, 1995). She coedited *The Handbook of the Sociology of Mental Health* (Kluwer Academic/Plenum, 1999), which was named as Best Publication by the Sociology of Mental Health Section, American Sociological Association.

About the Publisher

Pine Forge Press is an educational publisher, dedicated to publishing innovative books and software throughout the social sciences. On this and any other of our publications, we welcome your comments.

Please write to:

Pine Forge Press
An imprint of Sage Publications, Inc.
2455 Teller Road
Thousand Oaks, CA 91320-2218
(805) 499-0721
E-mail: info.pineforge@sagepub.com

Visit our World Wide Web site, your direct link to a multitude of online resources:

www.pineforge.com

To Gay and Clayton Meixel

Contents

The great tragedy of Science
—the ugly slaying of a beautiful hypothesis
by an ugly fact.

Thomas Henry Huxley

Series Foreword

The Pine Forge Press Series in Research Methods and Statistics, consisting of core books in methods and statistics and a series of satellite volumes on specialized topics, allows instructors the flexibility to create a customized curriculum. Authors of volumes in the series are seasoned researchers and teachers as well as acknowledged experts in their fields. In addition to the core texts in research methods and statistics, the series offers more compact volumes focusing on sampling, field research methods, survey research, and experimental design and analysis of variance.

We are proud to offer Carol Aneshensel's *Theory-Based Data Analysis for the Social Sciences* as the latest entry in the series. Drawing on and extending Morris Rosenberg's elaboration model, published in *The Logic of Survey Analysis* over 30 years ago, Aneshensel tackles the task of making inferences about cause and effect based on survey data.

The volume offers a blueprint for the craft of using relevant data and modern statistical techniques—multiple regression and logistic regression—to evaluate a theory. Assuming that the reader has a familiarity with regression analysis equivalent to an intermediate course in social statistics, the book focuses on the logic of theory-based data analysis. Beginning with evidence supporting a *focal relationship*, the one pivotal cause-and-effect relationship that is central to a particular theory, Aneshensel presents two general analytic tools: an *exclusionary strategy* for eliminating alternative explanations and an *inclusive strategy* for placing the focal relationship within a network of relationships among antecedent, intervening, and consequent constructs in the theory.

Instead of technically explicating the statistical techniques per se, the volume illustrates and explains the use of these techniques to test and inform a guiding theory. In keeping with the tradition of volumes in the *Pine Forge Press Series in Research Methods and Statistics*, Aneshensel draws on her extensive experience as a researcher and teacher, using real social data to model each step in the process.

The book is intended to guide student and professional researchers through the joint application of theory and statistical analysis of survey data in their own research. The book could serve as the primary text for a research practicum course, or together with Allison's *Multiple Regression: A Primer* as the toolkit for this research endeavor.

—*Kathleen S. Crittenden*
Series Editor

Preface

In writing this book I have attempted to answer a question often posed by graduate students in the social sciences, "How do I translate the theory guiding my research into a coherent plan for data analysis?" Answers to this question tend to be elusive because students usually learn theory separately from research methods in general and from statistics in particular. As a result, a student may have all the gear needed to undertake a scientific journey, but lack a map showing the routes to his or her destination.

I was fortunate to stumble upon an elegant answer to this question very early in my research career. A colleague asked if I was familiar with the *elaboration model* and, after hearing me admit, possibly for the first time, that there was something I didn't know, handed me *The Logic of Survey Analysis* by Morris "Manny" Rosenberg, written in 1968. I still wonder how I missed this classic during my doctoral studies, but remain grateful that this omission was put right because this approach has guided my research thereafter.

In *The Logic of Survey Analysis*, Rosenberg articulated for the first time a comprehensive model for systematically testing social science theory with correlational data. The central issue he tackled was the inference of cause and effect. This thorny issue remains challenging to social scientists because our theories usually involve causal explanation and because our data tend to be observations of social life as it naturally occurs. Rosenberg argued that the influence of one social characteristic on another should be tested indirectly using statistical manipulation because in real life it could not be tested directly using experimental manipulation. To attain this end, he proposed the elaboration model, an analytic strategy that clarifies the meaning of an empirical association between two variables by observing changes that occur when a "third variable" is added to the analysis.

As with most goods things, the end inevitably arrived and *The Logic of Survey Analysis* went out of print, forcing me to search for a replacement text. This task did not seem to be especially difficult because the course, applied multivariate data analysis, is taught in one form or another in most social science doctoral programs and in most professional schools. I found several excellent texts on multivariate statistical techniques, but the theory covered in these texts was largely and appropriately confined to statistical theory. Social theory appeared on occasion, but was usually limited to brief examples.

I searched without success for a systematic treatment of how to apply these statistical techniques to theory-based social research. For instance, existing texts explain how to interpret regression coefficients, but not the reasoning used to select independent variables for inclusion in the regression equation so that it operationalizes the theory one would like to test. It is not difficult to take students by surprise, then, by asking why they have included a given variable in their model. The most common answer, based on my long-standing practice of asking this question to unsuspecting students, is "to control for confounding." This answer turns out to be correct, but only some of the time. In many instances, the variable performs a very different function.

To shed light on these functions, I have devised the concept of a *focal relationship*, the one pivotal cause-and-effect type of relationship whose presence is indispensable to the integrity of the entire theoretical model. In this text, I present two analytic strategies for evaluating the internal validity of the focal relationship. Internal validity is the extent to which conclusions about cause and effect can be drawn from a research study. It is achieved through statistical analysis in studies of real life social processes, in contrast to experimental research for which internal validity is achieved by design. These strategies collectively bolster the inference that the focal independent variable influences the focal dependent variable.

The first analytic strategy is *exclusionary*: It eliminates alternative explanations for the empirical association between the focal independent and dependent variables. The goal of this strategy is finding that some meaningful portion of the original association remains when other explanations for it have been taken into consideration. This ruling-out function involves the multivariate analysis of control variables to eliminate spuriousness and additional independent variables to remove redundancy. This strategy is exclusionary in the sense that it concerns the covariation remaining between the focal independent and dependent variables when other potential sources of covariation have been eliminated.

The second strategy is inclusive and seeks to establish internal validity by placing the focal relationship within a network of relationships among other constructs. These other relationships are represented by antecedent, intervening and consequent variables. Antecedent variables are used to extend the causal process back in time to the determinants of the focal independent variable, intervening variables embody the causal mechanisms and processes that connect the focal independent variable to the dependent variable, and consequent variables extend the causal process forward in time to examine the subsequent impact of the dependent variable. These variables collectively explicate the functioning of the entire causal system of which the focal relationship is a part. When expected patterns of association do indeed materialize, the inference of relatedness is supported. This strategy is an inclusive approach to internal validity in the sense that other explanatory variables are brought into the analysis of the focal relationship.

I follow Rosenberg's lead and use existing research to illuminate scientific reasoning with regard to data analysis and to illustrate the interpretation of empirical findings. These examples have been drawn from a number of disciplines, including my own areas of research, social stress and mental health, caregiving, and aging and the life course. Several examples come from criminology. One example, for instance, analyzes the impact of crime rates on the racial composition of neighborhoods and vice versa; another study considers whether the status rankings of criminal and conventional occupations affect subsequent criminal behavior; and still another examines whether an employment intervention alters the risk of recidivism. Marriage and the family also contribute a number of examples. For instance, one group of studies illustrates the inclusive strategy over an extended causal sequence, using antecedent, intervening, and consequent variables. The impact of parental divorce on the risk of divorce in the next generation—that is, among adult sons and daughters—is assessed, along with potential mediators of this connection, such as interpersonal behavior problems; these second-generation divorces are then reconnected to subsequent relationships between these adults and their parents. Other examples are drawn from political science, demography and population studies, race and ethnic studies, and gender studies.

I also present an analysis journal that develops a single data analysis as it evolves over the sequence of the topics covered in this text. The data are from one of my own projects, the Los Angeles Survey of Adolescent Experience, and were collected from personal interviews with a community-based probability sample of 877 young people between the ages of 11 and 17. The focal relationship is between socioeconomic status (SES) and mastery, the belief that you control important aspects of your life. These data are analyzed to illustrate the exclusionary strategy, adding both control and other independent variables to the analysis of the focal relationship. The analysis then applies the inclusive strategy, using intervening variables to explain how SES influences adolescent mastery. Segments of the analysis journal recur throughout the text as the analysis develops. This journal emphasizes the interpretation of findings and the continuity of analysis from beginning to end.

Portions of this data set appear on the website for this text. This data set includes the variables used in the analysis journal. It also contains a parallel set of variables that allows students to conduct their own analyses but on more-or-less familiar ground. For instance, the example in the text concerns a focal relationship between family income and mastery, whereas the additional data contain similar variables, parental education and self-esteem. Thus, readers can replicate the results appearing in the text and then immediately apply the analytic principles to relevant unanalyzed data.

In chapter 1, I define data analysis and describe how it links social theory to multivariate statistical techniques. I also outline theory-based data analysis, introducing the elaboration model, the concept of the focal relationship, and the inclusive and exclusionary strategies to internal validity. The remainder of the text develops this approach. In chapter 2, I summarize some fundamental principles of logic as they pertain to the analytic interplay between social theory and statistics. This discussion contrasts the use of inductive and deductive reasoning in the complementary processes of operationalizing theory versus assessing its fit with empirical observations. In chapter 3, I discuss association, which is a prerequisite to relationship, and delineate the differences between association and relationship. Chapter 4 describes in detail the concept of the *focal relationship*: the single relationship at the center of one's theory. This description emphasizes the underlying goal for theory-based analysis: to determine whether an observed association is the result of one variable influencing another in the manner anticipated by theory. In chapter 4, I sketch out the data analytic steps used to attain in this goal.

The next several chapters examine the exclusionary and inclusive strategies in detail. In chapters 5 and 6, I describe how to use control variables and other independent variables to account for spuriousness and redundancy, respectively. I then describe the use of antecedent, intervening, and consequent variables in the inclusive strategy in chapter 7. Chapter 8 examines conditional relationships, that is, situations in which the focal relationship differs across situations or among subgroups of the population. In chapter 9, I provide an overall summary of this approach to theory-based analysis and discuss key comparisons that illuminate the meaning of the focal relationship.

This text was conceived at a student's preliminary doctoral exam, and its development has been a response to questions posed by students in the graduate course that eventually grew from this brainchild. I was struck, not for the first time, by a technically correct description of a series of statistical techniques that had little relevance to the theory to be tested in the proposed research. Lest students think they have been unfairly singled out, I should mention that this disconnection is also found in the proposals of more seasoned investigators. I was puzzled because the students who struggled most with their data analysis were uniformly bright, articulate in their understanding of theory, and, most perplexingly, well trained in the techniques of multivariate statistics. This pattern suggested that something was missing from the way we were training the next generation of social scientists.

With considerable chutzpah, I started a seminar on multivariate data analysis to rectify this problem. I soon discovered that I had no idea how to teach someone else how to translate his or her theory into a coherent plan for data analysis. Fortunately students in those first few years did not seem to realize this chaotic state of confusion and found that the seminar enabled them to integrate what they had learned over several years in other courses. I was pleased, of course, and more than ready to accept the credit for their astute insights. In retrospect, it is clear students were able to bring their ideas and their analyses closer together because they presented their analyses to their classmates, responded to their critiques, and offered the same in exchange. This book is the result of eavesdropping on their conversations.

Acknowledgments

This book has been in the works for a long time, leaving me with many intellectual debts, more than I can credit, much less repay. Foremost is Manny Rosenberg. His classic text, *The Logic of Survey Analysis*, schooled me in social analysis and inspired me to undertake this project. Coincidentally we share a dear friend and collaborator, Leonard I. Pearlin, whose influence on my work is unmistakable. In our collaborative work, I have touched the synergy of theory and data, learned the single-mindedness and fascination necessary to fully develop an idea, and discovered the fun that can be had in this line of work. My thinking has also been shaped by Blair Wheaton, whose work deftly translates theory into elegant analysis strategies, exemplifying the approach described in this text.

My principal debt, however, is to the community of social scientists who have collectively created a body of theory-based empirical research that has challenged me, sparked my imagination, and pushed me to ask questions. In particular, I am indebted to those working in the sociology of mental health, whose research has shed light on analytic issues that extend well beyond the boundaries of this substantive area. This is especially true for those contributing to the area of stress and mental health, in particular the question of the buffering role of social support. Findings from these studies have informed my own research, but, equally importantly, their reasoning and analytic strategies have shaped the approach I present here. This influence is evident, at least in part, in the citations throughout this text, but extends to a much longer list of unnamed scholars.

In addition, I have used the work of various social scientists to illustrate analytic strategies. Portions of these studies are reproduced in the text, and I would like to thank the authors and publishers for their permission to reprint this work.

Amato, P. R. (1996). Explaining the intergenerational transmission of divorce. *Journal of Marriage and the Family, 58,* 628–640. © 1996. Reprinted by permission of the National Council on Family Relations.

Broman, C. L. (1993). Race differences in marital well-being. *Journal of Marriage and the Family, 55,* 724–732. © 1993. Reprinted by permission of the National Council on Family Relations.

Hiday, V. (1995). The social context of mental illness and violence. *Journal of Health and Social Behavior, 36,* 122–137. © 1995. Reprinted with permission by the American Sociological Association.

Li, L. W., Seltzer, M. M., & Greenberg, J. S. (1997). Social support and depressive symptoms: Differential patterns in wife and daughter caregivers. *Journals of Gerontology: SOCIAL SCIENCES, 52B,* S200–S211. © 1997. Reprinted with permission of the Gerontological Society of America.

Link, A. E., Monahan, J., Stueve, A., & Cullen, F. T. (1999). Real in their consequences: A sociological approach to understanding the association between psychotic symptoms and violence." *American Sociological Review, 64,* 316–332. © 1999. Reprinted with permission by the American Sociological Association.

Mirowsky, J. (1997). Age, subjective life expectancy and the sense of control: The horizon hypothesis. *Journals of Gerontology: SOCIAL SCIENCES, 52B,* S125–S134. © 1997. Reprinted with permission by the Gerontological Society of America.

In other instances I have used published data as examples without reproducing the original form in which the data were published. I would like to thank these authors formally for this use of their work:

Cooksey, E. C., & Fondell, M. M. (1996). Spending time with his kids: Effects of family structure on father's and children's lives. *Journal of Marriage and the Family, 58,* 693–707.

Kanazawa, S. (2000). A new solution to the collective action problem: The paradox of voter turnout. *American Sociological Review, 65,* 443–442.

Lichter, D. T., McLaughlin, D. K., Kephart, G., & Landry, D. J. (1992). Race and the retreat from marriage: A shortage of marriageable men? *American Sociological Review, 57,* 781–799.

Liska, A. E., & Bellair, P. E. (1995). Violent-crime rates and racial composition: Convergence over time. *American Journal of Sociology, 101,* 578–610.

Matsueda, R. L., Gartner, R., Piliavin, I., & Polakowski, M. (1992). The prestige of criminal and conventional occupations. *American Sociological Review, 57,* 752–770.

Spitze, G., Logan, J. R., Deane, G., & Zerger, S. (1994). Adult children's divorce and intergenerational relationships. *Journal of Marriage and the Family, 56,* 279–293.

Turner, R. J., & Marino, F. (1994). Social support and social structure: A descriptive epidemiology. *Journal of Health and Social Behavior, 35,* 193–212.

Uggen, C. (2000). Work as a turning point in the life course of criminals: A duration model of age, employment, and recidivism. *American Sociological Review, 67,* 529–547.

I addition, I have reprinted text from the following sources because these authors made the point more elegantly than I could restate it:

Scientific knowledge: A sociological analysis, © Barry Barnes, David Bloor, & John Henry, 1996. © 1996. Used by permission of The University of Chicago Press.

Genius by James Gleick, copyright © 1992 by James Gleick. Used by permission of Pantheon Books, a division of Random House, Inc.

Keller, E. F. (1985). *Reflections on gender and science.* New Haven, CT: Yale University Press. © 1985. Used by permission of Yale University Press.

Lloyd, G. (1996). Reason, science and domination of matter. In Evelyn Fox Keller & Helen E. Longino (Eds.), *Feminism and science.* New York: Oxford University Press. Reprinted with permission from *The man of reason: Male and female in Western philosophy,* Genevieve Lloyd, p. 50. London: Routledge. © 1993.

I am also grateful for the institutional support that has come my way. The research reported in the *Analysis Journal* was supported by a grant from the National Institute of Mental Health (5 RO 1 MH40831). A 3-month sabbatical from the University of California, Los Angeles, enabled me to get this project off the ground and another 3-month sabbatical let me complete it.

I spent part of this leave at the Laboratory of Socio-Environmental Studies of the National Institute of Mental Health thanks to Carmi Schooler, its Director, and at the Department of Sociology, University of Maryland, College Park, courtesy of Leonard I. Pearlin. Carmi and Len provided me the stimulating intellectual atmosphere we all would like to have every day, a warm and supportive setting in which to work, and, best of all, good company. Manny Rosenberg was for a long time a distinguished member of the Laboratory and the sociology faculty at the University of Maryland and long-time friend of both Len and Carmi. I also had the opportunity to get to know Florence Rosenberg, Manny's wife and colleague, and talk over this project. These individuals and this setting were especially meaningful to me as I set about crafting a text that follows in this exceptional tradition of social analysis.

Support was also forthcoming from my teammates on the home field. Susan B. Sorenson, Dawn M. Upchurch, and Richard G. Wight urged me on when it seemed easier to quit, brought me back to earth when I was lost in a world of my own and found my sense of humor when I misplaced it. Yasmin Kusunoki, Dana Miller Martinez, and Joslan Sepúlveda Drew doctoral students in the Department of Community Health Sciences—persevered through multiple drafts of the text, meticulously scrutinizing it for errors and helping me achieve greater clarity and accuracy than I could manage on my own. Numerous other students in my seminar have contributed as well by asking questions that proved difficult to answer, producing findings that were unanticipated, and being willing to take this journey with me.

I am grateful to Stephen D. Rutter, former publisher of Pine Forge Press, for believing in this project and fostering its development. Steve entrusted me to Kathleen S. Crittenden, for which I am also appreciative. As editor of the series, Kathy provided a valuable critique of an early and unwieldy draft. Her review of the final draft provided polish and her backing carried me beyond the finish line.

Finally, I wish to thank my son and daughter whose unwavering support of a project so distant from their own interests has sustained me. It is to them that I dedicate this book.

CSA
Los Angeles, California
December 2001

1 Introduction to Theory-Based Data Analysis

Quantitative data analysis is as much a logical enterprise as it is a statistical one. Although few social scientists would debate this point, contemporary research emphasizes statistical technique to the virtual exclusion of logical discourse. This is not to say that the analyses are illogical, but, rather, that the connection of statistics to either theory or conclusion is often haphazard. This situation has developed, at least to some degree, from the ease with which complex and powerful statistical models can be estimated in today's computer-dominated research environment. Thus, it is likely to become even more pronounced as these tools become all the more accessible. This text offers an alternative that reemphasizes the role of theory in data analysis.

In this chapter, I introduce data analysis and comment briefly on its functions. I then link data analysis to theory on the one hand and to statistical technique on the other. In the third section I present an overview of theory-based data analysis, describing the *elaboration model*, a prototype for the translation of theory into a data analytic strategy, and introducing the concept of the *focal relationship*, the most central relationship in the theoretical model. With this approach I seek to establish that one construct is related to another by demonstrating that an empirical association between two variables is explained, at least in part, by theoretical processes and that alternative explanations do not account for the observed association. Although there are other strategies for achieving coherence in the analysis of quantitative data, the elaboration model is especially well suited to testing theory. Its advantages, therefore, are realized best in explanatory research. After introducing the elaboration model, I conclude with a brief discussion of the inherent subjectivity of analysis, even in its most quantitative and seemingly objective forms. These closing remarks introduce a cautionary theme: Data analysis provides insight into the workings of the social world, but this insight is inevitably shaped and constrained by our most fundamental assumptions about the nature of the social world, assumptions so basic they often are imperceptible.

The Connection Between Analysis, Theory, and Statistics

Definition of Data Analysis

Data analysis can be thought of as the systematic arrangement of information into meaningful patterns. The term *data* means information, or, more formally, facts and figures from which conclusions can be inferred. Although this phrase, "facts and figures," possesses an aura of objectivity that has scientific appeal, information does not possess intrinsic meaning. A set of data, by itself, is merely an accumulation of numbers and other symbols. The meaning of these facts and figures must be inferred. This attribution of meaning to data is accomplished through its systematic and logical analysis.

In this context, *analysis* refers to the dissection of a whole into its component parts for the specific purpose of ascertaining its nature. The whole in this instance is the accumulated body of information obtained during the data collection phase of the inquiry.[1] We refer to this body of information as a *data set*. It usually comprises measurements made for multiple units of observation. For a survey data set, for instance, the units of observation are people, typically a sample of some population, and the measurements are responses to survey questions. These measurements may be quite concrete, such as age, gender, height, or weight, or they may represent abstract concepts such as acculturation, religious beliefs, or powerlessness. The data analytic task is to make sense of these measurements as they are observed across the multiple elements of the sample.

The "nature" one seeks to uncover through analysis takes numerous forms. For example, an analysis may be concerned with the articulation of a construct, such as mastery, the belief that you control important aspects of your life. This type of analysis would entail procedures such as an assessment of internal reliability (e.g., Does the instrument used to operationalize mastery produce measurements that can be accurately reproduced?) and an evaluation of construct validity (e.g., Is mastery related to other constructs, such as socioeconomic status [SES], in the manner predicted by theory?). Alternately, analysis may be directed toward revealing the function or purpose of an entity (e.g., To what extent does mastery influence voting behavior?). In many applications, analysis concerns the manner in which a system functions (e.g., What are the processes or mechanisms that link mastery to whether a person votes?). Data analysis, therefore, is the sifting and sorting of a body of information about a concept to determine its meaning, to uncover its function, or to discern the mechanisms through which it operates.

Data analysis is conducted within the larger context of the research design, which is itself set within a theoretical framework The search for meaning that characterizes data analysis, therefore, is not blind, nor does it begin on a tabula rasa. Rather, the intent of the analysis is established during the design of the study, when the theory guiding the research is translated into a set of procedures that eventually generate the observations comprising the data set. The form and character of what one seeks to uncover from a set of information, therefore, are known at the outset. Hypotheses and research questions often evolve as the analysis proceeds, sometimes undergoing metamorphosis, but the original theoretical framework establishes the starting point for this journey of discovery. Similarly, it should be recognized that data analysis is one component of the overall research design and has meaning only within this context, that is, within the framework of the entire enterprise. Although this point may appear obvious, the integration of analysis with other components of research is often overlooked.

Explanatory Data Analysis

Research in general and analysis in particular may have *exploratory, descriptive,* or *explanatory* objectives or some combination of these aims.[2] Exploratory research generally is undertaken when very little is known about a phenomenon. It forms the foundation for subsequent descriptive and explanatory research. Descriptive research undeniably makes a valuable contribution to science. It serves to identify important areas of inquiry, addressing whether a phenomenon is a common occurrence or a rare event. For example, this type of research could be used to describe the population of eligible voters for national elections, the extent to which these persons are registered to vote, and their voting behavior in recent elections. A survey like this would reveal a low rate of participation in national elections, about 50% in years with presidential contests and less in off years, a finding indicating that voter abstention is worthy of further scientific investigation given that voting is an essential element of a democratic society.

Scientific inquiry usually does not end with description, however, but proceeds almost immediately to explanation. Establishing the presence of a phenomenon usually stimulates curiosity about why that phenomenon exists. For example, once the extent of voter abstention is known, one is likely to ask whether certain subgroups of the population are more likely to vote than others, and, if so, why. In other words, descriptive findings are likely to lead to the investigation of the factors associated with the outcome and to attempts to understand how these factors contribute to the occurrence of the outcome. The search for scientific understanding, therefore, tends to evolve in the direction of explanation.

This explanatory focus means that a basic goal of most data analysis is to estimate associations among variables and ascertain whether these associations can be interpreted as relationships. To say that two variables are associated with one another means that the values of one variable tend to coincide with the values of the other. To say that a *relationship* exists between these variables implies more. It means that the two variables share a causative connection to one another, specifically that one variable influences the other. Relationship implies dependency: The value taken by the independent variable affects the value taken by the dependent variable.

Establishing relatedness is an issue of *internal validity*. Internal validity refers to the extent to which conclusions about cause and effect can be drawn from the research. In experimental research, internal validity is usually achieved through design: Factors that could influence the outcome of interest are controlled or held constant during the conduct of the experiment. In nonexperimental research, internal validity is achieved in large part through analysis.[3] This distinction emerges because experimental research tends to be conducted in laboratory-type settings where strict control is feasible, whereas nonexperimental research is conducted within naturally occurring settings where control is not possible.

In this regard, Rosenberg (1968) argues that the introduction of test factors into survey analyses enables one to exploit some of the virtues of the experimental design while avoiding the inappropriateness of experimentation for many research questions. The elaboration model is a cogent method for evaluating the internal validity of a theory through data analysis. It starts with an observed association between two measured variables that we would like to interpret as a relationship between two constructs, one independent and one dependent. In these instances, internal validity is established with an exclusionary strategy, ruling out alternative explanations such as spuriousness. Internal validity is also established with an inclusive strategy, especially identifying the causal mechanism or process through which the independent variable influences the dependent variable. These analytic strategies are used to enhance the internal validity of research that uses correlational data.

Theory and Data Analysis

Analysis can be thought of as the intersection of theory and data. It is the use of information (data) to test theoretical predictions about what should be observed if a theory is valid. This procedure is not simply one of confirming or disconfirming a set of hypotheses. Rather, data analysis contributes to the development of theory. Aspects of a theory that are not supported empirically are likely to be reformulated or revised rather than merely being rejected and abandoned. Those facets that receive empirical support are likely to be refined, elaborated on, or specified with greater precision based on analytic results. Thus, analysis modifies theory as much as theory directs analysis. In the words of Rosenberg (1968), analysis is the "dynamic interplay between theory and data" (p. 217).

The chief function of data analysis is to connect the theoretical realm with the empirical world. *Theory* refers to a systematic statement of the principles involved in a phenomenon. These principles specify relationships among constructs in a hypothetical population. Theory describes an imaginary world. The presence of this world is inferred from observations made from the empirical or "real" world. This empirical world consists of direct experience— that which can be touched, tasted, seen, heard, or smelled. It is material, factual, and perceptible. It can be experienced firsthand.[4]

The attribution of *meaning* to these immediate sensations, however, is a theoretical construction. First, theory selects, sorts, and classifies direct observations. The essence of these observations is abstracted and conceptually interpreted. Then theory seeks to make sense of how various types of observations are connected to one another. In this manner, direct observation is transformed into theoretical constructs and hypothesized relationships. Thus, Barnes, Bloor, and Henry (1996) observe that, "The interaction of theory and observation reports may be regarded as an interaction between past observations [condensed in theory], and present observations [reported as such].... If observation is 'theory laden,' theory is 'observation laden'" (p. 92).

Data analysis presupposes that the theoretical and empirical realms are aligned with one another. For instance, theory typically posits relationships among two or more constructs operating within a population. These abstract notions are put to the test by estimating associations among measured variables within a specific sample. In other words, constructs are operationalized as observed variables, relationships are estimated as empirical associations, and populations are represented as samples. Findings from the concrete analysis of variables, associations, and samples are used to make inferences about general principles, which then contribute to the development of theory about constructs, relationships, and populations.

Theory and analysis constitute distinct components of social inquiry, and usually are taught separately, but nonetheless acquire meaning only in juxtaposition. Theory by itself is merely a collection of ideas. Analysis by itself is merely a set of tools. These analytic tools are no different from hammers, saws, and nails; shovels, rakes, and hoes; and, pots, pans, and knives. These objects become instruments only when used purposefully—in construction, in gardening, or in preparing dinner. Similarly, methods of analysis, including the statistical manipulation of data, are inert until used in the service of some goal. That goal, I submit, is to put theory to the test.

Statistics and Data Analysis

In contemporary social science research, data analysis usually entails the application of statistical procedures. This tendency arises because empirical research, including the most circumscribed and straightforward of inquiries, generates an enormous mound of information. The sheer volume of information makes it unlikely that it can be grasped solely by exercising one's intellect. When the number of observations is large, keeping track of even one piece of information can be challenging. Data analysis, therefore, requires statistical techniques simply to reduce the volume of information and to present it in a comprehensible summary form.

The analytic task becomes increasingly complex when two or more attributes are simultaneously considered. For example, a survey of voting behavior would probably also examine the extent to which such behavior varies according to characteristics such as age, gender, ethnicity, political party membership, political ideology, sense of powerlessness, and so on. Detecting such associations requires the simultaneous manipulation of numerous pieces of information, a task that is made possible through the application of various statistical procedures.

In addition, most research seeks to generalize results to some larger population, a goal that necessitates the use of inferential statistics. This aspect of statistics may be the most familiar, embodied in the ubiquitous test of significance or the almost equally common confidence interval. Inferential statistics are essential to generalization, a goal of most social science research.

These considerations have made data analysis virtually synonymous with the application of quantitative statistical procedures to numeric information. This tendency has emerged because research has increasingly relied upon quantitative rather than qualitative data and because statistics constitutes the most productive approach to quantitative data. This statement is not intended to devalue qualitative analysis, nor does it imply that the preponderance of quantitative research is necessarily desirable. It is a descriptive statement about the status quo.

Although statistics is an important tool, it is but one component of data analysis. Aspects of data analysis other than its statistical considerations, however, often are given short shrift, perhaps because statistical models have become so complex, technical, and powerful that they overwhelm other considerations. The analysis sections of research reports, for example, commonly identify the statistical techniques used to analyze data without mention of how these techniques correspond to the conceptual orientations motivating the research.

This tendency emphasizes the numeric component of data analysis at the expense of its logical component. It is unfortunate because data analysis is stripped of its most basic functions, namely the processes of inductive and deductive reasoning. Deduction refers to the translation of theory into predictions about the empirical world, whereas induction refers to the development of theories through observation of the empirical world. These forms of logical reasoning link the theoretical realm to the empirical world, the hypothetical to the real, and the abstract to the concrete (see Chapter 2). This link between the theoretical and the empirical has, unfortunately, atrophied through disuse.

The difficulty lies not with the application of quantitative statistics per se. Rather, the problem arises from the inadequate synthesis of theory with method. That is, theory does not sufficiently inform the application of statistical procedures and the results of quantitative analysis often are only tangentially relevant to conceptual models. The statistical manipulation of numbers has become largely separated from the logical manipulation of ideas.

This separation, in turn, impedes the cross-fertilization of theory and observation that is the catalyst for scientific discovery and explanation. On the one hand, theoretical principles are not tested as directly or as efficiently as they might be and, hence, cannot be fully refined or developed. On the other hand, powerful statistical techniques often address issues other than the core theoretical principles and, therefore, generate insight into the data, but insight that is somewhat off target. Under these conditions, research necessarily fails to accrue its full potential.

Statistical techniques often seem to be selected without regard to the nature of the research question being asked. Although research questions should inform the selection of statistical techniques, the reverse is a common occurrence: The selection of a technique comes to define the research question. The consequence is disembodied results—results whose connection to the underlying theory is at best tangential.

This unfortunate situation arises, I submit, because easily accessible statistical software packages calculate complex mathematical models almost instantaneously, making it is easy to become caught up in analysis and lose sight of its purpose. It is not necessary to give much thought to the specification of an analytic model when it is a simple matter to change the model in a subsequent run. This type of modification of an analytic model, however, usually becomes an empirical matter rather than a theoretical one. The model is refined based on initial results as distinct from the conceptual specification of the relationship being tested and its alternatives. The empirical modification of statistical models may inadvertently move the analysis further away from the theoretical model, subverting the purpose of the analysis. Although empirical modifications are appropriate in many instances, they do not originate in the theoretical specification of relationships among constructs and, hence, may only incidentally advance the interplay between theory and observation.

The issue here is not error in the application of various statistical procedures, faulty technique. Rather the problem lies with the selection of procedures that do not precisely operationalize research questions and hypotheses. In other words, the statistics chosen do not test theory-based hypotheses. To be sure, the statistical procedure tests some hypothesis, but not necessarily the hypothesis that operationalizes the research question.

Elements of Theory-Based Analysis

The Elaboration Model

Data analysis has not always relied so exclusively on statistics. Survey research, for example, has a rich tradition that clearly articulates the logic of analysis. Influential in this tradition is Morris Rosenberg's (1968) classic, *The Logic of Survey Analysis*, describing the *elaboration model* for the analysis of survey data, originally developed by Paul Lazarsfeld. Rosenberg elegantly delineated the logical structure of inferential analysis. In addition, he described procedures for conducting this type of analysis. Unfortunately, the statistics and illustrations in the book are now dated, and, hence, it is not read as widely nor appreciated as fully as it merits. Most textbook discussions of the elaboration model limit its application to cross-tabular analytic techniques for simple three-variable models. Although this application may be useful for expository purposes, it is of limited value to students whose own research employs a broader array of variables in one simultaneous multivariate model. Nonetheless, the elaboration model contains just about all of the basic elements necessary for the logical analysis of correlational data.

The elaboration model is an explanatory model. Its purpose is to account for an observed association between two variables, to explain *why* one variable is correlated with another. Although it has some utility in other applications, its power is realized most in instances in which cause-and-effect is an issue. The elaboration model is not the only approach to explanation, of course, but it has proven itself over time and over a broad spectrum of substantive applications. It is useful to outline here key aspects of the elaboration model now because it forms the foundation for the multivariate analytic strategy I present in this volume.

The core issue in the elaboration model is whether an observed association represents a relationship, whether it involves a necessary connection between two variables.[5] In other words, does one variable influence the other in the manner envisioned by theory? Answering this question entails comparing theory-based expectations about a relationship to observed associations. Accomplishing this goal entails systematically introducing "third variables" or "test factors" and assessing the impact on the original association.

Third Variables

Third variables specify the mechanisms or processes that produce the observed association between two other variables. As we shall see, placing this association within a theory-based system of interlocking variables strengthens the inference that one variable is related to the other. Third variables are also used to rule out alternative explanations for the observed association. For example, third variables are used to limit the possibility that the association is *spurious*, that it merely reflects the mutual dependence of both variables on the third variable. Demonstrating that the theoretical model is feasible while also ruling out alternative explanations for an empirical association constitutes strong evidence for inferring that a cause-and-effect type of connection exists between the two variables.

These two functions of third variables are the basis for the data analysis strategy described in this text. One additional function, however, should be identified at the outset. Third variables are also used to ascertain whether an association is universal or specific to particular conditions or groups. This task entails determining whether the association is contingent upon the particular value taken by the third variable. As we shall see, this type of specification can also enhance the interpretation of an association as a relationship to the extent that these contingencies are consistent with theory.

Empirical association can be demonstrated with bivariate analysis, but establishing relatedness necessitates multivariate analysis. The two-variable model shows only that the values of the two variables coincide. To demonstrate that this covariation can legitimately be interpreted as a cause-and-effect type of relationship, the model needs to be expanded to include at least one additional variable. This third variable is needed to rule out alternative interpretations or to test the causal mechanisms described by theory. In most applications, numerous third variables are included in the analysis using multivariate statistical techniques.

Although the assessment of relationship requires multivariate analysis, the widespread application of multivariate statistical techniques has inadvertently obscured the assessment of relatedness. This ironic situation results from the complexity of the technical procedures needed to simultaneously evaluate the effects of several variables. The large number of independent variables used in most analyses diverts attention away from the interpretation of any one association as representing a relationship between an independent and a dependent variable.

The Focal Relationship

To counterbalance this trend, I develop the notion of a *focal relationship*: the one relationship of primary significance—the heart of the theory.[6] This single relationship becomes the cornerstone for all subsequent analysis. The first analytic step is to establish that the focal relationship is feasible, that two variables may be related to one another. This goal is realized by demonstrating that the two variables are empirically associated with one another. After establishing association, further analysis serves to evaluate whether the focal relationship is indeed a relationship or merely an association.

The idea of a focal relationship is a natural extension of the elaboration model. Indeed, its presence is implicit in the original model insofar as third variables are used to enhance the interpretation of one basic association. Labeling this association as the focal relationship serves to move one independent and one dependent variable to the forefront of the analysis and to maintain this center of attention as other variables are added to the model. As we shall see, this device becomes more serviceable as the number of variables in the analysis increases.

Two types of analytic strategy are used to establish the focal relationship as a cause-and-effect type of relationship, as illustrated in Figure 1.1. The first is an exclusionary strategy: ruling out alternative explanations for the observed association to validate the focal relationship. The goal is to show that the association cannot be attributed to factors other than the hypothesized relationship. This strategy involves the analysis of control variables to eliminate spuriousness. It also entails the introduction of additional independent variables to take into consideration redundancy with alternative theories. These other explanatory variables are included in the analysis to demonstrate that they do not account for the observed association between the independent and dependent variables. This strategy is exclusionary in the sense that it concerns the covariation remaining when other potential sources of covariation have been excluded from the estimate of the focal relationship.

Other independent variables and control variables usually account for some of the variation in the dependent variable. These additional variables may also account for some of the covariation between the focal independent and dependent variables. That is, some of the focal relationship may in fact be spurious or the result of alternative causal processes. This outcome is satisfactory if some of the empirical association remains, but it disconfirms one's theory when these third variables fully account for the association between the focal independent and dependent variables. In other words, the inference of relatedness is supported when other explanations do not account for *all* of the covariation between the focal independent and dependent variables.

As illustrated in the bottom panel of Figure 1.1, the second approach seeks to establish internal validity by connecting the focal relationship to other constructs. This approach is useful when we think the focal relationship is embedded within a network of relationships with other constructs. These other relationships are operationalized as antecedent, intervening, and consequent variables. In brief, antecedent variables are used to extend the causal process back in time to the determinants of the focal independent variable, intervening variables operationalize the causal mechanisms linking the focal independent variable to the dependent variable, and consequent variables extend the causal process forward in time to examine the subsequent impact of the dependent variable. These variables are explanatory in the sense that they explicate the functioning of the causal system of which the focal relationship is a part. When expected patterns of association with the focal relationship do indeed materialize, the inference of relatedness is supported. This is an inclusive approach

Figure 1.1

Strategies to Establish the Internal Validity of the Focal Relationship

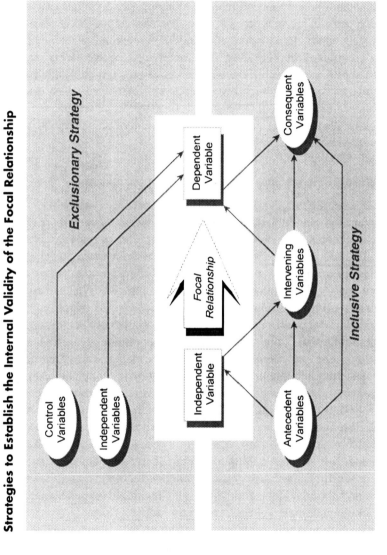

to internal validity in that it includes other explanatory variables in the analysis of the focal relationship.

The elaboration model is an inferential rather than a deterministic model. It does not directly demonstrate cause and effect; rather, it establishes such effects by systematically eliminating alternative explanations while conforming to theoretical expectations. Ideally, all possible reasons for the observed association would be identified, tested, and ruled out, and the researcher is left with only one explanation. However, the universe of potential explanations is infinite and cannot be exhaustively tested. In practice, then, one seeks to narrow down a broad range of alternatives to a select few that remain plausible. Thus, the meaning of an association is established by a process of elimination, but necessarily remains somewhat speculative.

Mental Illness and Violence: An Application

The use of third variables to elaborate a focal relationship is illustrated in a model of the connection between severe mental illness and violence proposed by Hiday (1995). Most persons with mental illness are not violent, but the rate of violence is somewhat higher among those with mental illness than among those who do not meet diagnostic criteria for mental illness. This modest association reinforces stereotypes and contributes to stigma and social isolation—conditions with adverse consequences for persons with mental illness. Previous research demonstrates that this association is not the result of spurious covariation with demographic or historical characteristics. The conventional interpretation of this association is that severe mental illness results in violent actions.

Hiday (1995) argues that this interpretation is overly simplistic because it does not take into account the social context within which violent acts occur. A slightly modified version of the causal model she proposes, illustrated in Figure 1.2, uses both exclusionary and inclusive strategies to challenge the conclusion that severe mental illness leads to violent acts. The inclusive variables in this model encompass (1) antecedents to mental illness, (2) intervening experiences that determine whether mental illness results in violence, and (3) consequences of exposure to violence. The exclusionary variables encompass two additional sets, (4) control variables to rule out spuriousness and (5) other independent variables to take into consideration alternative theories of severe mental illness and violence.

Figure 1.2

Causal Model of Severe Mental Illness and Violence

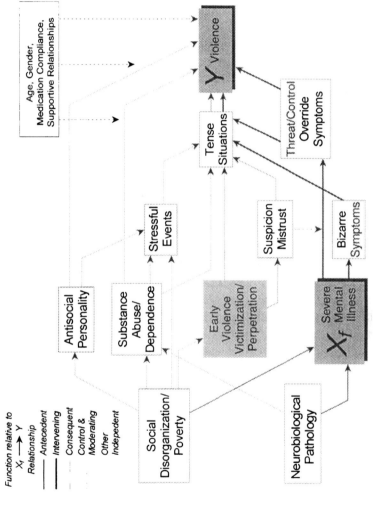

Source: Adapted from Hiday (1995).

Although this model is too complex to discuss in its entirety, several pathways are highlighted here to illustrate the uses of exclusionary and inclusive variables. With regard to antecedent variables, the model posits two broad antecedents to the focal relationship between severe mental illness and violence: social disorganization/poverty and neurobiological pathology. The connection between social disorganization/poverty and these outcomes is crucial to the model insofar as this type of hardship and deprivation is seen as creating the conditions under which mental illness is likely to result in violent acts. For example, a chaotic impoverished environment contributes to the development of specific psychotic symptoms, including those that entail feelings of personal threat or intrusive thoughts. According to Hiday (1995), this type of symptom is especially likely to override self-control and result in violent acts, either directly or by exacerbating tense situations. (See also the discussion of Link, Monahan, Stueve, & Cullen, 1999, in Chapter 4.) These variables are antecedents because they precede the focal independent variable, serious mental illness (X_f). They also represent alternative theories and, therefore, can be considered as other independent variables. In addition, control variables are included in the model, as shown in the upper right-hand corner of Figure 1.2. These exclusionary variables are used to remove covariation between severe mental illness and violence that is the result of their joint dependency on characteristics such as gender or medication compliance. (Hiday (1995) treats this set of variables as moderators; see Chapter 8).

This model also illustrates the use of intervening variables in elaborating a focal relationship. Specifically, Hiday (1995) argues that the connection between severe mental illness and violence is indirect, mediated by intervening conditions and experiences. A key intervening variable entails the presence of threat/control symptoms that override self-control and trigger violent acts. The existence of tense situations also serves as an intervening variable, mediating the impact of bizarre symptoms. This variable additionally mediates the impact of prior exposure to violence, substance abuse/dependence, antisocial personality, stressful events, and a suspicious/mistrustful worldview. The latter connections elaborate the focal relationship by placing it within a set of broader processes.

Finally, although the dependent variable in this model is violence, the model contains a segment that specifies some of the consequences of violence, specifically the consequences of early exposure to violence. Hiday (1995) contends that some of the causal connection between mental illness and violence occurs in the reverse direction insofar as victimization in childhood is associated with subsequent mental health problems. She argues that socialization into an environment tolerant of violence increases the likelihood that severe mental illness will trigger violent acts because it fosters suspicion and mistrust, which, in turn, contribute to the occurrence of tense situations in which violence is likely to erupt. This model traces forward in time the consequences of early exposure to violence, which includes its own subsequent perpetuation as violence directed toward others.

In concluding this example, it is important to note that the relative risk for violence for persons with mental illness is not nearly as great as the risk for those who are young, male, single, lower class, and substance abusing or substance dependent. Thus, Hiday (1995) is careful to caution that the association between mental illness and violence is small and indirect. This association should not be used, then, as evidence corroborating stereotypes of persons with mental illness.

The Inherent Subjectivity of Analysis

It is important to acknowledge at the outset that data analysis is never entirely objective. What one sees in a set of data is inevitably shaped by what one expects to see. The notion that data analysis is subjective runs counter to the traditional principles of science, which presume that research is conducted in an impartial manner. The image of the researcher as a neutral observer and reporter, however, is an ideal that cannot be fully actualized.

The inherent subjectivity of data analysis becomes self-evident when we recall that analysis is conducted within the context of theory, which is itself a statement of what one expects to find. Theory shapes the very questions that are asked, the data selected to answer these questions, and the methods applied to these data. The interpretation of analytic results, therefore, is necessarily affected by one's theoretical inclinations. Keller (1985) cogently articulates this viewpoint:

> Let the data speak for themselves, these scientists demand. The problem with this argument is, of course, that data never do speak for themselves.

It is by now a near truism that there is no such thing as raw data; all data presuppose interpretation. And if an interpretation is to be meaningful—if the data are to be "intelligible" to more than one person—there must be participation in a community of common practices, shared conceptions of the meaning of terms and their relation to "objects" in the real world ... it means sharing a more or less agreed-upon understanding of what constitutes legitimate questions and meaningful answers. Every explicit question carries with it a set of implicit (unarticulated, and often unrecognized) expectations that limit the range of acceptable answers in ways that only a properly trained respondent will recognize. Thus for every question such as "What accounts for X?" the range of acceptable answers is circumscribed by unspoken presuppositions about what counts as accounting—a circumscription that is assumed as a matter of course by members of a particular community. (pp. 121–130)

Thus, research in general and data analysis in particular are always conducted under a set of ceteris paribus conditions. These comments do not imply that the researcher has license to indulge his or her personal inclinations. On the contrary, acknowledging the pervasive influence of presupposition is a warning: One should be alert to implicit assumptions that limit analysis and constrict interpretation.

It is especially easy to lose sight of the impact of expectations when pouring over quantitative results produced by the application of sophisticated statistical procedures. Computer output crammed full of numbers and statistics creates an illusion of factual reality. The application of formal tests of statistical significance further embellishes this image. Despite the illusion of impartiality created by quantitative analysis, it must be recognized that implicit theoretical assumptions affect the selection of statistical procedures, the choice of variables entered into an analysis, and so forth. Although quantitative analysis may mask this type of subjectivity, it does not produce findings that are objective in the absolute.

The analyst is an artist. He or she observes a mass of information that dazzles with multifaceted possibilities. These impressions spark the imagination. The analyst–artist selects and arranges these images to communicate his or her vision to others. Some elements are pulled to the forefront and depicted in minute detail, whereas others form the middle ground or fade into the vagueness of background. This ordering of impressions is an act of creation: The vision being communicated is that of the analyst–artist. The same objects would appear differently if viewed from another vantage point: An element relegated to the background might well become the focal point. Alternately, shifting perspectives may reveal an object previously concealed from view. Representations of the same scene created by different artists often bear little resemblance to one another.[7] The act of observing and communicating is no less subjective because the analyst works with numbers, computers, and statistical output rather than sights, easel, and canvas.

This perspective is similar to Bacon's view of the ideal analogy for science (cited by Lloyd, 1996):

> Neither the activity of the ants, who merely heap up and use their store, nor that of the spiders, spinning out their webs; but rather that of the bee, who extracts matter from the flowers of the garden and the field, but who works and fashions it by its own efforts. (p. 50)

The strategies presented in this text are tools for transforming a set of observed associations into a coherent representation of theoretical causal processes. This method is capable of demonstrating that the observed data are consistent with theory but it falls short of demonstrating that the theory is factually true because there always remain alternative accounts for the same observed pattern of association. This caveat serves as a reminder that we should not confuse our representations of reality with reality.

Looking Ahead

The method of theory-based analysis described in this text (1) assesses whether one variable is associated with another in the manner described by theory and at a level beyond that expected by chance, (2) eliminates alternative explanations for the observed association through the use of control and other independent variables, and (3) demonstrates that this focal relationship fits within an interconnected set of relationships predicted by theory using antecedent, intervening, and consequent variables. Achieving these objectives strengthens the interpretation that the observed association represents a relationship, that the focal independent variable influences the dependent variable.

A good deal of this text is concerned with the impact of third variables on estimates of the association between the focal independent and dependent variables and with the interpretation of this association. These estimates are obtained from a variety of multivariate statistical models, including the commonly used multiple linear regression and logistic regression. Despite differences among these statistical techniques, the core issue across techniques concerns the extent to which the coefficient that operationalizes the focal relationship is *altered* by the addition of relevant third variables. The specifics of these changes are taken up in subsequent chapters. At this point, it is sufficient to note that the changes associated with the addition of third variables are used to evaluate whether an inference of relatedness is warranted.

This theory-based approach to the focal relationship represents an ideal analytic strategy, and, in practice, many applications fall short of this ideal. For example, the theory being evaluated may not be developed sufficiently to specify the mechanisms or processes that generate the focal relationship or measures of key third variables may be missing from the data set. Despite such limitations, this strategy is apt to move the analysis in theoretically relevant directions. This situation simply means that the analysis of internal validity is incomplete and that additional research is warranted.

In addition, there are other strategies for theory-based data analysis and even more techniques for data analysis in general. These approaches can supplement the approach described in this text or serve as productive alternatives. There is no one right way to analyze data. The focal relationship and the elaboration model are presented as starting points in the development of a coherent analysis plan for a specific research question, but only as starting points. The development of the analysis can and should go beyond the bare-bones scheme inventoried in this text.

Notes

1. In most applications, only a limited segment of a data set is analyzed at any given time; one rarely analyzes the entire data set simultaneously.

2. Some methodologists treat evaluation as a fourth distinct type of research, but evaluation can also be seen as a special case of explanatory research.

3. Quasi-experimental research, a hybrid type, often uses both strategies to establish internal validity: Threats to internal validity are controlled by design to the extent possible, and those that cannot be controlled by design are controlled through analysis.

4. This empiricism derives from the philosophy of John Locke, whereas the theory-testing perspective is consistent with the Cartesian tradition.

5. Often this entails a causal relationship, but Rosenberg (1968) correctly notes that causality is only one form of determination.

6. My idea of the focal relationship is similar to Ernest Schachtel's idea of "focal attention," described by Keller (1985) as man's "capacity to *center* his attention on an object fully, so that he can perceive or understand it from *many sides*, as fully as possible" (p. 165).

7. A striking example of this aspect of artistic vision appeared at an exhibit *Impressionists on the Seine: A Celebration of Renoir's "Luncheon of the Boating Party"* shown at the Phillips Collection, Washington, DC, September 21, 1996–February 9, 1997. This exhibit presented side-by-side paintings of the same subject painted simultaneously by two impressionist masters, Claude Monet and Auguste Renoir. Particularly striking is the difference in palette and composition for the two pairs of identically titled paintings, *Sailboats at Argenteuil* and *La Grenouillère* (Rathborne, Rothkopf, Brettell, & Moffett, 1996; see also White, 1996, for other fine examples). Monet (cited in Levine, 1994) also gives us a powerful image for the impact of theory on observation when he notes, "One is not an artist if one does not carry a picture in one's head before executing it" (p. 270). See also Rosow (1994) for a discussion of Monet's method of visually capturing the changing effects of light and in particular how it serves as a model for social science research, both controlled experiments and, the topic of this text, the analysis of interactions among multiple variables. In addition, Kemp (2000) provides an especially rich discussion of the shared motifs in the imaginary worlds of the scientist and the artist for whom the act of looking has the potential to become an act of analysis.

2 The Logic of Theory-Based Data Analysis

Theory and observation share a symbiotic existence. This union is illustrated in Figure 2.1 as the familiar yin-yang symbol. The theoretical universe contains abstractions such as constructs, relationships, and populations. The observed realm, in contrast, encompasses measured variables, empirical associations, and finite samples.

Data analysis is shown here as the boundary between theory and observation. This boundary serves as a point of exchange. First, abstract elements of theory are transformed to become observable in the real world. Constructs become measured variables. Populations are converted into samples. Relationships are translated into associations. This transformation makes the abstract concrete. We are now able to observe associations among measured variables in a sample.

Second, a stream of information about how well observations match theory flows in the reverse direction. Measured variables

Figure 2.1

Theory, Observation, and Data Analysis

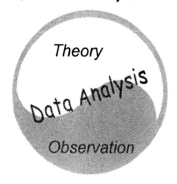

are compared to descriptions of abstract constructs. Associations among these variables are compared to ideas about how one construct affects another. Samples are generalized to populations. This procedure enables us to use observed associations among variables measured in a sample to make inferences about the probable nature of relationships among constructs in the population. In this manner, the degree of correspondence between theory and observation is used to formulate and develop theory.

This analytic movement back and forth between theory and observation is necessary because the theoretical realm exists only as an abstraction. We cannot directly observe constructs, relationships, or populations, but must instead make inferences about these entities. These inferences are based on that which *can* be observed—the surrogates of measured variables, associations, and samples. Consider the electron, to draw an example from the physical sciences. Barnes, Bloor, and Henry (1996) point out that the electron, a basic theoretical object, has been institutionalized in physics to the extent that this unobserved object is now treated as if it were a normal material object even though what is actually "seen" is the presumed effect of the electron, or, stated differently, the electron has *in effect* been seen. This reliance upon surrogates means that we can never be entirely certain that we have captured the unobservable. Accordingly, this chapter describes the ways in which data analysis enables us to connect unobservable ideas to empirical observations.

Inductive and Deductive Processes

Observation, Induction, and Theory

Theory is the abstract representation of reality. It originates in observation of the empirical world. As a phenomenon is studied, certain regularities about it are recognized and its peculiarities are noted. The theorist then constructs an explanation to account for these occurrences. In general, theory seeks to account for a phenomenon by describing the underlying processes that generate the observed regularity and any departures from it.

The real world is limitless, however, too expansive and complex to be observed fully. Observation, then, is necessarily incomplete. In addition, perception is selective: It filters, distills, and organizes the empirical world. As a result, theory may approximate reality but cannot reproduce it. In this regard, Keller (1992) maintains that no representation of nature can ever correspond to reality because nature is only accessible to us through representations, and these representations are necessarily structured by language and, hence, by culture. She refers to the scientific method as "a *method* for 'undoing' nature's secrets: for the rendering of what was previously invisible, visible—visible to the mind's eye if not to the physical eye" (p. 41). Barnes et al. (1996) similarly assert that any given set of empirical observations and experimental procedures must be interpreted, "Meaning must be attached to them and there is no unique way of reading their significance" (p. 194).

The dependence of theory on observation is illustrated in Figure 2.2. This figure depicts the development of theory through the process of *inductive reasoning*: deriving general principles by extending what is observed for a specific case to other cases of the same class. General principles are abstractions, ideas about how things work, and, consequently, cannot be observed first-hand. Instead, their existence is inferred through observation of their presumed effects. These presumed effects are the phenomenon as observed in the empirical world. The observed phenomenon is treated *as if* it is a manifestation of some unobservable concept.

An example of this process can be found in an investigation my colleagues and I have conducted with informal caregivers to spouses and parents suffering from dementia (Aneshensel, Pearlin, Schuler, & Levy-Storms, 2000). The baseline sample consisted of 555 primary family caregivers living in San Francisco or Los

Figure 2.2

The Reasoning Linking Observation and Theory

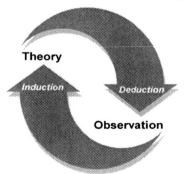

Angeles in 1988, the start of the study. All care recipients suffered from dementia and resided in the community at baseline (1988). Data were collected by means of a multiwave panel survey, with six face-to-face annual interviews. Caregivers were reinterviewed irrespective of whether they continued to provide care at home, found it necessary to place their relatives in institutions, or became bereaved. Over the course of the study, 273 of the care recipients were placed in long-term care institutions: 155 (57.0%) of these persons died before the end of data collection.

Mortality rates for elderly persons with dementia are high immediately following their relocation from home to nursing home and then drop to lower stable rates after roughly 6 months. We identified two competing explanations for the high rates of death in the immediate aftermath of admission. One is a social selection hypothesis that attributes excess mortality to the disproportionate admission of persons in extremely poor health: These deaths were imminent and would have occurred at home had the person not been institutionalized first. The second interpretation is a social causation hypothesis: Excess deaths occur as a result of admission, possibly because the transition itself is traumatic or because the nursing home environment is unhealthy or dangerous, especially for persons with dementia, who are easily confused by new surroundings.

In this example, we see how an empirical observation, high postadmission mortality, serves as the impetus for the development of two competing theories, social selection and social causation. Selection and causation are hypothetical processes. These processes cannot be observed firsthand. Instead, they can only be inferred by observation of their presumed effects, in this instance, high rates of postadmission deaths. Both theories are consistent with high mortality shortly after admission to a nursing home.

In developing theory, we construct a hypothetical explanation for a phenomenon by imagining the underlying processes that could generate what we have observed. Note the term "could." We are not able to directly observe that the phenomenon does indeed result from these processes; instead, we merely speculate that it does. Theoretical explanation, therefore, is hypothetical: If these principles operate, then we would observe something closely resembling what we have indeed observed. The logical leap is connecting observed phenomena to their hypothetical origins. In other words, the empirical world is treated as if it is a manifestation of imagined principles.

Theory, Deduction, and Observation

As soon as a theory is articulated, it becomes evident that it might account for the phenomenon, but it might not. In the preceding example, for instance, social selection might explain some or all of the deaths following nursing home admission, or all of these deaths may be the result of other processes. The possibility that other processes may account for the observed data provides the impetus for developing a testable form of the theory. For a theoretical formulation to be testable means that it is capable of being disproved, shown to be false. This test entails comparing theoretical predictions of what should be observed to new observations of the phenomenon.[1] This comparison is the essence of data analysis.

It should be noted in passing that not all theory can be disproved. For example, the concepts comprising the theory may not have been specified in sufficient detail to be operationalized and measured. Alternately, the theory may require types of data that simply cannot be obtained. Ideally, however, the theory contains at least some components that can be empirically tested. Testing a segment of a theory can be informative about the larger theory within which the segment is embedded, even though the theory cannot be tested in its entirety.

Developing a testable form of a theory entails the translation of abstract ideas into concrete statements about what should be observed if the theory is correct. Expectations about what should be observed are known as *hypotheses*. The formulation of hypotheses entails *deductive reasoning*: attributing to the particular case the qualities of the general class. As illustrated in Figure 2.2, deduction completes the logical circuit linking theory and observation.

In deductive reasoning, we assume that what is true of the general class is also true for the particular case. This assumption is tenable insofar as the particular case is element of the general class, in the sense that a whole is composed of its parts. The development of a testable form of theory proceeds by specifying hypotheses about what should be observed in the specific case if the theory about the general class is correct.

Let us continue the example of nursing home mortality. The observation of high postadmission mortality led my colleagues and me to posit two competing theories, social selection and social causation. Both of these theories are consistent with the observed pattern of deaths. Obviously, it makes a good deal of difference whether selection or causation processes are at work. If selection alone is operative, these deaths are not problematic—they would have occurred at home if the transfer to a nursing home had not occurred first. Deaths attributable to the stresses of moving, however, are deaths that could have been prevented as are deaths resulting from a confusing or hazardous new environment or from inadequate care.

We can clarify the association between admission and mortality by speculating about what *else* should be observed if one process or the other is operative. The stated reason for admission is helpful in this regard. Caregivers were asked why they placed their spouses or parents in nursing homes. Numerous reasons were given; indeed most caregivers cited several reasons for their actions, including prominently their own exhaustion, patient incontinence, and poor patient health. The latter provides us with the means of testing the selection hypothesis: If selection alone operates, then postadmission mortality should be high among patients admitted for poor health and *only* among these patients. In other words, mortality should not be high immediately after admission to a nursing home among persons who were admitted for reasons other than poor health.

This example illustrates the use of deductive reasoning to specify a testable hypothesis. If selection alone is operative, we anticipate one pattern of results. Moreover, this pattern of results is expected only if selection is the sole process at work. We do not expect this pattern if causal processes are working, either alone or in combination with selection processes. If social causation occurs, then mortality should be high even among patients whose caregivers placed them in nursing homes for reasons other than poor health. This empirical pattern would be inconsistent with the notion that all of the apparent elevation in postadmission mortality is due to the admission of patients whose deaths are about to happen anyway.

The Circuitous Link Between Theory and Observation

In developing a testable form of theory, we use the general class to make deductions about the particular case so that we can then use the particular to test the general. This circuitous approach is necessary because the general class is an illusion that cannot be directly observed. However, the particular case can be observed firsthand and we can ascertain whether it is consistent with our hypothesis. We then use the degree of correspondence between hypothesis and observation to draw conclusions about the general principles comprising our theory.

The basic question is, "How well do the observed data fit the theoretical model?" If observations and hypotheses are inconsistent, our theory is discredited. A theory cannot be valid for the general class if it is invalid for any member of that class. In this manner, the particular case serves as a test case. If our hypotheses are disproved for associations among measured variables in a sample, then our theory of relationships among constructs in the population is also negated.

If observations and hypotheses are consistent, our theory is supported, but not proved definitively. Although valid for the one particular case tested, our theory may nevertheless subsequently prove to be invalid for other cases of the general class. Our research has tested only one case, yielding one set of findings. A replication would constitute a second case; if it reproduces the original results, it increases confidence. The same would be true for a second replication and a third. Replication does not resolve the uncertainty, however, because the general class is infinite: No matter how many replications are examined, there remains at least one more untested case and this untested case may be the one that disproves our theory. Consequently, we must be content with failing to disprove our theory.

A historical footnote illustrates these points for a uniquely creative scientist, Galileo Galilei. His 17th century lifetime coincided with a cosmic conflict between Ptolemy's earth-centered theory of the universe, which was endorsed by the Roman Catholic Church, and Copernicus's sun-centered theory, which was consistent with emerging astronomical findings, but judged as heresy. Searching for proof positive of the Copernican system, Galileo developed a theory in which the motion of tides could not be explained by a stationary earth, but instead required a moving vessel to generate its ebb and flow. The two movements of the Copernican theory, the earth on its axis and its revolution around the sun, could explain the tides, he argued. The sun-centered worldview of Copernicus and Galileo was ultimately vindicated, of course, but Galileo's tidal proof was not. His biographer Sobel (1999), who provides this vignette, points out that the moon generates the tides, a body Galileo rejected as far too distant to exert this effect, and not the movement of the earth. Indeed, the tides would occur even if the earth stood still. A major paradigmatic shift, then, was built, at least in part, on a theory that was consistent with the available data, but incorrect.

We can now conclude the nursing home mortality example by comparing the selection hypothesis to the observed data. Recall that we expect mortality to be high in the immediate postadmission interval only for persons who were admitted specifically because of their poor health. Our findings are displayed in Figure 2.3, which plots the hazard of dying as a function of time since admission for those admitted for reasons of poor health versus those admitted for reasons other than poor health.

The social selection argument is validated, but only in part. The greatest hazard is seen in patients admitted specifically because they were in poor health. However, high mortality is also seen in patients admitted for reasons other than poor health immediately following their admission. The selection argument does not account for these deaths. Put another way, the admission of persons in poor health accounts for some of the apparent excess mortality

Figure 2.3

Postadmission Mortality Among Dementia Patients

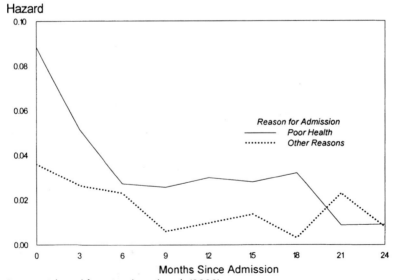

Source: Adapted from Aneshensel et al. (2000)

observed immediately after admission to a nursing home, but does not account for all of these extra deaths. Although selection appears to be operative, it does not seem to be the sole process at work.

Social selection and causation are hypothetical processes; they cannot be observed firsthand but must instead be inferred by observation of their presumed effects. Specifically, we infer selection is at work because persons with dementia who are admitted to nursing homes because of poor health are especially likely to die soon afterwards. We conclude that processes other than selection must also be at work because other relocated patients are also dying at a high rate at this time. In this manner, the observed pattern of deaths between these two groups of patients is treated as evidence concerning the extent to which selection and causation processes are at work.

To recap, this example was used initially to illustrate how empirical observation leads to the development of theory through inductive reasoning: high postadmission mortality served as the impetus for developing two competing theories, social selection and causation. We then extended the example to demonstrate how theory is operationalized into a testable hypothesis using deductive reasoning. Finally, we see the empirical test of this hypothesis, which leads to conclusions about theory, again using inductive reasoning.

Operationalization and the Assessment of Fit

This two-way exchange between theory and observation entails two key processes, *operationalization* and *the assessment of fit*. In this context, operationalization refers to the translation of theory into explicit expectations or hypotheses that can be tested via empirical observation. The assessment of fit is the evaluation of how well theory-based expectations and observations correspond. As illustrated in Figure 2.4, these basic procedures, operationalization and the assessment of fit, go hand-in-hand with one another, in the same way that induction complements deduction.

This pairing, operationalization and fit, takes three major forms. One form involves constructs and measured variables. Another aligns relationships with associations. The third connects populations and samples. From this perspective, data analysis asks the following questions: Are constructs adequately manifest in measured variables? To what extent do the relationships predicted by theory

Figure 2.4

Operationalization and the Assessment of Fit

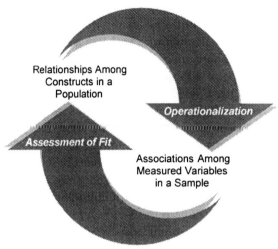

match observed associations? Do expectations about the population materialize within the sample? Most of this text is concerned with associations and relationships, but drawing conclusions about relationships from associations entails assumptions about constructs and measured variables, on the one hand, and populations and samples, on the other hand. Consequently, it is instructive to look at each of these pairings.

Constructs and Measured Variables

In theory-based research, we are interested in drawing conclusions about how one construct influences another construct, conclusions made on the basis of observed associations among various measured variables. Constructs are abstractions: mental images or representations of intangible things that are thought to exist but not in a material or physical form. For example, in personality theory, constructs refer to imagined qualities of a person, such as introversion-extroversion. Although these terms are widely understood in contemporary Western society, these qualities are not tangible. Instead, their existence is inferred from observations of how a person behaves, especially the extent to which his or her behavior is consistent across various settings, and, hence, indicative of some general propensity to act. For example, we label as an extrovert the person who talks to strangers, seeks out the company of others, organizes social gatherings, and acts like the life of the party even though he or she sometimes enjoys solitude.

Constructs apply not only to individuals, but to other entities as well. For example, interpersonal interactions may be characterized as reciprocal versus unilateral or competitive versus cooperative, and we speak of groups in terms of solidarity or cohesion. Constructs are also used to describe societies or populations, for example, to distinguish between developed and technically less developed regions of the world or to describe "national character." In addition, constructs, despite their ethereal nature, are essential elements of the physical sciences and, indeed, help to define the physical world. For example, the ionization of subatomic particles is not visible; its presence must be inferred from a characteristic trail of visible droplets in a cloud chamber. Likewise, canaries were once used in coal mines to detect dangerous levels of methane gas, which is tasteless, odorless, and colorless. Overcome by low levels of methane, dead canaries alerted miners to toxic levels of the gas and the risk of explosion.

A construct cannot be observed directly precisely because it is intangible, which explains its synonyms of *unobserved variable* and *latent variable*. Instead, a construct is inferred from its presumed manifestations, referred to as *observed variables* or *measured variables*. The measured variable is, in effect, a surrogate or proxy for the construct. Scores on the measured variable are seen as being produced by the underlying construct, the assumption that links the theoretical realm to the empirical world. This process of operationalization entails deductive reasoning: The conceptual description of the construct is transformed into a measurement instrument. This tool is then used to make observations, generating a set of measurements, which we call a measured variable.

For example, depression is an emotional state encompassing negative feelings, such as being sad, downcast, and forlorn; confused thinking, including difficulty concentrating and extreme negativity; and uncharacteristic behavior, such as losing interest in things that are usually enjoyed, having trouble sleeping or eating, or moving very slowly. Becker (1974) describes depression as a mood state that is never directly observed and must always be inferred or interpreted from objectively observed signs and symptoms that covary in a specific manner. The covariation criterion means that multiple signs and symptoms have to present for a person to be depressed; if only a few appear and most are absent, the person is unlikely to be depressed. Depression is inferred when a person conveys being sad, thinks that life is not worthwhile, is unable to get out of bed, and so on.

The key point is that the underlying state of depression is not directly visible to another person. Others may notice behavioral changes, but feelings and thoughts are experienced internally and are not apparent to others unless communicated. Thus, depression cannot be directly observed, but is instead inferred from its manifest signs and symptoms, which usually involve a person describing how he or she is feeling. This self-disclosure might be made informally to family or friends, be part of a diagnostic interview with a clinician, or, for our purposes, be a response to a standardized measure administered by a researcher.

The degree of correspondence between the observed measurements and the theoretical description of the construct, the assessment of fit, is shown in Figure 2.4 as movement from right to left. The primary dimensions of fit assessed for constructs are *validity* and *reliability*. Validity refers to how well the measured variable corresponds to the concept. Reliability asks whether repeated measurements of the construct yield the same observed value or at least highly similar values. A reliable instrument, like a reliable person, tells the same story from one occasion to the next, or in the words of Lewis Carroll in 1910 in *The Hunting of the Snark,* "What I tell you three times is true."

Validity and reliability are necessary for the accurate estimation of associations among measured variables and, by extension, to the inference of relationships among constructs. Measures that lack reliability attenuate estimates of association among measured variables, as discussed later in this chapter. Furthermore, reliability is necessary (although not sufficient) for validity; a measure that lacks reliability inherently lacks validity. When validity is lacking, the measured variable is assessing something other the theoretical construct, meaning that observed associations cannot be indicative of theoretical relationships. These empirical associations may reflect causal processes, but not the processes contained in the conceptual model because the measured variable is not what it purports to be. Continuing the depression example, if the symptom inventory assessed anxiety rather than depression, then the correlation of inventory scores with a count of stressful life events would misrepresent the impact of this type of stress on depression.

ANALYSIS JOURNAL: Reliability and Validity

These concepts can be illustrated with data from the Los Angeles Survey of Adolescent Experience, a survey of depressive symptoms in adolescents that my colleagues and I conducted with a large (N = 877), community-based sample of adolescents living in Los Angeles County (Aneshensel & Sucoff, 1996; Siegel, Aneshensel, Taub, Cantwell, & Driscoll, 1998). These data are used as a continuing example throughout this text to provide continuity in illustrating key points. To support these analyses, additional information about the study is provided in this section.

Sample

Adolescents were selected from a multistage area probability-sampling frame of Los Angeles County: census tracts, blocks, and households. Listed households were screened to determine whether an adolescent between the ages of 12 and 17 lived there as a permanent resident. If so, that adolescent was recruited for participation in the study. In households with more than one teen, a single adolescent was randomly selected using the next birthday method. The response rate of 77.1% yielded a sample of 877 adolescents.

As shown in the table, the ethnicity of the sample is diverse with almost half of the adolescents being of Latino origin or descent, which is especially characteristic of the children of this region. More than half of the adolescents in the sample live in an intact nuclear family, but a quarter live in single-parent households. The sample has, on average, a low-middle family income, but one in four lives in a family with income below the federal poverty line.

Data Collection

Interviews were conducted in person in English or Spanish at the respondent's home. The Spanish instrument was a verified translation and back-translation of the English version. On average, interviews lasted 2.2 hrs. They were conducted between October 1992 and April 1994. Resident mothers (N = 728) and fathers (N = 447) or other parental figures were also interviewed. Respondents were reinterviewed an average of 12 months after the baseline interview.

Weighted Sample Characteristics, Los Angeles Survey of Adolescent Experience

Characteristic	Percent or *Mean* (N = 877)[a]	Standard Deviation
Gender		
Male	53.5	
Female	46.5	
Ethnicity		
White	25.8	
African American	11.4	
Latino	48.6	
Asian American	10.6	
Other	3.6	
Family structure		
Intact nuclear family	58.0	
Parent and stepparent	15.9	
One parent	26.1	
Family income (thousands of $)[b]	*32.29*	*21.87*
Age (years)	*14.49*	*1.63*

[a]N varies slightly due to missing data.
[b]Means and standard deviations in italics. Standard deviations estimated without weights and cluster adjustment.

Technical Information

Sample weights adjust for variability in selection probabilities resulting from subject nonparticipation and for households containing multiple adolescents. The Huber White sandwich estimator of variance is used to adjust for the complex sample design. Data were analyzed with Stata Version 6.0.

Measurement of Depression

Depression was measured with the Child Depression Inventory (CDI), a 21-item self-report symptom inventory (Kovacs & Beck, 1977). Symptoms are scored from 0 to 3 for increasing severity; for example, "I do not feel sad; I feel sad sometimes; I am pretty sad all the time; I am so very sad that I can't stand it." These inventory scores are used to make inferences about the true level of depression experienced by these adolescents. Inventory scores are merely indicators of depression, however, not depression itself; it is an inference, not a direct assessment. These scores are affected not only by the underlying construct of depression, but also by other influences including, for instance, the person's awareness of internal states, willingness to self-disclose these states and social desirability response sets. Thus, discrepancies between the construct and the measured variable are inevitable and reflect problems with reliability, validity, or both.

The scale demonstrates very good internal consistency reliability, as assessed with Cronbach's alpha ($\alpha = .86$). Adolescents also rated themselves on a second measure of depression, the Stony Brook Child Psychiatric Checklist 3R (Gadow & Sprafkin, 1987). It asks how often 11 depressive symptoms have been experienced, with response categories of (1) for never through (4) for very often. It too demonstrates very good reliability ($\alpha = .80$). The CDI appears to be a valid self-report measure of depressive symptoms among adolescents because it correlates strongly with this second measure of the same construct ($r = .61; p < .001$).

Relationships and Observed Associations

Once again, it is useful to distinguish between the theoretical and empirical realms. As mentioned previously, constructs are inherently unobservable because they are hypothetical abstractions, part of the theoretical realm. Consequently, relationships among constructs also are unobservable. The presence of a relationship, therefore, must be inferred from an association. This association is observed among the measured variables that serve as proxies for constructs.

Measured variables are used in data analysis to estimate associations, which are then used to draw inferences about relationships among constructs. This process entails both operationalization and the assessment of fit, as illustrated earlier in Figure 2.4. The first step is deductive: the translation of theoretical statements about relationships among constructs into hypotheses about associations among measured variables. If theoretical relationships among constructs do indeed exist, then measures of these constructs should be associated with one another in the manner described by theory. The second step ascertains how well theory-based expectations conform to observed data. Referring once again to Figure 2.4, this is an inductive process, in which the pattern of observed association between two measured variables is used to draw conclusions about a probable relationship between two constructs.

If the measured variables are not associated with one another, then the theory is disconfirmed; if the theory does not apply to this one particular case, then it cannot be an accurate account of the general class. On the other hand, when data correspond to theoretical expectations, theory gains credibility. However, it is not definitively proven: Demonstrating association between two variables in one empirical case does not mean that this correspondence exists for all cases in the general class. The data are consistent with this possibility, but do not prove it.

Measured Variables and Observed Associations

The correspondence between associations and relationships depends upon the accuracy achieved in the assessment of constructs with measured variables. First, as noted above, a lack of validity nullifies the entire enterprise. Second, a lack of reliability attenuates observed associations among measured variables and, therefore, yields estimates of relationships among constructs that are smaller than they would be if measurement error were not as great.[2] This situation is illustrated in Figure 2.5.

As discussed in the preceding section, our theoretical concern is with the relationship between two constructs. In Figure 2.5, these constructs are marked with an asterisk to distinguish them from

Figure 2.5

Reliability and Estimates of Relationships

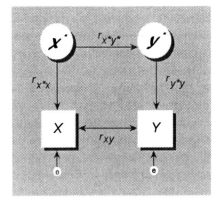

the measured variables that serve as their proxies. Thus, the construct X^* is measured by X and Y^* is similarly measured with Y. The unidirectional arrows linking constructs to measured variables signify that constructs are assumed to influence scores on measured variables. Measures of constructs, however, are always imperfect. Accordingly, each measured variable in Figure 2.5 reflects the influence of measurement error (e) as well as the influence of the underlying construct. Constructs, in contrast, are "error free." This line of reasoning leads to the familiar equation[3]:

$$\begin{array}{ccc} \text{Observed} &=& \text{construct} + \text{error} \\ \text{variance} & & \text{variance} \quad \text{variance.} \end{array} \tag{2.1}$$

The reliability coefficient (shown in Figure 2.5 as r_{x^*x} and as r_{y^*y}) represents the correlation between the measure and an equivalent measure or the correlation of a measure with itself (r_{xx} or r_{yy}). The square root of the reliability coefficient is the correlation between the variable as measured and the unmeasured construct (Cohen & Cohen, 1975).

The true relationship between the constructs ($r_{x^*y^*}$) is estimated by the association (r_{xy}) between the two measured variables. This estimate, however, is constrained by the amount of error present in each variable (Nunnally, 1967, pp. 203–204), such that

$$r_{xy} = r_{x^*y^*} \sqrt{r_{xx}} \sqrt{r_{yy}} \; . \tag{2.2}$$

This equation can be rearranged to give the true value of the association between the constructs adjusted for measurement error:

$$r_{x^*y^*} = \frac{r_{xy}}{\sqrt{r_{xx}} \sqrt{r_{yy}}} . \tag{2.2b}$$

The amount of attenuation increases as reliability decreases. Thus, measurement error conceals a portion of the true relationship that exists among constructs.

Notice that the relationship between X^* and Y^* is represented in Figure 2.5 as a unidirectional arrow whereas the association between X and Y is shown as a bidirectional arrow. This distinction signifies the difference between relatedness and association, in other words, the inference of cause and effect among constructs that we hope to make from the empirical association between the measured variables.

Clearly, a lack of reliability compromises the assessment of associations among measured variables, yielding values that are smaller than the true relationship among the constructs. Alternately stated, poor reliability increases the chance of a Type II error—failing to reject the null hypothesis when it should be rejected. In this instance, the null hypothesis is that the two variables are independent of one another. Thus, we may fail to observe a true relationship between two constructs because of poor reliability in the measured variables.

ANALYSIS JOURNAL: Attenuation in Estimates of Relationships

For example, depression and anxiety are states of psychological distress that tend to co-occur: Persons who are depressed often experience elevated symptoms of anxiety, and the anxious are often downhearted. The relationship between these constructs was estimated with data from the Los Angeles Survey of Adolescent Experience. As before, depression was measured with the CDI; anxiety was measured with a subset of items from the Hopkins Symptom Check List (Derogatis, Lipman, Rickels, Uhlenhuth, & Covi, 1974). Reliability for both measures is estimated as $\alpha = .86$ and the two measures have a moderate positive correlation, $r = .45$. Applying Equation 2.2b, the hypothetical correlation between the two constructs is $.45/(.86 \times .86)^{1/2} = .52$. This adjusted value is about 15% greater in strength than the value observed with the two imperfect measures of the constructs. The true association, thus, is substantially larger than the observed association even though both measures are reasonably reliable.

Populations and Samples

The observations that are used to assess fit typically have been made for a sample of some population. The conclusions we wish to draw about constructs and relationships, however, are for populations not samples. Most populations cannot be observed directly because they are defined abstractly and cannot be enumerated. For example, the population of the United States changes before it can be completely listed because births, deaths, and immigration continuously alter its composition. Consequently, samples are used as proxies for populations. In this regard, populations resemble constructs and relationships: Each abstraction is known only through its tangible manifestations. Observed data, in the form of variables measured within a sample, are analyzed as associations to draw conclusions about relationships among constructs within a population.

Referring back to Figure 2.4, the population of interest is first operationalized as a sample, the deductive step. This step entails specifying a sampling plan for randomly selecting a subset of elements from the population and occurs before data collection. During analysis, operationalization entails stating hypotheses about the sample data. For theory-based research, these hypotheses usually assert expectations about associations. As should be familiar by now, the second step is inductive: the sample is used to draw inferences about the population. From the perspective of testing theory, the inference of most interest usually concerns relationships among constructs in the population.

The null hypothesis for explanatory research typically states that there is *no* association between variables. In the case of the correlation coefficient, for instance, the usual null hypothesis is H_0: $r = 0$, the value indicating no linear association between the two measured variables. (Values of -1.00 up to but not including 0 signify an inverse or negative linear association, whereas values above 0 through 1.00 denote a positive linear association). In most cases, we hope to reject the null hypothesis. This goal is so common because theories specify the presence of relationship much more frequently than they specify its absence.

Although the sample yields an exact value of the empirical association, this value is only an estimate of the true population value, which is unknown. The accuracy of the sample estimate, however, is uncertain. Inference from sample to population, therefore, necessitates the use of probability theory and inferential statistics. Basically, one calculates the probability of observing the empirical association if in truth no association exists in the population. Other things being equal, this probability decreases as the magnitude of the empirical association increases.

For example, the test statistic for the correlation coefficient is t with degrees of freedom $(N - 1)$. If t is large (relative to its degrees of freedom), its associated p value is small, and the null hypothesis is rejected. We would conclude that it is unlikely that the two constructs are independent of one another in the population. In contrast, we would fail to reject the null hypothesis if t is small and its p value is large. Note that we do not accept the null hypothesis; we merely fail to reject it, a sometimes confusing idea for reasons that are discussed in the next section. Earlier we saw that anxiety and depression are correlated at $r = .45$ for a sample of adolescents. We conclude that anxiety and depression are unlikely to be independent among the population of adolescents because $t = 10.099$ and $p < .001$.

As noted earlier, data analysis and statistics are distinct components of scientific inquiry, even though these tools are often used in conjunction with one another and just as often tacitly equated with one another. The distinction between the two can be confusing, especially given that analytic and statistical information tends to be calculated simultaneously. These values appear together in the computer output generated by various software programs and, thus, appear to be the same.

To continue with the correlation coefficient, p values for t tests are often printed underneath correlation coefficients. This convention obscures the fact that the coefficient has a known, exact value for the sample. The t test and p value pertain to inferences about the probable value of the coefficient in the population. If we were interested only in the sample, the test statistic and its p value would be unnecessary. The population value, however, is unknowable. Thus, inferential statistics are essential whenever we wish to draw conclusions about population parameters from sample data.

Recall that the magnitude of the association is distinct from its probability level. A large association is more likely to be statistically significant than a small association (other things being equal). However, in a small sample, a very large association may not be statistically significant. Similarly, a small association will attain statistical significance given a large enough sample. Consequently, the substantive importance of an association merits attention equal to that usually reserved for tests of statistical significance.

In summary, data analysis is concerned with the assessment of fit between theoretical expectations and observed data. Expectations or hypotheses are formulated with deductive reasoning. We apply our theory to a particular case, making guesses about what should be observed if our theory is correct. This process of operationalization is followed by the analysis of fit, which determines how closely observations match expectations. The degree of fit is used to make inferences from measured variables, associations, and samples to constructs, relationships, and populations. The function of inferential statistics, in this context, is to estimate the likely correspondence between sample statistics and population parameters.

The Roundabout Route of Failing to Reject

This chapter has presented data analysis as the evaluation of how well theory-based expectations fit observed data. Close correspondence tends to support the underlying theory, whereas pronounced deviations disconfirm some or all of it. This perspective does not mean that a researcher conducts a search to uncover information that aligns well with his or her expectations. This evidentiary strategy makes for lively debate in law, politics, and religion, but is nonscientific. Instead, one determines in advance the types of observations that would be consistent or inconsistent with one's theory, makes observations using methods that are free of one's theoretical predilections, and then objectively compares observations with expectations. In other words, the standards for what constitutes correspondence and deviation are established in advance of examining the data.

The assessment of fit between theory and data is organized according to an analytic strategy that at first glance seems convoluted: Instead of searching for data that confirm theory, one seeks disconfirming information, hoping to fail in this quest. To put it differently, the basic analytic task is to demonstrate that theory-based expectations are *not* met, that is, to reject one's hypotheses. Although it may be gratifying to reject someone else's theory, there is no satisfaction in rejecting one's own theory. Hence, the analyst vigorously tests the fit between theory and data, searching diligently for information that shows the theory to be incorrect, all the while hoping that these tests will fail, leaving his or her theory intact.

Demonstrating that theoretical expectations are met, the seemingly more straightforward approach, unfortunately, does not establish the veracity of the theory. Observations that are concordant with one's expectations support, but do not prove, the underlying theory. This limitation emerges because our observations are necessarily imperfect and incomplete. It is not possible to enumerate the entire population, measure the full spectrum of content implicit in a construct, or evaluate all instances in which two constructs may be related to one another. Because our observations are never exhaustive, we cannot be certain about what the next observation might reveal, or the following observation, ad infinitum. Accordingly, data analysis should be thought of as reducing uncertainty rather than incontrovertibly providing proof.

This situation is analogous to the legal concept of "beyond a reasonable doubt."

In his biography of atomic physicist Richard Feynman, Gleick (1992) describes the provisional nature of scientific knowledge even within the "hard" sciences:

> Physicists made a nervous truce with their own inability to construct unambiguous mental models for events in the very small world. When they used such words as *wave* or *particle*—and they had to use both—there was a silent, disclaiming asterisk, as if to say: "*not really.*" As a consequence, they recognized that their profession's relationship to reality had changed. Gone was the luxury of supposing that a single reality existed, that the human mind had reasonably clear access to it, and that the scientist could explain it. It was clear now that the scientist's work product—a theory, a model—interpreted experience and construed experience in a way that was always provisional. Scientists relied on such models as intensely as someone crossing a darkened room relies on a conjured visual memory. (p. 243)

In summarizing Feynman's views, Gleick (1992) writes, "He believed in the primacy of doubt, not as a blemish upon our ability to know, but as the essence of knowing. The alternative to uncertainty is authority, against which science had fought for centuries" (pp. 371–372).

Given that certainty is illusive, science generally settles for a lesser goal, minimizing uncertainty. As we shall see, this goal plays a pivotal role in theory-based data analysis.

Summary

Data analysis is a means of linking theory with observation. Theory is operationalized into a set of expectations or hypotheses about what should be observed if the theory is correct. This process utilizes deductive reasoning: applying general principles to a particular case. From the perspective of testing a focal relationship, we are primarily interested in hypotheses about associations among measured variables observed for a finite sample.

These hypotheses are then tested using various data analytic techniques, as described in subsequent chapters. These statistical procedures enable us to draw conclusions about the theoretical world. In particular, inferential statistics are used to draw conclusions about the probable nature of relationships among constructs in the population. This inference is based upon the degree of fit between the data expected under the theoretical model and the observed data. This aspect of data analysis relies upon inductive reasoning: deriving general principles from observations of a particular case.

A close correspondence between observed and expected data, however, does not prove that the theory is indeed correct. Although this one study produced results that are consistent with theory, a subsequent study may well produce results that deviate from these theoretical expectations. In these circumstances, the theory would be discredited, despite its one successful test, because it cannot be true for the entire set if it is invalid for any member of the set. Successful replication enhances confidence in the theory being tested, but there always remain untested cases, meaning that some uncertainty is inevitable.

Notes

1. Theory usually cannot be tested with the same set of observations that was used to formulate the theory: The information contained in those initial observations has, in effect, been used up. The assessment of how well theoretical predictions fit the empirical data, therefore, usually entails additional observation, referred to as *data collection*. Whereas the initial observations may have been made under a variety of circumstances, including situations of fortuitous happenstance, scientific data collection exclusively concerns observations that are purposeful, methodical, and standardized.
2. This statement assumes that measurement error is random. Systematic error can generate artifactual associations.
3. This equation may be more familiar as total score = true score + error.

3 Associations and Relationships

bivariate relationships

In preparation for the analysis of relationships, we start with a prerequisite: determining whether two variables are empirically associated with one another. This bivariate analysis ascertains whether the values of the dependent variable tend to coincide with those of the independent variable *in the manner predicted by theory*. This last phrase is critical. Not any association between the two variables will do: We are only interested in one particular association, the one predicted by theory. If we expect to find a linear association, for example, but find instead a U-shaped one, then our theory is discredited even though the two variables are empirically associated with one another. An essential consideration, then, is ensuring that the statistical and theoretical models are aligned with one another.

Association: The Basic Building Block

Association is an integral component of the logic used to establish causality. Two variables are causally related to one another if and only if the values of one variable regularly co-occur with those of the other variable (Little, 1991). As we shall see, other conditions are also required to sustain a causal argument, but these other conditions are relevant only in the presence of covariation between the independent variable and the dependent variable.[1] Similarly, empirically establishing association is a prerequisite to analyzing that association as a relationship. The analytic strategies described in this text assume that the focal independent and dependent variables covary. The first step in theory-based analysis is to put this assumption to the test.

Starting Small: Association Between the Two Focal Variables

The importance of bivariate analysis is sometimes overlooked because it has been superseded by multivariate analysis. This misperception is reinforced by scientific journals that report bivariate associations in passing, if at all. This practice creates the misleading impression that analysis begins at the multivariate level. In reality, the multiple-variable model rests upon the foundation laid by the thorough analysis of the two-variable model. The proper specification of the theoretical model at the bivariate level is essential to the quality of subsequent multivariate analysis. Similarly, univariate analysis forms the foundation for bivariate analysis. Variable distributions are crucial considerations in the selection of appropriate bivariate and multivariate statistical techniques. Finally, although there are exceptions to this generalization, it usually is not productive to conduct multivariate analysis in the absence of a bivariate association.

The reasonableness of beginning with bivariate analysis is so self-evident that it hardly seems to merit much comment. Indeed, most investigators start with bivariate analysis. Yet, most analyses that go off track are derailed at this junction.

These detours occur because numerous bivariate associations are typically estimated at the beginning of analysis, not just the one representing the focal relationship. Associations are estimated between the dependent variable and other independent variables, potential control variables, and so forth. One's eye is easily drawn to the strongest associations, which may or may not involve the variables of prime theoretical interest. In this manner, the focus of the analysis can shift subtly and unintentionally toward subordinate issues. This side trip is occasionally serendipitous, uncovering a hidden gold mine. More often, the resulting analyses are technically correct, but unfocused. The idea of a focal relationship helps to counterbalance this analytic drift.

Association as Covariation

Figure 3.1 illustrates the bivariate association between the focal independent and dependent variables as two overlapping circles. By convention, independent variables are designated as X and dependent variables as Y. The subscript f is used here to

Figure 3.1

Covariation in the Bivariate Model

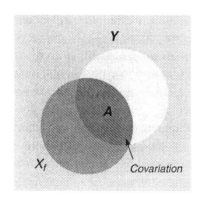

distinguish the focal independent variable (X_f) from other independent variables. Each circle represents the variation in one of these variables (expressed as a standard variance of 1 for convenience). The overlap (A) represents variation shared between the two variables, that is, their covariation, or the extent to which the values of one variable correspond to the values on the other variable. This quantity is often called the amount of the dependent variable that is "explained" or "accounted for" by the independent variable.

In assessing whether two variables are associated with one another, it is customary to designate one of these variables as independent and the other as dependent. Independent means that the variable is presumed to influence an outcome; it is capable of effecting change. Dependent variables are the outcomes we seek to explain. Dependent implies a cause-and-effect type of relationship. The idea that there is a connection between these variables is also conveyed by comparable terms such as "explanatory variables" and "outcomes" (Afifi and Clark, 1984, p. 17) or "causal variables" and "affected variables" (Judd, Smith, & Kidder, 1991, p. 28). This terminology emphasizes that the empirical association represents a dependency: The values on the two variables tend to coincide *because* one brings about the other.

Researchers are sometimes hesitant to apply the labels "independent" and "dependent" to variables because they are wary of imputing a causal interpretation to correlational data. Although circumspect, this cautious course may inadvertently obscure the correct line of analysis. As presented in this text, a central goal of most theory-based analysis is to ascertain whether an association can legitimately be interpreted as a relationship. This goal is impossible to attain if one is unwilling to posit a relationship—to treat one variable as dependent and one variable as independent.

The analytic strategies described in this text emphasize the area of covariation between the focal independent and dependent variables (*A* in Figure 3.1), specifically the extent to which this covariation is explained by various "third variables." This emphasis differs from the usual approach of explaining variation in the dependent variable *Y*. It emphasizes instead explaining the dependent variable's covariation with the focal independent variable. This distinction is subtle but crucial. The analytic strategies developed in this text place the focal relationship in the spotlight rather than the dependent variable. To put it differently, we are primarily interested in the connection between the focal independent and dependent variables rather than the dependent variable itself.

The usual approach, accounting for variation in the dependent variable, is well developed in numerous statistical and data analytic texts and does not require further explanation here. The same cannot be said for the elaboration of a single potential causal connection, hence the emphasis in this text on explicating the focal relationship. However, our interest in the focal relationship often flows from a fundamental concern with understanding the occurrence of the outcome or dependent variable. Thus, even within the framework presented in this text, explaining the dependent variable remains a vital goal.

Linear Associations

The association between two variables can take numerous forms. Often we mean that one variable increases as the other variable increases (referred to as a positive association) or, the reverse, that one variable decreases as the other variable increases (referred to as an inverse or negative association). This is the form of the simple correlation coefficient, the most frequently used measure of association when both variables are interval. The correlation coefficient assumes that the association approximates a straight line, which means that it is *linear*: A unit increase in the independent variable is accompanied by a fixed increment in the dependent variable, which is given by the slope of the line. Linear associations are illustrated in Figure 3.2 (See Analysis Journal: Linear Associations.).

Figure 3.2

Linear Associations: Mastery, Depressive Symptoms, and Income

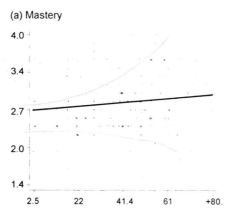

(a) Mastery

(b) Depressive Symptoms

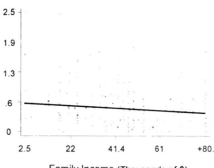

Family Income (Thousands of $)

Nonlinear Associations

The variables in an association need not be numeric, but may reflect instead a correspondence among qualities.[2] When the independent variable is composed of several categories, its association with the dependent variable necessarily takes a nonlinear form because the differences among categories are qualitative not quantitative. The idea of a unit increase, which is essential to the definition of linearity, implies equal intervals, a concept that simply does not apply to qualitative differences among categories.

For example, in the study of family caregivers to elderly persons suffering from dementia mentioned in Chapter 2, the relationship

ANALYSIS JOURNAL: Linear Associations

The data in Figure 3.2 are from the Los Angeles Survey of Adolescent Experience, introduced in Chapter 2. The independent variable in each graph is family income, and the two dependent variables are mastery, or a person's sense of being in control of what happens in his or her life, and symptoms of depression. Socioeconomic status (SES), mastery, and depression are key elements in our running empirical example, making it useful to introduce now their theoretical connections. One of the most consistent associations in psychiatric epidemiology is the inverse association between SES and various manifestations of a psychiatric disorder, including symptoms of depression. This association has been demonstrated repeatedly in studies spanning more than 50 years and using a variety of research methodologies. This inverse association has been attributed to both differences in exposure to stress and to differences in the impact of stress. Specifically, people with low levels of education, income, and occupational status are likely to be depressed because they are exposed to high levels of stress or because they have limited access to economic, personal, and social resources, assets that might otherwise offset the adverse impact of stress, or so the theory goes (Aneshensel, 1992).

Mastery refers to the perceived ability to bring about sought after outcomes and to avoid undesirable states. Success and failure are attributed to one's own personal characteristics rather than to outside influences such as fate: What I achieve in life is a result of my talent and hard work, not luck. The concept of mastery is quite similar to those of self-efficacy, internal locus of control, perceived control, perceived control of the environment, and instrumentalism, and opposite in meaning to fatalism, external locus of control, powerlessness, and learned helplessness (Mirowsky & Ross, 1984). Although mastery is a personal attribute, it is shaped, at least in part, by experiences that are connected to a person's status within society, including class-based opportunities, assets and achievements, and obstacles such as inadequate resources and opportunities, restricted alternatives, and jobs that limit autonomy (Pearlin & Radabaugh, 1976; Ross & Mirowsky, 1989). This line of reasoning is substantiated by numerous studies documenting a positive association between SES and mastery.

For the example in Figure 3.2, mastery was measured with a seven-item scale, including statements such as "I often feel helpless in dealing with the problems of life" and "What happens to me in the future mostly depends on me" (Pearlin & Schooler, 1978). Response categories were (1) strongly disagree, (2) disagree, (3) agree, and (4) strongly agree. Responses were reversed for negatively worded items so that a high score indicates a strong sense of mastery. The summated score was divided by the number of items to maintain the metric of the original response categories. In this sample of teens, the scale demonstrates very good internal consistency reliability ($\alpha = .76$); evidence of validity was presented previously (Pearlin & Schooler, 1978). The measure of depression is the Children's Depression Inventory, described in Chapter 2. SES is assessed here as annual family income in thousands of dollars.

The associations among these variables are shown as scatter plots. Each dot represents the observed values of the independent and dependent variables for a single teen. Although there are 877 adolescents in this study, only a few of the data points are shown because displaying all points makes the plot too cluttered. The estimated value of the dependent variable (mastery or depression) is plotted as a straight line based on its simple regression on the independent variable (family income). As can be seen in Figure 3.2, both mastery and depression are associated with family income, but in opposite directions. Compared to those of less advantaged economic backgrounds, teens living in families with higher incomes are more likely to feel in control of important events in their lives, on average, and are less likely to feel depressed.

The inverse association between depression and SES is sometimes attributed to social selection rather than to causation and is referred to as "social drift": Persons with psychiatric impairments are often unable to function well in social and occupational roles and, as a result, may experience downward social mobility. In general, there is little empirical support for this interpretation, except for severe impairments such as schizophrenia. In any event, this interpretation can be ruled out in this case because the social status of these adolescents is in reality the social status of their parents. If there is a causal connection, therefore, it necessarily goes from parental SES to adolescent depression and not in the reverse direction.

between the caregiver and care recipient is a qualitative variable; its possible values—husband caring for wife, wife caring for husband, daughter caring for mother, and so forth—differ in kind rather than in amount. These categories may be assigned a number score for convenience (e.g., 1 = husband, 2 = wife, 3 = daughter), but these codes do not have a numeric meaning. The same is true for the reasons these caregivers gave for relocating their relatives from home to a nursing home, for example, "Dad was too aggressive to handle at home." The association between these two variables entails assessing whether the percentage of caregivers citing aggression as a reason for admission differs from one category of relationship type to another, as illustrated in Figure 3.3.

Here we see that wives caring for husbands were more likely than other caregivers to give aggression as a reason for nursing home admission. Estimates of the association between reason for admission and caregiver type would not be affected by reordering the categories of relationship type in Figure 3.3 to (1) daughter-mother, (2) husband-wife, and (3) wife-husband: Physical aggression would remain most common among wives. The notion of linearity clearly does not apply to this association because caregiver type is not ordered from small to large.

The issue of nonlinear associations arises most clearly for interval variables because a nonlinear form is assumed for lower forms of measurement. For interval independent variables, however, linear models are often used automatically, by default, without much consideration of whether the theoretical relationship is expected to be linear. This tendency arises, at least in part, because theoretical models are often not specified in sufficient detail to make clear predictions about the form of the focal relationship.

Figure 3.3

Example of Association Between Qualitative Variables

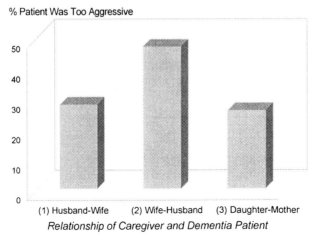

% Patient Was Too Aggressive

(1) Husband-Wife   (2) Wife-Husband   (3) Daughter-Mother

Relationship of Caregiver and Dementia Patient

An informative example of nonlinear association appears in the results of an epidemiological survey of a community sample of adults (aged 18 to 55) living in Toronto (Turner & Marino, 1994). This study describes the overall prevalence of depression in the community and the extent to which depression is more common among some subgroups of the community than among others. Age is a particularly interesting characteristic. Most research finds relatively high levels of symptoms among young adults, but results for the older population are inconsistent. Some researchers maintain that depression is especially common among the oldest old (over age 85) whereas other researchers disagree.

Some of the inconsistency across previous studies has been attributed to differences in the conceptualization and measurement of depression. Specifically, some studies have taken a psychiatric diagnostic approach, assessing major depressive disorder as either present or absent. Other studies have examined depression as a continuous rather than a discrete condition, using symptom inventories. The Toronto study used both approaches. Figure 3.4 shows a graph of the association of each of these measures of depression with age.

The observed age trend for depressive symptoms (Figure 3.4a) is distinctly nonlinear. Symptoms are most common among the youngest age group and least common in the oldest age group, but do not follow a pattern of steady decline between these extremes. Instead, there is a plateau in average symptom levels between the two middle-aged groups. The observed age trend for major depressive disorder (Figure 3.4b) also is distinctly nonlinear, although the pattern differs somewhat from the pattern for symptoms. Like symptoms, disorder is most common for the youngest adults and least common for the oldest adults. Unlike symptoms, however, a decline with age is apparent across the two middle-aged groups. Despite the continuity of decline, the trend is nonlinear because the rate of decline during the youngest period is noticeably steeper than the rate of decline thereafter. In other words, the slope of the line is not constant across all values of the independent variable, the defining characteristic of a linear association.

This study does not support the hypothesis that depression is especially prevalent among the elderly. Instead, it is most common among young adults. Several explanations have been given for the elevated levels of depression among young adults, including the extensive exposure of young people to social stressors. This period

Figure 3.4

Nonlinear Associations Between Depression and Age

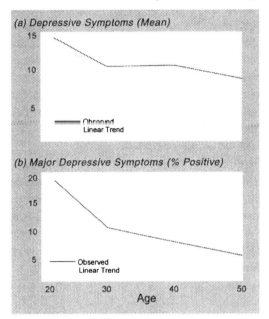

Source: Adapted from Turner and Marino (1994).

of the life course is characterized by transitions in many domains of life—ending education and beginning work life, starting a family of one's own, becoming financially independent, and so on. The sheer amount of stress makes this a difficult period. Moreover, young people have relatively little experience in coping with major stressors and may be more affected by these occurrences than older adults who have had more experience, in general, in coping with adversity.

Statistical Models of Association

Numerous statistical procedures are available to estimate the association between two variables. This variety reflects a key consideration in the selection of a method of analysis—the measurement properties of the independent and dependent variables. For example, correlation is the method of choice for analysis of two interval variables (when the association is thought to be linear), but it is not suitable for the analysis of two categorical variables. There are as many analytic techniques as there are combinations of variable types; indeed, there are more when sample size is added as a consideration. The bulk of bivariate analysis in the social sciences, however, is conducted with three techniques: χ^2 analysis of contingency tables for categorical variables; analysis of variance (ANOVA) for the assessment of mean differences between groups, especially if there is reason to expect a nonlinear association; and correlation coefficients for linear associations between numeric variables. The popularity of these three methods of analysis is due, at least in part, to their conceptual continuity with two of the most common methods of multivariate analysis, multiple linear regression (correlations and ANOVA) and logistic regression (contingency tables).

The selection of an analytic technique is also driven by a second criterion, the type of association one expects to find. For instance, do we think the association is linear or should it more closely resemble another form? Mirowsky (1985), for example, reports a U-shaped or parabolic association between emotional distress and the balance of power in marital decision-making. Husbands and wives are most distressed when their partners make all the decisions and least distressed when decision-making is shared. However, they also experience high distress when they are the ones making all the decisions. As decision-making moves from one extreme toward balance, distress decreases, but it increases again as decision-making moves from balance to the other extreme.

Although the first criterion, level of measurement, is empirical, the second, functional form, is theoretical. The expected functional form for marital decision-making was based on equity theory, whereas a simple self-aggrandizement model posits linear patterns. The theoretical model may not give information about the expected shape of the relationship between the focal independent and dependent variables, but asking whether theory predicts a linear association often opens the door to considering other possibilities.

Establishing Relatedness: The "Third Variable"

Although association does not necessarily imply relatedness, the presence of an empirical association often invites speculation about its possible causal meaning. Before attributing this meaning to an association, however, it is necessary to explore other possibilities. In general, we would like to eliminate these alternative interpretations of the focal relationship and thereby strengthen the interpretation that the covariation between X_f and Y signifies a relationship. In addition, we would like to connect the focal relationship to a more encompassing set of relationships to show that it fits theory-based expectations. Accomplishing these objectives requires multivariate analysis because third variables are essential to ruling out alternative explanations on the one hand and to explicating how the focal relationship fits within a more encompassing network of relationships on the other hand.

The most important aspect of the multivariate analysis, given our concentration on the focal relationship, is the extent to which the addition of a third variable alters the magnitude of the association between the focal independent and dependent variables. The addition of a third variable introduces a fundamental reorientation in how we think about the focal relationship. The bivariate association estimates the *total* association between the focal independent variable and the dependent variable. With the addition of another independent variable, this component becomes the *partial* association, the contribution of the focal independent variable *net* of the contribution of the third variable. This partial association is sometimes referred to as the effect of the variable with other factors "held constant," "being equal," "statistically controlled," or simply "controlled."

The Three-Variable Model

The addition of a second independent variable converts the bivariate analysis into a three-variable analysis. The three-variable model provides an estimate of the association between X_f and Y net of the effects of the other independent variable on Y and net of the association of the other independent variable with X_f. The latter point means that the analysis takes into consideration potential covariation among the independent variables.

The three-variable model is the basic building block of multivariate analysis. Larger models add terms that are, in most cases, repetitions of the three-variable model.[3] Furthermore, the analysis of the three-variable model is a necessary intermediate step in the development of a comprehensive model that simultaneously includes all relevant third variables. The impact of a single third variable is difficult to discern when numerous third variables are simultaneously added to the bivariate model. Consequently, each third variable that is earmarked for inclusion in a more comprehensive model should first be examined as part of a simple three-variable model.

The dynamics of the three-variable model are illustrated in Figure 3.5.[4] As before, Y is the dependent variable, and X_f is the focal independent variable. X_i is a second independent variable that functions as a third variable. The overlap among circles represents their covariation.

Note that each of the circles overlaps with the other two circles. One area of overlap $(A + B)$ corresponds to the total association between the focal independent variable and the dependent variable (which corresponds to area A in Figure 3.1). This association is now subdivided into a portion that is unique to $X_f (A)$ and a portion that is shared with $X_i (B)$. The latter, then, is covariation that is common to all three variables. This shared covariation occurs because the two independent variables are associated with one another $(B + D)$ and because the dependent variable is associated with both the focal $(A + B)$ and the other $(B + C)$ independent variable.

The total or zero-order association between X_f and Y is area $A + B$. The independent effect of X_f is A. The reduction in the total association that can be attributed to the third variable is B. This reduction can be expressed as a proportion of the original bivariate association, $B/(A + B)$. The combined area of $A + B + C$ represents the extent to which the dependent variable is explained by the two independent variables.

From the perspective developed in this text, we are particularly interested in area A. This is the portion of the focal association that

Figure 3.5

Covariation in the Three-Variable Model

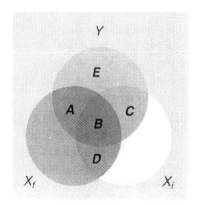

remains when the impact of the third variable is excluded from the impact of the focal independent variable. The three-variable model shown here, then, is a simple version of the exclusionary strategy for evaluating the internal validity of the focal relationship.

Figure 3.5 portrays one possible result from the analysis of the three-variable model. Here we see that each independent variable is associated with the dependent variable, but that about half of each of these associations is shared rather than separate. This large area of overlap (B) is the consequence of the moderate association ($B + D$) that exists between the two independent variables.

There are innumerable possible results for the analysis of the three-variable model. Two extreme possibilities are shown in Figure 3.6. To the left, the area of common covariation (B) is almost equal to the total covariation between the dependent variable and the focal independent variable ($A + B$). The two independent variables are so highly associated with one another ($B + D$) that neither variable has much of an independent effect on the dependent variable (A and C). This model illustrates a case of severe multicollinearity: One independent variable is almost indistinguishable from the other independent variable. Consequently, X_i accounts for most of the association between X_f and Y, but it does not add much to the explanation of Y beyond that attained by X_f.

At the other extreme (Figure 3.6b), each of the independent variables has a substantial separate effect on the dependent variable (A and C). Although the two independent variables are associated

Figure 3.6

Examples of Extreme Covariation in the Three-Variable Model

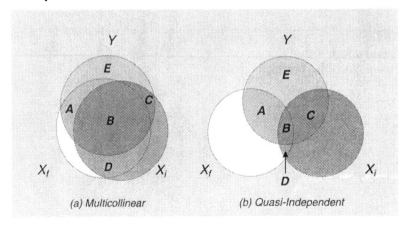

(a) Multicollinear   (b) Quasi-Independent

with one another, this association is weak $(B + D)$. As a result, most of their association with the dependent variable is not shared in common. In this model, X_i has limited potential to account for the relationship between X_f and Y. However, X_i makes a substantial contribution to explaining the occurrence of the dependent variable Y beyond that achieved by X_f.

The two examples shown in Figure 3.6, then, have opposite implications for explaining the focal relationship versus explaining the dependent variable. These are both valid and important analytic goals. Some variables, as we have just seen, attain one goal to the virtual exclusion of the other one.

The Multiple Variable Model

In most applications, we are concerned with the potential effects of several independent variables, not just one (bivariate model) or two (three-variable model) independent variables. When it is reasonable to suppose that a third variable alters the focal relationship, there are usually several potential third variables. Explanatory analysis, therefore, inevitably moves toward models containing multiple independent variables.

This situation is illustrated in Figure 3.7, which shows the intersection of the dependent variable (Y) with the focal independent variable (X_f) and with several other independent variables

Figure 3.7

Covariation in the Multiple Variable Model

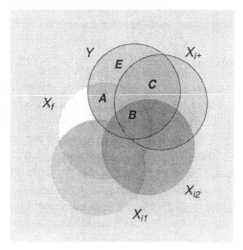

$(X_{i1}, X_{i2}, \ldots, X_{i+})$. The covariation exclusively attributable to the focal independent variable is given by area A, that part of the focal relationship that is not shared with any of the other independent variables. This area is smaller than that in the three-variable model (see area A in Figure 3.5) whenever X_f is correlated not only with X_{i1}, but also with $X_{i2}, \ldots, X_{i+}$. These additional variables encroach on the covariation that was initially attributed to X_f (see area A in Figure 3.1).

With regard to the exclusionary strategy for inferring related-ness, area A is crucial. It represents the impact of the focal independent variable on the dependent variable when the impact of other independent variables is excluded. Its presence, then, is essential to inferring relatedness. If A shrinks to zero, then this inference cannot be sustained. All of the original association would be due to covariation with other independent variables.

From the perspective of explaining Y, rather than the focal relationship between Y and X_f, E gives the "unexplained" portion of Y. It too is smaller than the area in the three-variable model because the additional independent variables are contributing to the explanation of Y.

The addition of a set of independent variables may alter the estimate of the focal relationship or leave it unchanged. The impact of adding several independent variables is an empirical question that can be answered only by estimating the multivariate model. The set of additional variables may reduce or eliminate the focal relationship, leave it unchanged, or, under some circumstances, increase it.[5] The actual outcome is a result of how strongly the independent variables are correlated with the dependent variable and of how strongly the independent variables are correlated with one another.

Contingent Relationships

Before concluding our discussion of third variables, it is necessary to consider at least briefly the functional form connecting these third variables with the focal relationship. The discussion so far is quite consistent with a linear, additive model. However, some third variables modify the effect of the focal independent variable on the dependent variable. This particular type of third variable is called an *effect modifier, moderator,* or *moderating variable*—equivalent terms. The general principle defining this class of contingent or conditional relationships is that the magnitude of the focal relationship varies across values of the modifying variable.

The third variables we have considered up to this point have altered the magnitude of the association between the focal independent and dependent variables, but the magnitude has been fixed or constant across all values of the third variable. The conditional relationship has a distinctively different impact on the focal relationship. Instead of changing the magnitude of the focal relationship from one size to another, the effect modifier enables the magnitude of the focal relationship to vary according to the values of the third variable.

An example of this type of interaction is found in a recent analysis of the impact of employment on criminal recidivism. The identification of effective means for deterring recidivism is of utmost social policy concern because of the large numbers of offenders who are released from custody and subsequently commit crimes at high rates. Work is thought to deter crime, at least in part, because the informal social controls of the workplace encourage conformity, and because stability and commitment are associated with working. Uggen (2000) recently examined whether a large-scale experimental employment program, the National Supported Work Demonstration Project, affected recidivism. The intervention offered minimum-wage jobs, mainly in the construction and service industries, in supervised crews of 8 to 10 workers.

Uggen reported an age-by-employment interaction. For the younger group, those in their teens and early twenties, the percentage who have not been arrested after 2 years is similar for the control group (55%) and the treatment group (54%), indicating no treatment effect as illustrated in Figure 3.8. For those 27 years or older, in contrast, there is a substantial difference between the control (54%) and treatment (65%) groups, indicating a meaningful and statistically significant employment effect.

As illustrated in Figure 3.8, the intervention, the focal independent variable, has an impact on recidivism, the dependent variable, for one value of the third variable, age, but not for the other. This pattern means that the impact of the focal independent variable is conditional on age. In this example, age is an effect modifier. Uggen points out that the significant impact of the job treatment program among older offenders contrasts sharply with the stylized cultural image of the "hardened criminal" and concludes that work appears to be a turning point in the life course for older, but not younger, offenders because work has different meanings at these stages of the life course.

Figure 3.8

Age and Employment Interaction for Criminal Recidivism

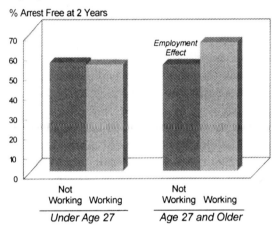

Source: Adapted from Uggen (2000).

Association and Causality

The familiar maxim, "correlation does not imply causality," means that not every correlation (or other form of association) can be interpreted as a relationship. Some correlations represent happenstance, for instance, and others are artifacts. This cautionary saying is sometimes misunderstood to mean that *t c* correlations can be causally interpreted. This belief is an overgeneralization of the limits of correlational research. By itself, a correlation might signify causation or it might signify any one of numerous alternatives. Eliminating alternatives to causality enables one to tentatively infer causality. From the perspective developed in this chapter, internal validity is strengthened when there is covariation remaining between the focal independent and dependent variables net of the influence of other independent variables (see A in Figure 3.7).

A thorough treatment of the philosophical grounds for claims of causality is beyond the scope of this volume, but a few points are essential to the analytic framework developed in this text. The concepts of necessary and sufficient are tacit components of intuitive or common sense understandings of the term "cause." In the extreme case, Y occurs if and only if X occurs; that is, X is both necessary *gt* sufficient to produce Y. This type of deterministic approach is derived from everyday experience in the physical world, a model that is generally not suitable for the explanation of human behavior.

Anyone who has ever felt compelled to act in a seemingly irrational manner, who has discovered unconscious motivations, or who finds himself or herself acting like his or her parents knows that human behavior is shaped by multiple factors that combine in complex ways, sometimes reinforcing and other times negating one another. In methodological terms, human behavior is *overdetermined*: multiple conditions are separately capable of bringing about an event, so that none of the circumstances is singly necessary, even though one of the set of circumstances is necessary (Little, 1991, p. 26). In other words, there are multiple routes to an outcome. Similarly, a set of conditions may be collectively sufficient even though no one member of the set is singly sufficient.

As a result, causation in the human sphere is inherently probabilistic rather than deterministic. Deterministic relationships follow the one-to-one correspondence embodied in the concepts of necessary and sufficient: A given condition always results in one specific outcome, which never occurs in the absence of this antecedent. The outcome in the probabilistic relationship, in contrast, is uncertain. Given a particular value of the independent variable, some values of the dependent variable are more likely to occur than others, but these values do not necessarily occur, and other values are possible, albeit less likely. In other words, the occurrence of X increases the probability that Y will occur, but does not guarantee that Y will occur.

I emphasize this point because our common sense understanding of cause and effect is deterministic and differs markedly from the probabilistic approach of the social sciences. The deterministic approach entails a one-to-one connection between independent and dependent variables. The value taken by the independent variable produces one and only one value on the dependent variable. In the probabilistic approach, this value is more likely to occur than other values, but other values, although less likely, may indeed occur.

One difficulty remains with the probabilistic model. It is never possible to rule out all conceivable alternatives to a causal interpretation: There always remains at least one more alternative not yet imagined. Consequently, we must be satisfied with eliminating alternatives that are most likely. The possibility of unknown and hence untested alternatives means that we must be content with a science built on degrees of uncertainty as distinct from absolute certainty. This impasse is not limited to data analysis in the social sciences, but permeates the entire scientific enterprise. In the words of physicist Richard Feynman (Gleick, 1992):

> Science is a way to teach how something gets to be known, what is not known, to what extent things are known (for nothing is known absolutely), how to handle doubt and uncertainty, what the rules of evidence are, how to think about things so that judgments can be made, how to distinguish truth from fraud, and from show. (p. 285)

Summary

The analysis of cause-and-effect relationships among constructs starts with the estimation of associations among measured variables. Numerous bivariate statistical techniques are used to determine whether association is present, that is, whether the values of one variable tend to correspond to the values of a second variable. The level of measurement of the two variables is one consideration in the selection of a technique, especially whether they are numeric or categorical. Equally important is the kind of association that is anticipated, a consideration that often centers upon the question of linearity. Specifying the correct form of association during bivariate analysis is essential because it forms the foundation for all subsequent multivariate analysis. Although bivariate association is insufficient to demonstrate causality, its presence is a stimulus for conducting the types of multivariate analyses that can sustain a causal inference.

These multivariate analyses introduce various third variables to clarify the meaning of the empirical association between the focal independent and dependent variables. From this perspective, third variables perform two complementary functions: they rule out explanations other than relatedness, and they shed light on how the focal relationship fits within a more encompassing set of theoretical relationships. The most crucial aspect of the analysis is the extent to which the addition of these third variables alters the estimate of the association between the focal independent and dependent variables. In addition, third variables are used to specify contingent relationships: the possibility that the focal relationship operates differently under some conditions or for some subgroups of the population. The following chapters consider in more detail the use of various types of third variables to strengthen the inference that the focal independent variable influences the dependent variable.

Notes

1. This covariation is not always immediately apparent. For example, it may be concealed by a suppressor variable, as discussed in Chapter 5.

2. The analysis of associations may also mix types of variables; for example, differences in quantities may be assessed across groups that differ qualitatively from one another.

3. This point is somewhat ambiguous for categorical variables because they are typically operationalized as a series of dummy variables in regression analysis. For example, the categories of ethnicity might be converted into a set of dichotomous dummy variables indicating whether the person is (1) African American, (2) Latino, (3) Asian American Pacific Islander, or (4) non-Latino White (or is in the excluded reference category of "other"). Although this technique uses four analytic variables, these variables represent only one construct and are most appropriately thought of as a single conceptual variable. Although this distinction may appear to be splitting hairs, it reduces confusion about the focal relationship when more than one term is used to operationalize the focal independent variable.

   Contingent relationships (see Chapter 8) also appear to be exceptions to this generalization because they are often modeled as interaction terms, which seem to constitute an additional variable, in our terminology, a "fourth variable." For instance, two independent variables might be multiplied and the product used to specify synergism in their effects on the dependent variable (see Chapter 8). This additional analytic variable (i.e., the product term) models the contingency between the two independent variables, but does not represent an additional construct. Thus, the theoretical model continues to have only two explanatory constructs even though three analytic variables are needed to operationalize their joint effects on the dependent variable.

4. Cohen and Cohen (1975, Chap. 3) use a similar Venn diagram in an excellent discussion of the partitioning of variance in multiple linear regression.

5. An increase in the estimate of the focal relationship typically means that one or more of the added variables acts as a suppressor.

4 The Focal Relationship: Demonstrating Internal Validity

Theories often revolve around a single hypothesized relationship that I refer to as the focal relationship. This relationship may not be immediately apparent because researchers typically articulate complex systems of interlocking relationships among numerous constructs. In other words, it is hidden among many other relationships. A brief perusal of any theory-based research journal demonstrates this complexity. Within its pages, one is likely to find at least one flowchart or path diagram whose convoluted interconnections are difficult to trace, much less comprehend. The emergence of computer graphics and color printers has intensified this trend. Nevertheless, one pivotal relationship can often be found within an intricate theory—a specific causal connection whose presence is indispensable to the integrity of the entire conceptual model.

The idea of a single focal relationship might be misinterpreted as simplistic. In actuality, the reverse is the case: Establishing that a *single* association is indicative of a *causal* relationship is a much more challenging task than demonstrating simultaneous associations among dozens of variables. The latter is a straightforward empirical task that requires only technical knowledge of multivariate statistics. The former requires, in addition, a plan of analysis that logically establishes relatedness. This chapter describes one technique for achieving this end, the strategic manipulation of "third variables."

The intricacy of large theoretical systems often camouflages the importance of any single association simply because there are multiple associations with which to contend. It is easy to be caught up in the specification of third variables and lose sight of the core relationship of theoretical interest. To minimize this possibility, I use the idea of the focal relationship to single out one independent variable as primary. The purpose of this focal independent variable is to capture the cause-and-effect relationship that is most central to the theory being researched. In this context, other independent variables can be seen as serving a single purpose—elucidating the focal relationship.

In this Chapter I consider the inference that a particular empirical association represents a cause-and-effect type of relationship, developing the underlying principles that guide the theory-based analysis of a focal relationship. I develop the rationale for including various types of third variables and the interpretation of their effects on the focal relationship. I then present an overview of the strategies for the analysis of the focal relationship. First, the exclusionary strategy seeks to rule out alternative explanations for the focal relationship, that is, explanations other than relatedness. Second, the inclusive strategy specifies the mechanisms or processes that link the focal relationship to other cause-and-effect type relationships. Having a glimpse of the entire analytic model is essential to understanding each of its component parts. These components are then taken up in detail in subsequent chapters.

Coincident Associations: The Exclusionary Third Variable

Third variables are used to evaluate the possibility that the empirical association between the focal independent and dependent variables does not represent a causal relationship. I refer to this type of alternative as *coincident* to emphasize the essential aspect of this explanation, namely that the two variables just happen to occur at the same time. The key feature to coincident associations is the absence of any connection between the two variables: they tend to co-occur, but their joint appearance is not the result of the focal independent variable influencing the dependent variable. Of the many sources of coincident association, the possibilities listed in Table 4.1 account for the preponderance of these kinds of associations.

Chance

The first possibility is that the two variables have been observed to co-occur simply by chance. This possibility is usually addressed

Table 4.1

Coincident Associations

- Chance
- Spuriousness
- Redundancy

with tests of statistical significance for the null hypothesis that there is no association between the two variables. In most applications, we hope to reject this hypothesis because theories tend to posit relationships rather than the absence of relationships. That is, we are hoping for a large test statistic, which corresponds to a very small probability level. This test gives the probability of rejecting the null hypothesis when it is true (Dixon & Massey, 1969, p. 82). This result means that it is extremely unlikely that the pattern of correspondence between the two variables would be observed in the sample if in truth the two variables were independent of each other in the population.

The specific null hypothesis varies from one statistical procedure to another, which tends to obscure the similarity in its function across procedures. For example, in analysis of variance (ANOVA), the null hypothesis is $H_0 : \mu_1 = \mu_2 = \cdots = \mu_j = \mu$, where μ is the mean of the dependent variable and j is the number of groups, which is the number of categories on the focal independent variable X_f. Similarly, for χ^2 it is $H_0 : p_1^+ = p_2^+ = \cdots = p_j^+ = p^+$, where p^+ is the proportion positive on the dependent variable and j is the number of categories on X_f.[1] For the correlation coefficient, the null hypothesis is $H_0 : r = 0$ where r is a measure of the linear association between the focal independent and dependent variables. Although these null hypotheses look very different, they perform the same basic function: Each declares that the independent and dependent variables are not associated with one another, a statement we usually hope to reject. When we cannot reject the null hypothesis, the focal relationship fails on the first criterion for relatedness—the presence of covariation.

Tests of statistical significance are statements about probabilities, however, not fact. Consequently, we inevitably remain uncertain. Chance always remains an alternative to relationship. In this sense, uncertainty can be seen as a reality of data analysis, not a deficiency of any particular analysis.

Spuriousness

The second type of coincident association is spuriousness, or the possibility that the observed association exists because both variables depend upon a third variable as illustrated in Figure 4.1. In other words, the values of the two variables coincide because they share a common cause. This common cause is X_c, where the subscript c signifies a *control variable* or *confounder*.[2] The empirical association between X_f and Y is shown here as a two-headed line to indicate that some or all of the original bivariate association between these variables is coincidental not causal.

The dashed line signifies that some portion of the empirical association between the focal independent and dependent variables is accounted for by the influence of the control variable on both of these variables. In the extreme case, the association between the focal independent and dependent variables disappears when the third variable is statistically controlled. This result means that these variables are independent of one another and only appear to covary when the control variable is not taken into consideration. At the other extreme, the addition of the control variable does not alter the estimate of the focal relationship, meaning that none of the original association is spurious.

Most analyses will contain more than one control variable because multiple sources of spuriousness must be considered. In the analysis of spuriousness, we usually hope that some or all of the focal association remains when all relevant control variables are included in the statistical model. Remember that we are interested in evaluating whether the focal relationship can be interpreted as a relationship. That interpretation fails if all of the association can be attributed to spuriousness. Thus, left over covariation between the focal independent and dependent variables strengthens the inference of relatedness because an alternative explanation for the observed association, spuriousness, has been dismissed.

Figure 4.1

The Case of Spuriousness

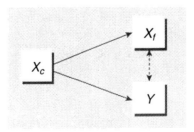

Matsueda, Gartner, Piliavin, and Polakowski (1992) provide an ingenious example of the use of control variables to address spuriousness in an analysis of whether the prestige of criminal occupations influences criminal behavior, an outcome of interest to most law-abiding citizens. The researchers note that seemingly high-prestige crimes share many features of high-prestige legitimate jobs, such as specialized technical skills, long-term commitment, ambition, reliability, high monetary returns, and connections to powerful people. This similarity, they contend, supports an occupational view of crime. Critics of this perspective, however, assert that the concept of a prestige hierarchy among criminal occupations is untenable. According to this critique, crime is caused by a lack of self-control, a personality trait that prevents criminals from developing stable organizations, including organized occupational roles and alternative status hierarchies.

To test this assertion, Matsueda and associates (1992) analyze data from a 1975 to 1978 panel survey of a sample of drug addicts and ex-offenders whose involvement in criminal activities offers a unique subcultural perspective. Respondents were asked how much respect they held for persons in each of 20 occupations using a thermometer scale ranging from 100 points, "very highly respected, looked up to and admired," to 0 points, "looked down on, very low." The average ratings for the 10 legal occupations included: doctor at 91, teacher at 85 through car washer at 54 and prison guard at 46. The ratings for illegal occupations were, for example, numbers banker at 43, hustler at 39 through pimp at 24 and purse snatcher at 10.

All of the criminal occupations were rated, on average, below the lowest ranked legal occupation. The ratings within the illegal occupations, however, follow a pattern similar to that seen within the legal occupations. Specifically, illicit occupations that produce more income and require more skill receive more respect (e.g., numbers banker) than occupations that lack these qualities (e.g., purse snatcher).

Matsueda and colleagues (1992) also examine whether the status accorded criminal occupations influences criminal behavior, the focal relationship. They find that status rankings are positively associated with subsequently engaging in unlawful activities (at least among persons who have previously engaged in criminal activity). However, the researchers point out that this association may be biased by spuriousness or by social desirability.[3] Their analytic strategy seeks to rule out these alternate explanations and thereby enhance their conclusion that attributing prestige to criminal activity increases the likelihood of engaging in such activity.

The investigators note that the same exogenous forces that cause individuals to assign high prestige to criminal occupations may also compel them to engage in illegal activity. To counter this objection, they include a set of characteristics known to affect criminal activity: select demographic characteristics, peer influences, and prior criminality. As shown in Figure 4.2, the focal relationship (*a*) between prestige and criminal behavior may be spurious if these control variables influence both the status accorded criminal occupations (*b*) and criminal behavior (*c*).

One control variable plays an especially important role in this analysis, prior criminality. Matsueda and associates (1992) argue that the inclusion of prior criminal behavior controls for unobserved individual heterogeneity, which refers to unmeasured confounders. The universe of potential confounders is infinite, making it impossible to measure all potential sources of spuriousness, which inevitably leaves some uncertainty about the focal relationship. Although unmeasured and unknown confounders obviously cannot be included explicitly in the model, their effects

Figure 4.2

An Example of Potential Spuriousness: Prior Criminal Behavior

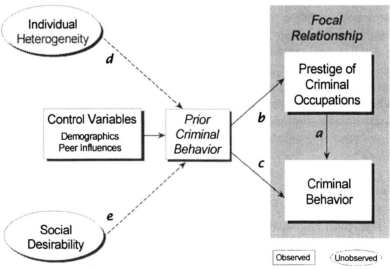

Source: Adapted from Matsueda et al. (1992).

can be removed from the estimation of the focal relationship. The procedure used in this analysis assumes that these confounders influence not only future criminal activity, but past criminal activity as well (d); their effects operate indirectly through the continuity of criminal behavior over time (c). Thus, the inclusion of prior criminality removes the effect of unmeasured confounders even though these variables themselves are not included in the model. This strategy is desirable because unmeasured individual heterogeneity is inevitable.

In addition, Matsueda and associates (1992) contend that the inclusion of prior criminal activity also controls unobserved social desirability effects, the tendency to give answers that are perceived to be desirable to others irrespective of whether the answers are true. The investigators argue that social desirability effects on contemporaneous reports of prior illegal activity (e) should be as high as or higher than their effects on future reports of subsequent illegal activity. Because social desirability effects are indirect through prior criminality, the inclusion of prior criminality controls social desirability. This aspect of the analysis illustrates the use of control variables to remove the effects of methodological artifacts other than spuriousness.

Demonstrating that the association between prestige and behavior persists net of prior criminal activity thus diminishes the likelihood that the focal relationship is either spurious or a product of social desirability reporting. Matsueda and colleagues (1992) demonstrate this outcome for both criminal activity and for earnings from these activities, findings that buttress their contention that the status accorded criminal occupations by persons who have previously engaged in criminal activity influences their propensity to engage in additional criminal behavior.

Redundancy

In spurious associations, the appearance of relatedness is deceptive, an illusion created by the simultaneous occurrence of two variables. Similar sorcery is at work with redundant associations. In this situation, the appearance of relationship is the result of covariation between two independent variables, only one of which influences the dependent variable. Figure 4.3 illustrates the redundant association.

In the redundant association, the third variable X_i acts as another independent variable, hence the subscript i. The redundant

Figure 4.3

The Case of Redundancy

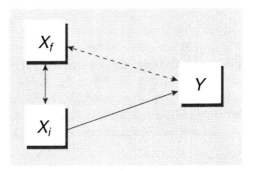

variable is X_f, which appears to influence Y because it covaries with X_i. The association between X_f and Y overlaps with the relationship between X_i and Y. This redundancy is the result of the tendency for X_f and X_i to co-occur. The two-headed arrow between X_f and X_i signifies that no causal influence is attributed to the covariation between these two variables. In other words, redundant associations are the result of independent variables that just happen to be correlated. In this instance, an extraneous variable is mistaken for an independent variable because it is associated with another independent variable. The dashed line between X_f and Y signifies that some or all of the original association between these variables has been accounted for by the addition of X_i. In excluding the influence of X_i, we hope that some or all of the focal association remains. If the estimate of the focal relationship is unchanged by the addition of the other independent variable, then X_f is not redundant with X_i.

The other independent variable X_i often represents a theoretical explanation that competes with the theory being tested. This type of influence should be taken into consideration in estimating the impact of the focal independent variable because we are concerned with its unique contribution to explaining the dependent variable. In this context, other independent variables serve to identify aspects of the dependent variable that are accounted for by other cause-and-effect relationships, that is, alternatives to the focal relationship.

Multiple independent variables are used in most analyses because there usually are several aspects of alternative theories that need to be taken into consideration. The use of multiple independent variables enhances the inference of relatedness by demonstrating that the focal relationship persists when several other causal influences are taken into account.

   In addition, these variables usually help to account for variation in the dependent variable irrespective of whether they alter the focal relationship. Although we are primarily interested in evaluating the focal relationship, this objective should not obscure the allied goal of explaining the occurrence of the dependent variable.

   The study of the status of criminal occupations conducted by Matsueda and colleagues (1992), just used as an example of spuriousness, also illustrates the concept of redundancy. This research tests two theories that make distinctly different predictions about associations between status rankings and behavior. Subcultural theory contends that criminal behavior depends only upon the status accorded criminal occupations, not the status accorded conventional occupations. Individuals who consider criminal occupations to be prestigious are thought to be more immersed in a criminal subculture, more likely to adopt a criminal lifestyle, and thus, more motivated to achieve status by engaging in criminal activity. Conventional occupations, especially high-status ones, are seen as being irrelevant to criminal activity because disenfranchised persons lack legitimate opportunities for success. As illustrated in Figure 4.4, only one positive association is predicted.

   Pseudo-cultural theories, in contrast, predict that criminal behavior is unrelated to the rankings of criminal occupations but varies inversely with the status accorded conventional occupations.

Figure 4.4

An Example of Redundancy: Alternative Theories of Criminal Behavior

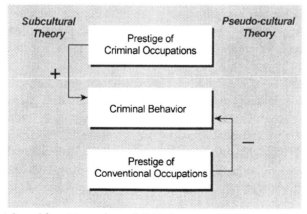

Source: Adapted from Matsueda et al. (1992).

This perspective negates the concept of a prestige hierarchy among criminal occupations, contending that criminal subgroups are merely pseudo-cultures, too disorganized to constitute a viable alternative to mainstream culture. However, prestige rankings of conventional occupations should have a negative correlation with criminal behaviors because these rankings represent a commitment, albeit weak, to mainstream culture—a commitment that should act as a deterrent to rule-breaking behavior.

This study provides a clear illustration of the explanatory efficacy gained by the specification of an alternative theory. Each theory predicts that criminal behavior is associated with only one type of occupational prestige ranking, and the type differs between theories. Equally important, each theory predicts an absence of association for the other type of occupational prestige ranking, directly contradicting the prediction of the other theory. It is somewhat unusual to predict the absence of association, but this strategy pays large dividends in this instance because it makes the theoretical predictions mutually exclusive. Results that are consistent with the subcultural perspective are necessarily inconsistent with the pseudo-cultural perspective and vice versa.

Notice that both of the status rankings are necessary to rule out the alternative theory. If we adopt the perspective of subcultural theory, the focal relationship is between the status of criminal occupations and criminal behavior. The status of conventional occupations operationalizes the competing pseudo-cultural theory and acts as an additional independent variable. Although a positive association between the status of criminal occupations and criminal behavior is consistent with subcultural theory, the inference of relatedness is strengthened if the alternative theory is ruled out by showing no effect of the status ranking for conventional occupations on behavior. The reverse holds if we adopt the perspective of pseudo-cultural theory.

The empirical results from this study support the subcultural theory. Net of background and experience variables, participation in crime, operationalized as any illegal earnings, increases as the prestige of criminal occupations increases. The same result is found for the frequency of criminal activity, operationalized as the amount of illegal earnings. Participation in unlawful activities is independent of the status given to conventional occupations, however, as is the frequency of participation. These results not only support the subcultural perspective, they disconfirm the pseudo-cultural perspective, at least among this sample of unemployed drug addicts and ex-offenders. These associations are net of relevant control variables as described above in the section on spuriousness. The investigators conclude that those who accord greater prestige to criminal occupations are more likely to engage in crime and to reap greater returns from it. However, they caution that other processes may operate among conventional populations in which opportunities for legitimate success are available.

Criteria for an Effective Exclusionary Variable

As noted above, our primary analytic interest is the impact on the focal relationship of adding an additional independent variable. The added variable will *not* alter this estimate unless both of the criteria in Table 4.2 are met.[4] In practice, many of the third variables that are considered in applied multivariate analysis meet one criterion, but not the other. Additional independent and control variables often turn out to be associated with the dependent variable, but separate from the focal independent variable or vice versa.

The addition of variables that meet only one of these criteria *cannot* alter the estimate of the focal relationship. Third variables associated with Y but not with X_f help to account for the occurrence of the dependent variable Y, but do so without altering the focal relationship. These variables perform a valuable function, enhancing our understanding of the outcome under investigation; however, this explanatory function is distinct from the goal of establishing the focal relationship as a cause-and-effect type of relationship.

Third variables that are associated with X_f but not with Y do not contribute to the explanation of the dependent variable. These variables are superfluous, then, because they do not advance our understanding of either the focal relationship or the outcome. They merely consume degrees of freedom and statistical power without

Table 4.2

Criteria for an Effective Exclusionary Variable

1. The added variable (X_c or X_i) must be associated with the dependent variable (Y), and
2. The added variable (X_c or X_i) must be associated with the focal independent variable (X_f).

improving the analysis. However, their inclusion in the analysis is sometimes justifiable to maintain comparability with previous research or to demonstrate that the variable is immaterial.

A variable that meets the two criteria for an effectual third variable may alter the estimate of the focal relationship, but this result is not a necessary consequence of its association with the other two variables. In other words, the added variable may be associated with both the focal independent variable and the dependent variable, but not appreciably alter the connection between these two variables.

Whether this result occurs or not is an empirical question. The additional variable may reduce or eliminate the focal relationship, leave it unchanged, or, under some circumstances, increase its magnitude. Thus, the two criteria for an effective exclusionary variable are necessary but not sufficient to produce spuriousness or redundancy. Determining whether additional third variables alter the estimate of the focal relationship is the raison d'être for the analysis plan described in this text.

Spuriousness and redundancy pose a difficult analytic challenge. The difficulty concerns the proper selection of third variables. For every empirical association between an X_f variable and a Y variable, there exist not one but many X_c and X_i variables. Testing every potential third variable inappropriately capitalizes on chance associations. Moreover, the list of potential third variables is limitless, making it impossible to conduct an exhaustive test. At the same time, the failure to specify a true confounder is a serious specification error insofar as a spurious association then gives the appearance of being a plausible relationship. The same holds true for redundancy. The selection of appropriate control and other independent variables, therefore, is of utmost importance. As we shall see, this selection is based on the results of previous research and on theory.

In summary, establishing that an empirical association can be interpreted as a relationship requires first that the possibility of a coincident association be addressed. In addition to tests of statistical significance, this task entails the systematic analysis of potential confounders to deal with spuriousness and other independent variables to sort out redundancy. Although it is not possible to rule out every alternative, systematic and rigorous analysis usually can eliminate the most plausible alternatives to relatedness. Each time a potential alternative is eliminated as the source of the empirical association between the focal independent and dependent variables, the case for its causal interpretation becomes that much stronger.

Causal Connections: The Inclusive Third Variable

Elements of the Inclusive Strategy

The elaboration model is inclusive in the sense that additional variables are brought into the analytic model to clarify the meaning of the focal relationship. The inclusion of these additional variables helps to establish internal validity, that is, the inference that the focal independent variable influences the focal dependent variable. These additional variables fall into three broad categories: *antecedent, intervening,* and *consequent.* These variables clarify the focal relationship by explaining, respectively, the occurrence of the focal independent variable, the connection between the focal independent and dependent variables, and the sequelae of the dependent variable. The intervening variable, which delineates the causal mechanism connecting the focal independent and dependent variables, is the most critical and has received by far the most attention in the research literature. Antecedent and consequent variables are seen less frequently, but also facilitate the interpretation of the focal relationship. The inclusive strategy seeks to establish that the focal relationship can be interpreted as a cause-and-effect relationship by linking this one relationship to a network of other cause-and-effect relationships.

The reference point for these terms—antecedent, intervening, and consequent—is the focal relationship. As can be seen in Figure 4.5, the focal relationship lies at the center of a causal nexus: antecedent variables occur before both X_f and Y; intervening variables occur between X_f and Y; and consequent variables occur after both X_f and Y. These variables are included in the analytic model to ascertain whether the association between the focal independent and dependent variables fits within a system of other relationships that is consistent with the theory guiding the analysis.

Antecedent, Intervening, and Consequent Variables

An antecedent variable logically precedes X_f, the independent variable of interest, as indicated in Figure 4.5. It does not explain away

Figure 4.5

Inclusive Variables

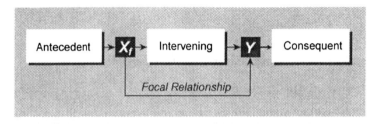

the focal relationship between X_f and Y, but instead clarifies the influences that precede it. For antecedent variables, the dependent variable is X_f, not Y. The antecedent variable, therefore, need not be associated with Y. The analytic goal for antecedent variables is to validate the focal relationship by demonstrating that the occurrence of X_f is associated with its theoretical origins. Establishing this connection entails procedures identical to those described for the focal relationship. Specifically, covariation is necessary and the alternatives of spuriousness and redundancy should be dismissed. The antecedent variable is summarized in Table 4.3.

Consequent variables similarly help to establish the internal validity of the focal relationship by demonstrating that Y produces effects anticipated by the theoretical model. Consequent variables logically succeed the dependent variable and clarify the continuation of the causal sequence within which the focal relationship is embedded. The focal dependent variable influences the occurrence of the consequent variable, as indicated in Figure 4.5, meaning that these two variables need to covary with one another. Moreover, this

Table 4.3

Functions of Inclusive Variables

Type of Variable	Conceptual Placement	Expected Impact on the Focal Relationship	Necessarily Associated With X_f	Necessarily Associated With Y
Antecedent	Before X_f	Unchanged	■	
Intervening	After X_f and before Y	Decreased	■	■
Consequent	After Y	Unchanged		■

covariation should not be the result of spuriousness or redundancy. Given that Y functions as the independent variable with regard to the consequent variable, the consequent variable does not need to covary with the focal independent variable X_f. Like the antecedent variable, the inclusion of a consequent variable does not alter the focal relationship, but rather enhances our understanding of it.

Intervening variables decipher how the focal relationship works. These variables specify the causal mechanisms that generate the observed association. As can be seen in Figure 4.5, the intervening variable is simultaneously a dependent and an independent variable: It both depends upon X_f and influences Y. The intervening variable, therefore, needs to be associated with both variables in the focal relationship, as shown in Table 4.3. It differs, then, from the antecedent and consequent variables and, in this regard, resembles the third variables used in the analysis of spuriousness and redundancy. Intervening variables mediate the focal relationship and help to explain how the relationship operates. These variables are used to assess the extent to which the observed association between the independent and dependent variables is produced by theoretical mechanisms.

The analytic goal with regard to intervening variables is diametrically opposite to the goal for spuriousness or redundancy. For intervening variables, the goal is to explain away some or all of the empirical association between the focal independent and dependent variables. The inclusion of intervening variables, therefore, should reduce the magnitude of the focal relationship and may fully account for it.[5]

The focal relationship is diminished in magnitude because we have taken into consideration the pathways through which the focal independent variable influences the focal dependent variable. This procedure enhances our understanding of the meaning of the association between the focal independent and dependent variables. To the extent that these causal mechanisms are consistent with the theoretical model, the inference of relatedness for the observed association is enhanced.

It must be emphasized that the labels identifying the functions of variables—independent, dependent, control, antecedent, intervening, and consequent—have meaning only within the context of a specific theoretical model and research question. Function is not inherent to the variable. For example, a variable that serves as a dependent variable in one analysis might well be treated as an independent variable in another analysis.

This point can be illustrated by a recent analysis of potential reciprocal relationships between the racial composition of cities and crime rates. Liska and Bellair (1995) point out that research generally has examined crime as something to be explained, not as the explanation of something, which in this case is the racial composition of neighborhoods. Most previous research has assumed that crime is influenced by racial composition because crime is the outcome of social disorganization, which happens to be more common in areas in which racial minorities reside. Other research has assumed that economic deprivation leads to frustration and crime, with deprivation being more common among nonwhites or that some subcultures are more prone to violence than others. The two-headed arrows at the left of Figure 4.6 suggest these possibilities, without specifying any causal interpretation among these variables.

In contrast, Liska and Bellair (1995) argue that crime, especially violent crime, influences people's decisions about where to play, work, and live, and, thus, shapes the social, economic, and racial composition of residential areas. In their model, racial segregation is the dependent variable, not the independent variable, whereas violent crime is conceptualized as being independent rather than dependent. Their empirical analysis demonstrates that violent crime shapes the racial composition of cities by affecting migration, especially flight of whites from central cities. The researchers conclude that previous research may have overestimated the effect

Figure 4.6

Violent Crime and the Racial Segregation of Cities

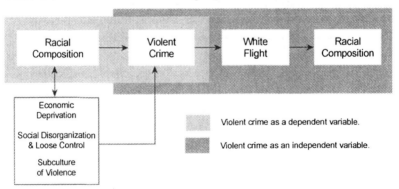

Source: Adapted from Liska and Bellair (1995).

of racial composition on violent crime by failing to take into account the reciprocal effects of crime rates on racial composition.

This example illustrates that the designation of variables as independent or dependent is based on the theory guiding the analysis. Similarly, classifying some variables as antecedent, intervening, or consequent is contingent upon selecting one relationship as the focal relationship. Moreover, it should be evident that the identification of one relationship as focal is a theoretical matter. In other words, the analytic function of a variable is not inherent but emerges from the theoretical placement of one variable relative to another. The focal relationship is a useful device because it provides a structure for interpreting the connections among the multiple variables in the analysis but it should not be reified.

An Example of Exclusionary and Inclusive Third Variables

For an example of the use of third variables to establish internal validity, we return to the association between mental illness and violence introduced as a theoretical model in Chapter 1 (see Figure 1.2). Link, Monahan, Stueve, and Cullen (1999) contend that this association arises when mental illness leads to experiences of feeling threatened or being under the control of some superior force, for example, a divine directive to kill someone. These situations prompt a violent response or override internal controls on the expression of violence because the situations are experienced as real despite being aspects of delusions and hallucinations, that is, not experienced as real by others. Link and colleagues (1999) argue that if one disregards the irrationality of psychotic symptoms, then violence unfolds in a rational or at least understandable fashion. In the absence of "threat/control-override" symptoms, other severe psychotic symptoms, such as hearing one's thoughts spoken out loud, although extremely disturbing and disruptive, are not likely to lead to violence.

To test these ideas, the researchers analyzed data from a psychiatric epidemiological survey of young adults ($N = 2,678$) conducted in Israel. Diagnostic data were from a structured clinical interview and symptoms were assessed in an earlier screening interview. Although these assessments are associated, many persons who do not meet diagnostic criteria experience symptoms, and most people who experience symptoms do not meet diagnostic criteria. The analysis begins with the estimate of the focal relationship shown in Table 4.4, Model 1, as an odds ratio. The focal independent variable is mental illness, operationalized here as having a psychotic/bipolar disorder (D+) versus not having this type of disorder (D−).[6] There are two dependent variables—fighting and use of a weapon—both assessed as present or absent and analyzed with logistic regression. The odds of being violent are the number of persons who were violent divided by the number who were not violent. The odds ratio is the ratio of these odds for two groups, those with disorder and those without disorder. The formula for this odds ratio, then,

Table 4.4

Psychiatric Disorder and Violence: An Example of Adding Several Third Variables

Independent Variables	Odds Ratios[a]					
	Fighting			Weapon Use		
	Model 1	Model 2[b]	Model 3[b]	Model 1	Model 2[b]	Model 3[b]
Psychotic/bipolar disorder (/no)	3.35***	2.94***	1.62	6.82***	5.99***	2.01
Female (/male)	—	.38***	—	—	.27***	—
North African (/European)	—	1.65***	—	—	.77	—
Age (years)	—	.90***	—	—	.90*	—
Education (years)	—	.90***	—	—	.83**	—
Social desirability scale	—	.49*	—	—	.21**	—
Substance abuse disorder (/no)	—	2.75***	—	—	3.56*	—
Antisocial personal disorder (/no)	—	2.59**	—	—	3.56*	—
Threat/control override symptoms (count)	—	—	1.86***	—	—	2.03***
Other psychotic symptoms (count)	—	—	1.02	—	—	1.07

Source: Adapted from Link et al. (1999).
[a]$N = 2,678$.
[b]Adjusted odds ratios.
*$p < .05$. **$p < .01$. ***$p < .001$.

is $(N_{D+}^{Violent}/N_{D+}^{Not\ Violent})/(N_{D-}^{Violent}/N_{D-}^{Not\ Violent})$. An odds ratio of 1.00 indicates no association because the odds ratio is a multiplicative measure of association and because $a \times 1.00 = a$. Values between 0 and 1.00 indicate an inverse or negative association whereas values greater than 1.00 indicate a positive association.

Compared to persons without these disorders, those with psychotic/bipolar disorders have about three times greater odds of having been in a fight and almost seven times greater odds of having used a weapon (Model 1). The p values test the null hypothesis that mental illness is not associated with acts of violence, which, in this instance, is equivalent to the assertion that the odds ratio equals 1.00. The small p value means that the null hypothesis is rejected with a high level of confidence. Thus, the hypothesized focal relationship is empirically supported.

To establish this association as a relationship, several alternatives should be considered. The empirical association may be spurious, the result of the joint dependency of psychotic/bipolar disorder and violence on shared characteristics, such as gender. Then again, the association may merely reflect a tendency to give socially desirable answers to survey questions—to deny both symptoms and violent acts. The last possibility considered by the investigators is that the association is not causal in nature, but reflects instead comorbidity, the simultaneous occurrence of substance abuse or antisocial personality disorder. In this instance, violence may be due to the comorbid conditions, not to the psychotic/bipolar disorder.

To rule out these alternatives, Link and associates (1999) introduced several third variables, as shown in Table 4.4, Model 2. In these multivariate models, the odds ratios for the focal independent variables are adjusted for the effects of all other variables in the equation. All of the background variables are significantly associated with each dependent variable, with the exception of national origin for weapon use. Fighting and weapon use are more common among males, among young persons, and among those with little education. Moreover, persons who tend to give socially desirable answers also tend to report that they have not been in a fight and have not used a weapon. Finally, violence is much more likely to occur among persons who are substance abusers or who have antisocial personality disorder.

Although these third variables contribute to the explanation of the dependent variables, these variables leave most of the disorder-violence association intact. They produce only a 12.2% reduction in the size of the odds ratios for fighting [(3.35 − 2.94)/3.35] and weapon use [(6.82 − 5.99)/6.82]. For each dependent variable, the adjusted odds ratio remains large and highly statistically significant. Thus, sociodemographic characteristics, social desirability responding, and comorbidity are indeed associated with violent acts, but these attributes explain only a small portion of the association between psychotic/bipolar disorder and violence. This exclusionary strategy enhances internal validity by demonstrating that the association persists when several alternative explanations are taken into consideration. This test cannot be definitive, however, because other possibilities necessarily remain untested.

The investigators also tested the mechanism by which mental illness purportedly results in violence, illustrating the inclusive strategy. Two types of symptoms—"threat/control override" and "other psychotic"—were added to the original bivariate model as intervening variables, as shown in Model 3 of Table 4.4. The adjusted odds ratio for psychotic/bipolar disorder is substantially reduced and is not statistically significant for either dependent variable. The adjusted odds ratio is statistically significant for threat/control override symptoms, but not for other psychotic symptoms. This pattern of results means that disorder increases the risk of violent behavior only to the extent that the person feels threatened or under the control of external forces. These results bolster the internal validity of the focal relationship because it is empirically accounted for by the hypothesized causal mechanism.

Notice the difference in results between Model 2 and Model 3. The addition of control and other independent variables in Model 2 leaves most of the focal relationship intact, whereas the addition of intervening variables in Model 3 fully accounts for the focal relationship. These are the results we expect with exclusionary versus inclusive strategies. Both of these findings support the inference that the focal relationship is a relationship, even though they differ with regard to impact on the effect of the focal independent variable.

One seemingly peculiar finding should be pointed out: For weapon use, the odds ratios are about the same size for psychotic/bipolar disorder and threat/control override symptoms, but only the coefficient for the latter is statistically significant. This discrepancy is clarified by comparing the units of measurement. A single symptom is a much smaller unit of measurement than the presence of a diagnosed disorder, meaning that these odds ratios signify effects of very different magnitudes.

To recap, for our purposes, this investigation into mental illness and violence demonstrates key features of theory-based data analysis. First, the bivariate association in Model 1 demonstrates that the hypothesized focal relationship is feasible because the independent and dependent variables covary with one another in a way that is unlikely to be a chance occurrence. Second, most of this empirical association remains when alternative explanations for the association are statistically controlled (Model 2). Third, the empirical association appears to be entirely due to the hypothesized causal mechanism (Model 3). In combination, these analyses provide support for the inference that there is a relationship between mental illness and violence and that this relationship is the result of the specific mechanism described by theory.

Substantively, Link and associates (1999) conclude that these findings counter the damaging social stereotype that persons suffering from mental illness are violent, a stereotype that produces rejection, exclusion, and stigmatization. In particular, they note that only psychotic/bipolar disorders are associated with increased risk of violent acts. Furthermore, the elevation in risk appears to be limited to instances when the person feels threatened or subject to external dominance.

Explaining Y Versus the Focal Relationship

Figure 4.7 shows the difference between explaining the outcome or dependent variable and explaining the focal relationship. The outcome Y is represented here as a pie chart. The shaded portion of the pie chart signifies the variation in Y that is accounted for by the entire set of independent variables (including X_f). The unshaded portion of the pie chart is the variation in Y that remains unexplained.

In this illustration, only a moderate amount of the variation in the dependent variable has been explained by the entire set of independent variables. Most of the outcome is left unexplained (the unshaded area of the pie chart). This result does not mean that the explanatory model is a failure. Most multivariate models in the social sciences account for well under half of the variation in the dependent variable. This incomplete explanation is consistent with the idea that explanation is probabilistic not deterministic.

Figure 4.7

Explaining Versus the **Focal Relationship**

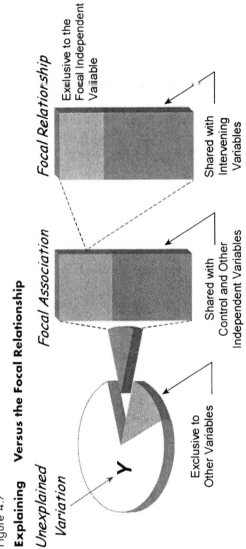

Unexplained Variation

Focal Association

Focal Relationship

Exclusive to the Focal Independent Variable

Shared with Intervening Variables

Shared with Control and Other Independent Variables

Exclusive to Other Variables

Y

The extracted slice of the pie chart represents the total association between the focal independent and dependent variables. This association has two components, as illustrated by the first column: a part that is exclusively due to the focal independent variable and a part that the focal independent variable shares with other independent and control variables. The exclusionary analytic strategy is designed to ascertain how much of this column is accounted for by the covariation of the focal independent variable with these other variables and how much remains. The remainder is the portion of the association that is neither spurious nor redundant, the portion we would like to interpret as a cause-and-effect type of relationship.

Aside from their shared association with the focal independent variable, the other variables are also independently associated with the dependent variable. This shaded slice is not extracted from the pie chart because it is not part of the focal relationship. It indicates that these other variables contribute to the explanation of the outcome in ways that have nothing to do with the focal relationship. These associations usually are of considerable substantive interest in their own right because an allied goal of the analysis is, after all, to account for Y.

The portion of the focal association that is not accounted for by the control and other independent variable is extracted from the first column and becomes the second column. The term "relationship" is applied to this column because the covariation it represents is neither spurious nor redundant and, therefore, seems to reflect a cause-and-effect type of relationship. It too encompasses two components. The first is covariation with the dependent variable that the focal independent shares with intervening variables. In accounting for some or all of the focal relationship, these intervening variables explain how the focal independent variable exerts its impact on the dependent variable. We hope that this component is relatively large because it shows that the mechanisms and processes described by theory do indeed produce the expected effects. This element of the inclusive strategy fills in the causal sequence separating X_f and Y, and in doing so, strengthens internal validity. The second component is covariation unique to the focal independent variable, that is, effects that are not mediated by intervening variables, at least the ones included in the analysis.

In practice, the goals of explaining Y versus explaining the focal relationship have diametrically opposed implications for the desired pattern of covariation among the independent variables. If the goal is solely to explain as much of the dependent variable as possible, then the independent variables should be minimally associated with one another in addition to being correlated with the dependent variable. If, in contrast, the goal is to explain the focal association, then the other independent variables should covary with the focal independent variable.

Summary

The focal relationship is a device for directing attention toward a critical test of theory. It is a means of imposing order on a large body of data. It should be evident that the selection of a focal relationship is idiosyncratic, dictated by the goals of the research. One researcher's focal relationship may play only a supporting role in another researcher's analysis of the same constructs. Indeed, this is often the case for complex social processes.

Treating one empirical association as the focal relationship helps to organize a strategy for evaluating whether that association can legitimately be interpreted as the relationship anticipated by theory. This evaluation has two components.

First, the exclusionary strategy seeks to rule out alternative explanations, leaving relatedness as the sole viable interpretation. This goal is accomplished when the empirical association between the focal independent and dependent variables is not entirely accounted for by other independent and control variables. If no covariation remains when these other variables are taken into consideration, the claim of relatedness is discredited. The exclusionary strategy provides only a provisional test, however, because there are always untested alternatives.

Second, the inclusive strategy seeks to bolster the causal interpretation by demonstrating that the focal relationship fits within an encompassing system of relationships. Explanatory variables—antecedent, intervening, and consequent variables—are used to trace out a network of relationships that clarify the nature and meaning of the focal relationship. Especially important are intervening variables, which specify the mechanisms through which the independent variable affects the dependent variable. Although antecedent and consequent variables leave the focal relationship intact, intervening variables should account for some or all of the empirical association between the focal independent and dependent variables.

With the exception of intervening variables, then, the general expectation is that the inclusion of third variables will not alter appreciably the estimated size of the focal relationship if the focal relationship is indeed the relationship anticipated by theory. For intervening variables, the expectation is reversed: The focal relationship should be diminished because its components have been specified.

Notes

1. If the dependent variable is not dichotomous, this null hypothesis is more complicated, taking into account the multiple rows and columns of the contingency table. This simplified version is presented because we are primarily interested in the case of the dichotomous dependent variable because it parallels the logistic regression model.

2. The terms "control variable" and "confounding" are frequently also used with regard to a variety of other situations, generating considerable confusion.

3. A third possibility—that the association is merely a specific instance of a general effect of occupational prestige ratings on income from any source rather than a specific effect on illegal income—is considered as well. This possibility is also ruled out during analysis but is omitted here because it deals with a distinctly different set of issues than those covered in this chapter.

4. An apparent exception to this generalization is effect modification: X_i may alter the association between X_f and Y even in the absence of bivariate covariation with these variables. In this instance, however, the third variable is not performing an exclusionary role but is instead specifying the conditional nature of the focal relationship. In addition, omitted suppressor variables may conceal covariation in bivariate analysis.

5. In some instances, the magnitude of the focal association increases when an intervening variable is added, which usually indicates suppression.

6. Not having a disorder is a composite category of no diagnosed disorder and diagnosed disorder other than psychotic/bipolar disorder. "Other" disorders are combined with "no" disorders because these other disorders do not elevate the risk of violence in bivariate analysis; that is, the elevation of risk is confined to psychotic/bipolar disorder.

political → party
views

5 Ruling Out Alternative Explanations: Spuriousness and Control Variables

A crucial goal of theory-based data analysis, as emphasized repeatedly in preceding chapters, is to evaluate whether an empirically observed association can legitimately be interpreted as a relationship. This goal is achieved using multivariate statistical techniques, such as multiple linear regression and logistic regression, to estimate whether two variables are associated with one another in the manner predicted by theory, at a level beyond that expected by chance and net of the influence of relevant "third variables." This chapter examines one of two exclusionary strategies for establishing internal validity: the use of control variables to rule out spurious covariation.

Spuriousness: The Illusion of Relationship

As mentioned in Chapter 4, spuriousness means that the association observed between two variables is the result of their joint dependence on a third variable and not the result of an inherent connection between the original two variables. Values on the independent variable tend to coincide with values on the dependent variable because these variables change in unison in response to a third variable. The independent and dependent variables are not related to one another; rather, both are related to a common antecedent. This possibility is illustrated in Figure 5.1.

The top panel represents our hypothesized focal relationship: the independent variable X_f is associated with dependent variable Y *because* X_f influences Y. The next panel represents the spurious explanation for the empirical association between X_f and Y; this

Figure 5.1

The Focal Relationship and Spuriousness

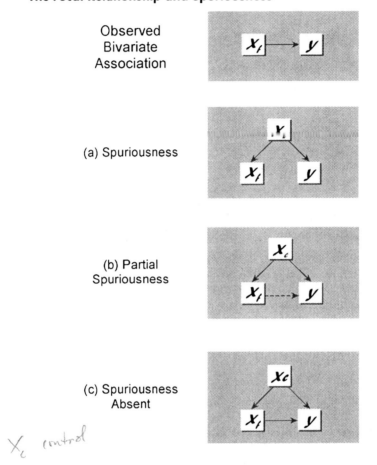

Observed
Bivariate
Association

(a) Spuriousness

(b) Partial
Spuriousness

(c) Spuriousness
Absent

association does not signify a cause-and-effect type of relationship, but rather the connection of these two variables with the control variable X_c. When X_c is included in the analysis of Y, the original association between X_f and Y disappears.

The influence of the control variable on the other two variables is the mechanism that produces spuriousness. These two variables appear to be related to one another only in the absence of X_c. To generate spuriousness, X_c must be associated with the independent variable X_f and with the dependent variable Y. As suggested in Figure 5.1a, these associations reflect the causal influence of the control variable on the other two variables.

The most important aspect of the analysis of potential spuriousness is the extent to which the addition of the control variable alters the magnitude of the association between the focal independent and dependent variables. There are four possible outcomes. First, the original association may be eliminated. This result means that the original bivariate association is completely due to the joint dependency of the focal independent and dependent variables on the control variable (Figure 5.1a).

Second, the control variable may account for only some of the association between the focal independent and dependent variables, as illustrated in Figure 5.1b. The dashed line signifies that the introduction of the control variable into the analysis reduces the magnitude of the focal association but leaves some covariation remaining. This result means that only some of the association between X_f and Y can be attributed to their joint dependency on the control variable X_c.

Third, the association may remain unchanged, as shown in Figure 5.1c. X_f and Y both depend upon X_c, but this joint dependency does not account for the covariation between X_f and Y. In this case, none of the original association can be attributed to the spurious effect of the control variable.

Fourth, it is not uncommon to add a third variable and find that the magnitude of the association between the focal independent and dependent variables has increased in size, the exact opposite of what is expected with spuriousness. Not only is classic spuriousness absent, but its mirror opposite, *suppression*, is present. Whereas spuriousness creates the illusion of a relationship, suppression creates the illusion of independence.

In the extreme, no association between the independent and dependent variables is observed at the bivariate level, as illustrated in the top panel of Figure 5.2. This association emerges only when the third variable is added to the analysis, as illustrated in the bottom panel. In less extreme cases, what first appears as a weak bivariate association is intensified by the addition of the control variable. The bold line in this figure signifies the magnifying effect of a suppressor variable. Usually this happens when X_c is positively associated with one of the variables in the focal relationship and negatively associated with the other.

Recall that our basic goal is to establish that the focal relationship can be interpreted as a relationship by ruling out spuriousness as an alternative explanation. In this context, we hope that the test

Figure 5.2

The Focal Relationship and Suppression

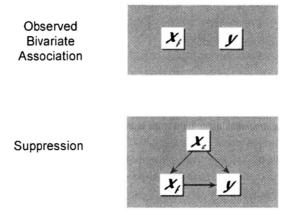

Observed
Bivariate
Association

Suppression

for spuriousness fails—that the independent variable continues to be associated with the dependent variable when the control variable is included in the analysis.

The Analysis of Simple Spuriousness

The empirical assessment of spuriousness is based on differences between simple and multivariate regression equations. Specifically, the relative size of the regression coefficient for the focal relationship between models connotes spuriousness. The influence of the control variable on the focal relationship, therefore, is not apparent from the multivariate model alone, but becomes evident only when the multivariate model is compared to the bivariate model. The following sections present this strategy for two common forms of statistical analysis: multiple linear regression and logistic regression.

Simple Spuriousness for Numeric Outcomes

When the dependent variable is numeric, spuriousness is often analyzed with multiple linear regression. The first step is the estimation of the simple regression of the dependent variable on the focal independent variable. This model is referred to as "simple" because there is only one independent variable. It gives the "zero-order" or bivariate association between focal variables—the total association

Figure 5.3

Simple Regression

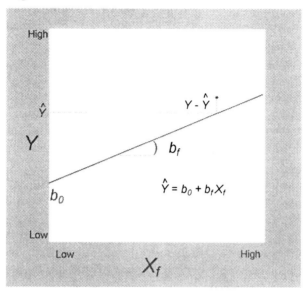

that we attempt to explain through the addition of third variables. The simple regression model is:

$$\widehat{Y} = b_0 + b_f X_f,\qquad\qquad(5.1)$$

where $\widehat{Y}$ is the estimated value of the dependent variable, b_0 is a constant, and b_f is the unstandardized regression coefficient for the focal independent variable. The constant b_0 is the intercept, the expected value of Y when X_f is equal to 0, as illustrated in Figure 5.3.[1] The unstandardized regression coefficient (b_f) assesses the zero-order association between the independent and dependent variables. This coefficient is a useful gauge of the magnitude of the association because it is expressed tangibly in the units in which the component variables have been measured. Specifically, it is the slope or the expected change in Y with each unit increase in X_f, as also shown in Figure 5.3. This association is assumed to be linear as reflected in the fact that the regression equation defines a straight line; there is a constant rate of change in Y across all values of X_f, or, stated differently, each unit increase in X_f produces the same increase in Y.[2] $Y - \widehat{Y}$ is the difference between the observed and estimated values of the dependent variable. The explanatory efficacy of this equation is evaluated with the multiple correlation coefficient R, which is equivalent to the correlation r in the case of simple regression. R^2 is interpreted as the amount of variance in the dependent variable that is "accounted for" or "explained by" the focal independent variable.

The relevant null hypothesis, H_0: $b_f = 0$, asserts that there is no linear association between the focal independent and dependent variables, which means that the slope of the regression line is horizontal. The test statistic is the F ratio with degrees of freedom of k, the number of independent variables (1 in this case), and $n - k - 1$. As usual, we hope to reject the null hypothesis. Because there is only one variable in the equation, the test of the regression equation performs the same function as the test of the individual regression coefficient (although this is not the case when there are multiple independent variables, as discussed below). If we fail to reject the null hypothesis, there is no need to proceed further with the analysis because the fundamental prerequisite, the presence of an association, has not been met. If instead the null hypothesis is rejected, we can proceed because there is an association between X_f and Y to examine for spuriousness.

As a preliminary step, the correlations of X_c with X_f and Y are estimated to determine whether X_c is a viable candidate for the role of control variable. If X_c is not correlated with both of these variables, there is no need to continue because X_c cannot produce spuriousness. Otherwise, the analysis of spuriousness proceeds.

Spuriousness is addressed by adding the control variable X_c to the simple regression model to ascertain whether it accounts for some or all of the bivariate association between X_f and Y:

$$\widehat{Y} = b_0 + b_f X_f + b_c X_c. \tag{5.2}$$

The regression coefficient b_f is now the expected change in Y with each unit increase in X_f when the value of the control variable X_c is held constant. Similarly, the regression coefficient b_c is the expected change in Y with each unit increase in X_c when the value of the focal independent variable is held constant. Thus, the meaning of the regression coefficient changes substantially from the simple regression to the three-variable regression. The constant b_0 is the expected value of Y when both X_f and X_c are equal to 0.

From the perspective of explaining the focal relationship, the coefficient b_f continues to be in the spotlight. The null hypothesis remains the same as above, H_0: $b_f = 0$, but is now tested in two steps. The first step tests the regression equation with its usual null hypothesis, H_0: $b_f = b_c = 0$, which is evaluated with the F ratio as described above. If this hypothesis cannot be rejected, there is no need to proceed because neither coefficient significantly differs from 0. In most analyses, however, this null hypothesis will be rejected because we have already ascertained that there is statistically significant covariation between Y and X_f and between Y and X_c (see above). Although the null hypothesis for the equation will be rejected if $b_f \neq 0$, it will also be rejected if only $b_c \neq 0$, meaning it is not sufficient to test only the regression equation. Instead, the individual regression coefficient b_f must be tested separately using the t test with degrees of freedom $n - k - 1$.

If b_f is reduced to 0, then the entire bivariate association between X_f and Y can be attributed to spuriousness resulting from their joint dependency on X_c. No part of the original correlation between X_f and Y can be interpreted as a relationship.

Suppose instead that only some of the correlation between X_f and Y is spurious. In this instance, the size of the regression coefficient for the focal independent variable would be reduced from its value in the simple regression (i.e., b_f would be smaller in Equation 5.2 than in Equation 5.1), but would still differ significantly from 0. This result means that spuriousness accounts for some of the bivariate correlation between X_f and Y. The remainder of this association can tentatively be attributed to a relationship between these variables, pending further analysis.

If the magnitude of b_f is not changed appreciably by the addition of X_c, then none of the original correlation may be attributed to spuriousness with X_c. Note that the test factor may be associated with Y ($b_c \neq 0$). This association, however, is not sufficient to demonstrate spuriousness; it must be accompanied by a reduction in b_f. When b_c differs from 0, but b_f is not altered by the addition of X_c, then none of the focal relationship can be attributed to the spurious impact of X_c even though X_c itself influences Y (see Figure 5.1c).[3]

In the three-variable model, the multiple correlation coefficient R is the correlation between the dependent variable and the optimal linear combination of the two independent variables, that is, $\widehat{Y}$ from Equation 5.2. R^2 is the variance "explained by" both independent variables, expressed as a proportion of the total variance of the dependent variable Y.

ANALYSIS JOURNAL: Simple Spuriousness
for Numeric Outcomes

The empirical association between family income and mastery was presented in Chapter 3 as an illustration of linear association. In this section, we ask whether this association is observed because income and mastery share common origins. Family income serves as an indicator of the adolescent's relative location within a stratified society. Socioeconomic disadvantage appears to generate experiences that discourage a person from feeling in control. For example, inferior schools make learning and valuing learning difficult, limiting academic success, and constricting future opportunities. Socioeconomic status (SES) also influences the ways in which parents socialize their children. For instance, parents who work under close supervision with little autonomy and no decision-making leeway—jobs that erode mastery—tend to emphasize conformity and obedience to external authority, whereas parents working with jobs that are self-directed and cognitively complex tend to encourage innovation in their children.

As shown in the table, there is an empirical basis for these lines of reasoning because family income is positively associated with mastery among the teens in this study. Although statistically significant, this

Regression of Mastery on Income and Ethnicity

Independent variables	Regression coefficients[a]		
	Model 1	Model 2	Model 3
Family income	.003***		.003***
(thousands of $)[b]	*(.001)*		*(.001)*
Ethnicity[c]			
African American		−.041	.037
		(.071)	(.083)
Latino		−.149***	−.070
		(.038)	(.044)
Asian American/Other		−.133*	−.123*
		(.057)	(.059)
Constant	2.731***	2.936***	2.783***
	(.029)	(.032)	(.056)
R^2	.028***	.021**	.041***

[a]Numbers in parentheses are robust standard errors.
[b]Focal relationship is in italics.
[c]Omitted reference category is white.
*$p \leq .05$. **$p \leq .01$. ***$p \leq .001$.

coefficient is small even though income is measured in thousands of dollars. A \$10,000 difference in income, for example, is associated with only a .03 unit change in mastery, which is measured on a four-point scale.

Perhaps this association is not due to SES, however, but reflects instead cultural orientations that differ across subgroups of the population. The idea that the individual is in control of his or her life is a decidedly Western and American worldview. Individuals from some ethnic and immigrant subcultures may ascribe greater power to external forces, for example, attributing success and failure to the will of some powerful being or to the ebb and flow of fate. In addition, experiences of prejudice and discrimination may erode mastery. Model 2 provides some support for these ideas. Although there is no significant difference in mastery between whites and African Americans, whites have a significantly higher level of mastery, on average, than teens who self-identify as Latino, as Asian American, or as being of some other background.

Ethnicity may contribute to mastery, but if it is to account for the association between income and mastery, ethnicity must also be associated with income. Moreover, if this connection represents spuriousness, then ethnicity must not only be associated with income, it should also be a determinant of income, and not merely happen to covary with income. This linkage could take several paths. For example, historical differences in education among ethnic groups could produce differences in earnings among the adult population. Alternately, ethnic segregation of the workplace and discrimination in hiring and promotion decisions may operate. Among the adolescents in this study, family income is significantly ($p < .001$) greater among whites (\$48,000) than among African Americans (\$24,600) or Latinos (\$24,000), who tend to have similar economic backgrounds; family income in the Asian American/Other group (\$43,500), however, does not differ significantly from that of the white group. Ethnicity can potentially account for some of the association between income and mastery because income and mastery are both highest among white teens and because Latinos tend to score low on both characteristics. Asian American and other teens, however, tend to come from relatively high-income families, but have low levels of mastery, whereas African Americans tend to be from low-income families, but have relatively high levels of mastery. Thus, ethnicity may account for some of the focal association because it is associated with both income and mastery, but it seems unlikely to account for all of the focal association because the patterns of group differences for income and mastery are not identical.

Model 3 shows the impact of adding ethnicity to the simple regression of mastery on income. The coefficient for income does not change appreciably from that in Model 1, suggesting that ethnicity does not generate a spurious association between income and mastery.

The coefficients for the impact of ethnicity on mastery differ somewhat depending upon whether income is included in the model. The greatest change concerns the Latino group. Controlling for income cuts this coefficient in half, and it is no longer statistically significant. In other words, the lower mastery scores of Latino adolescents compared to white adolescents appear to be entirely due to the lower incomes of Latino compared to white families. In contrast, taking income into account does not explain the lower mastery scores of adolescents from Asian American/Other backgrounds relative to those of whites. The explanation should be apparent: these two groups do not show significant differences in income (see above), meaning that income cannot account for their difference in mastery.

In sum, although ethnicity is associated with both family income and mastery, ethnicity does not account for the association between these two variables. Controlling for income, however, does account for differences in mastery between Latino and white adolescents. Notice that the R^2 value for Model 3 is nearly as large as the sum of the R^2 values for Models 1 and 2, which is another indication that the influence of income is largely separate and distinct from that of ethnicity.

Simple Spuriousness for Dichotomous Outcomes

The analytic strategy for dichotomous dependent variables parallels the strategy just described for numeric dependent variables. However, the statistical model changes to the logistic regression model because the dependent variable is dichotomous not numeric. Although the statistical form and estimation of these techniques differ, both are regressions that model an outcome as a linear function of multiple independent variables. As a result, the same analytic strategy can be used for both techniques (Hosmer & Lemeshow, 1989).

The logistic regression model takes two equivalent forms. One form models the *log odds* of being positive on the dependent variable ($\log \hat{o}^{Y^+}$) as an additive function of a set of independent variables. This form resembles the multiple linear regression model, except that the dependent variable in the logistic model is operationalized as $\log \hat{o}^{Y^+}$ rather than Y. This resemblance highlights the similarity of technique with that just described for multiple linear regression. Specifically, the total linear association between the focal independent and dependent variables is given by:

$$\log \hat{o}^{Y^+} = b_0 + b_f X_f, \qquad (5.3)$$

where $\log \hat{o}^{Y^+}$ is the natural logarithm of the expected odds of being positive on the dichotomous dependent variable Y, b_0 is a constant, and b_f is a regression coefficient that gives the expected change in the log odds with a one-unit change in X_f. As shown in Figure 5.4, b_0 is the expected value of $\log \hat{o}^{Y^+}$ when X_f equals 0, and b_f is the slope of the regression line specified in Equation 5.3. The difference between observed and predicted values is given by $\log o^{Y^+} - \log \hat{o}^{Y^+}$.

Once again, we are primarily interested in b_f, specifically the null hypothesis, H_0: $b_f = 0$, which asserts that there is no linear association between X_f and the log odds of being positive on Y. This hypothesis specifies a horizontal regression line. It is evaluated with the model χ^2 test (which is analogous to the F test used in multiple linear regression), with degrees of freedom equal to the number of independent variables in the model, in this case 1. The

Figure 5.4

Simple Logistic Regression

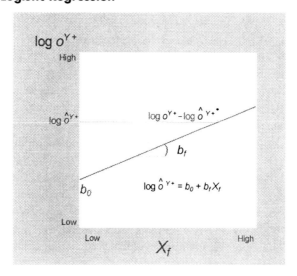

model χ^2 test is the difference between two values of the likelihood function (log L): $-2 \log L0$ for the intercept-only model minus $-2 \log L1$ for the full model, which in the case of simple regression is the model with both the intercept and b_f. The degrees of freedom equal k, the number of independent variables, which in this case, is 1. A significant test means that b_f is not equal to 0. For logistic regression, the individual test of the null hypothesis, H_0: $b_f = 0$, is evaluated with the Wald's χ^2 test, with 1 degree of freedom (comparable to the t test in regression). If we fail to reject the null hypothesis, there is no need to proceed further with the analysis because the fundamental prerequisite, the presence of an association, has not been met. Otherwise, the analysis can proceed because there is an association between the focal independent and dependent variables to examine for spuriousness.

If the association between the focal independent and dependent variables is spurious, then the coefficient for the focal independent variable should be reduced when the control variable X_c is added to the simple logistic model:

$$\log \hat{o}^{Y^+} = b_0 + b_f X_f + b_c X_c. \tag{5.4}$$

The addition of X_c alters the meaning of the coefficient for the focal relationship. This coefficient (b_f) now represents the partial effect of the focal independent variable when the control variable is "held constant" or "controlled." Likewise, b_c is the partial effect of the control variable net of the impact of the focal independent variable. The constant b_0 is the expected log odds of being positive on Y when both X_f and X_c are equal to 0.

As before, we are primarily interested in how the focal relationship changes with the addition of the control variable.[4] In particular, we are interested in whether b_f continues to differ from 0. As was the case with multiple linear regression, this test occurs in two steps. First, the logistic regression equation is tested with the null hypothesis, H_0: $b_f = b_c = 0$, which is evaluated with the model χ^2, which has degrees of freedom equal to the number of independent variables (in this case 2). The null hypothesis is rejected if either coefficient or both coefficients differ significantly from 0.

When the overall null hypothesis is rejected, a second step tests the regression coefficients separately, because the test of the regression equation is not informative about which coefficient differs from 0. The test statistic is Wald's χ^2 with 1 degree of freedom. Two individual null hypotheses can be tested for this model, H_0: $b_f = 0$ and H_0: $b_c = 0$, although we are primarily interested in b_f. If the logistic regression equation is not statistically significant, then the coefficients for the individual variables are not tested separately because the individual tests are subsumed by the overall test.

Once again, we are interested in the difference in b_f with the addition of X_c (i.e., between Equation 5.3 and Equation 5.4). A decrease in this coefficient is consistent with spuriousness. The association is completely spurious if b_f is reduced to 0 and partially spurious if b_f remains significantly different from 0. If b_f is essentially the same in Equation 5.3 and Equation 5.4, then none of the association between the focal independent and dependent variables can be attributed to the spurious effect of the control variable. (An increase in this coefficient is consistent with suppression.)

There is no exact equivalent to R^2 in the logistic regression model, but several approximations have been suggested (Hosmer & Lemeshow, 1989; DeMaris, 1995). One approach is based on the log likelihood and analogy to the sum of squares in multiple linear regression: $R_L^2 = [-2 \log L0 - (-2 \log L1)]/(-2 \log L0)$, often referred to as pseudo-R^2. The term $-2 \log L0$ applies to the intercept-only model, whereas $-2 \log L1$ pertains to the comprehensive model containing all independent variables (as well as the intercept). This statistic does not really have an "explained variance" interpretation because the log likelihood is not really a sum of squares (DeMaris, 1995) and because fitted values under two models are compared rather than fitted values to observed values (Hosmer & Lemeshow, 1989). DeMaris (1995) interprets R_L^2 as the relative improvement in the likelihood of observing the sample data under the hypothesized model relative to the model containing only the intercept. Like R^2, R_L^2 goes from 0, complete independence between the independent and dependent variables, to 1, the independent variable completely determines the dependent variable.

Although the additive version of the logistic regression model demonstrates comparability with the multiple linear regression model, it is somewhat difficult to interpret substantively, because effects are expressed in terms of the log odds of being positive on the dependent variable, which lacks an intuitive reference for many researchers. The multiplicative expression of the logistic model may be easier to interpret because effects are expressed in terms of odds and odds ratios, quantities that are more familiar.

The multiplicative expression of the logistic regression model for spuriousness is obtained by taking the exponent of the log odds model (see Equation 5.3):

$$\hat{o}^{Y+} = e^{b_0} e^{b_f X_f},$$

(5.5)

where $\hat{o}^{Y+}$ is the estimated odds of being positive on the dependent variable Y and e^{b_0} gives this value when the focal independent variable equals 0. The total association between the focal independent and dependent variables is given by e^{b_f}. This value is the expected multiplicative change in the odds of being positive on Y for a 1-unit increase on the independent variable. The percentage change in the odds of being positive on Y is given by $100(e^b - 1)$. This is a multiplicative model, meaning that a coefficient of 1.00 indicates no association (rather than the value of 0 in the additive model), because $e^0 = 1$ and because $a \times 1 = a$. A coefficient greater than 1.00 indicates a positive association, whereas a coefficient between 0 and 1.00 (i.e., a proportion) indicates an inverse association.

When a control variable is added to the model, the equation becomes:

$$\hat{o}^{Y+} = e^{b_0} e^{b_f X_f} e^{b_c X_c},$$

(5.6)

which is obtained by exponentiation of the additive model (Equation 5.4). In the simple regression model (Equation 5.5), e^{b_f} is the odds ratio for being positive on Y for a 1-unit increase in X_f. With the addition of the control variable X_c, e^{b_f} is the partial odds ratio for a 1-unit increase in X_f. In other words, it is the expected multiplicative change in the odds of being positive on Y for a 1-unit increase in the focal independent variable with the control variable held constant.

We are most concerned with changes in e^{b_f}. These changes are evaluated as movement toward 1.00 (as distinct from movement toward 0 in the additive model). A decrease in the size of e^{b_f} from Equation 5.5 to Equation 5.6 is indicative of spuriousness. Specifically, if e^{b_f} moves closer to 1.00, then at least some of the focal relationship is due to spuriousness with the control variable. This spuriousness is complete when e^{b_f} does not differ from 1.00. Movement in e^{b_f} away from 1.00 is consistent with suppression. In contrast, none of the focal relationship can be attributed to spuriousness with the control variable X_c if e^{b_f} is essentially unchanged from its value in the bivariate model.

The multiplicative form of the logistic model is especially convenient when the independent variable is dichotomous.[5] In the simple logistic regression (Equation 5.3), e^{b_f} is the ratio of the odds of being positive on Y given a positive value on X_f, relative to the odds of being positive on Y given a negative value on X_f. In other words, the total association between X_f and Y is expressed as an odds ratio. In multivariate logistic regressions, e^{b_f} is interpreted as a partial odds ratio.

Complex Sources of Spuriousness

Multiple Control Variables

As mentioned above, we usually hope that the focal relationship survives the test for spuriousness. This result means that significant covariation between the independent and dependent variables remains after the control variable is entered into the analysis. Ideally, we would like to interpret the remaining covariation as relatedness. However, it may instead be indicative of additional sources of spuriousness. If it is reasonable to speculate that an association between two variables is due to their joint dependency upon a third variable, there usually are several candidates for the role of third variable. The analysis of spuriousness, therefore, typically entails the analysis of multiple control variables rather than analysis of a single control variable, as illustrated in Figure 5.5.

In Figure 5.5a, each of these control variables is associated with both the focal independent (X_f) and dependent (Y) variables. In combination, the set of control variables fully accounts for the focal relationship, even though each individual control variable by itself may leave some covariation remaining between the focal independent and dependent variables.

This illustration shows one of numerous possible results from the analysis of multiple control variables. In practice, some potential control variables may turn out to be related to only the focal independent variable, to only the dependent variable, or to neither variable. Even if the set is limited to control variables that have bivariate associations with both the focal independent and dependent variables, some of these variables will prove to be unimportant in multivariate analysis because of covariation among the control variables. Figure 5.5b illustrates this type of result.

Figure 5.5

Complex Spuriousness

(a) Multiple Sources of Complete Spuriousness

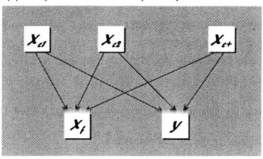

(b) Mixed Case of Partial Spuriousness

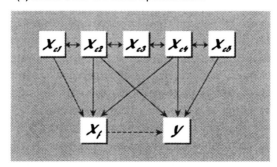

Only two of the variables in this set, X_{c2} and X_{c4}, generate spuriousness between the focal independent and dependent variables. The other variables cannot produce this effect because they are related to only the independent variable (X_{c1}), to only the dependent variable (X_{c5}), or to neither of these variables (X_{c3}). Although the last three variables are part of a set that collectively produces spuriousness, they are not contributing to that spuriousness. Thus, the set as a whole may generate spuriousness without each component variable contributing to this result. In this instance, spuriousness can be attributed to only some of the variables in the set (in this example, X_{c2} and X_{c4}).

The use of multiple control variables, however, does not necessarily account fully for the association between the focal independent and dependent variables. As was the case with a single control variable, there may be covariation remaining after these multiple control variables have been introduced into the analysis. The dashed line connecting the focal independent and dependent variables in Figure 5.5b suggests this possibility.

We would like to infer that the remaining covariation represents a cause-and-effect type of relationship. However, despite the use of multiple control variables, the covariation remaining between the focal independent and dependent variables may nevertheless be spurious. In practice, we often lack measures of some variables we think should be controlled. Even when all reasonable controls are taken into consideration, however, there remains the possibility that some unknown third variable has produced a spurious association. The set of potential controls is endless and, therefore, cannot be exhaustively tested. As a result, the specter of spuriousness continues to haunt estimates of the focal relationship, even in analyses with lengthy lists of control variables. However, despite this uncertainty, we can now have more confidence that a relationship probably exists because we have eliminated at least some of the most compelling alternatives to this inference.

Considerations in the Selection of Control Variables

The selection of the set of potential control variables is of obvious importance to the quality of the test of spuriousness. When no test factors are considered, the bivariate case, we have little confidence that any of the association merits a causal inference. Our confidence increases as the number of relevant control variables included in the model increases. Although it might seem desirable to throw in everything, including the well-known kitchen sink, this slapdash approach tends to obfuscate interpretation because there are too many variables with which to contend.

The set of control variables should include all those variables and *only* those variables that reasonably are expected to satisfy the criteria for spuriousness. In practice, this list is often shorter than suggested at first glance. Many candidates for the role of control variable fail to meet the requirements for spuriousness. In many applications, the control variable is associated with only the independent variable *or* the dependent variable. This situation violates the requirements for an effectual exclusionary variable, namely that a test factor be associated with both of these variables. A control variable that is associated with only the independent variable or only the dependent variable cannot generate spuriousness. It need not, therefore, be included in the analysis of spuriousness. In general, it is advisable to include control variables that turn out to be related only to the dependent variable because they enhance our explanation of that outcome. Although the inclusion of these variables does not serve the purpose of ruling out spuriousness, they do serve the equally important goal of explaining the dependent variable.

The Analysis of Complex Spuriousness

Complex Spuriousness for Numeric Outcomes

The analysis of one control variable (Equation 5.2) is easily extended to the analysis of multiple control variables ($X_{c1}, X_{c2}, \ldots, X_{c+}$) in multiple linear regression:

$$\widehat{Y} = b_0 + b_f X_f + b_{c1} X_{c1} + b_{c2} X_{c2} + \cdots + b_{c+} X_{c+}, \qquad (5.7)$$

where b_0 is the expected value of the dependent variable when the focal independent variable and all of the control variables equal 0. The contribution of the entire set of control variables is assessed as the increase in R^2 obtained by adding $X_{c1}, X_{c2}, \ldots, X_{c+}$ to the regression equation containing only X_f (Equation 5.1). The statistical significance of this increment is assessed with an F test.[6]

Once again, our focus is on the regression coefficient for the focal relationship, b_f. This coefficient is the expected change in Y with each unit change in the focal independent variable when the values of all of the control variables are held constant. The impact on the focal relationship of controlling for the entire set of control variables is given by the change in b_f from the simple regression (Equation 5.1) to the multiple variable regression (Equation 5.7).

Once again, the relevant null hypothesis is $H_0: b_f = 0$, tested first as part of the test of the regression equation and then as an individual regression coefficient. If b_f is reduced to 0, then the total association can be attributed to the spurious effects of the set of control variables. If instead b_f is unchanged by the addition of the set of control variables, then none of the focal relationship can be considered spurious. Between these two extremes, spuriousness accounts for some but not all of the covariation between X_f and Y. In this instance, the addition of the set of potentially spurious variables reduces b_f in size, but the coefficient continues to differ from zero.[7] The remaining nonzero component of b_f appears to be indicative of a relationship. This outcome means that the joint dependency of the focal independent and dependent variables on one or more of the control variables accounts for some of their covariation with one another, but some of this covariation seems to be indicative of a relationship between these two variables (see, for example, Figure 5.5b).

The explanatory efficacy of the entire set of control variables and X_f is quantified by R^2. The portion of R^2 that can be attributed exclusively to X_f is of particular interest from the perspective of explaining the focal relationhip. This quantity equals the increment in R^2 obtained by adding X_f to a regression equation containing the entire set of control variables. Notice that this assessment reverses our model-building strategy. We start with the comprehensive model (Equation 5.7) and delete the focal independent variable. The second model is a nested subset of the first model, meaning that the difference in R^2 is the increment associated with X_f, net of the contribution of all of the control variables. The statistical significance of this increment is assessed with an F ratio.[6]

When there are multiple control variables, we usually wish to know which specific variables generate spuriousness. Spuriousness may be limited to one control variable, extend to several variables, or encompass the entire set of controls. It is altogether possible that the entire impact of the set of control variables is due to the influence of a single control variable, even though it has been observed through the introduction of several control variables. For this reason, it is desirable to analyze a series of three-variable models (one control variable) before moving on to the multiple control variable extension. These small models help to locate more precisely the source of the spuriousness and are indispensable to the interpretation of more complex models.

In many instances, variables that generate spuriousness in these preliminary three-variable models are not significantly associated with the dependent variable in the more comprehensive model. This result is most likely to occur when two or more control variables are highly associated with one another. When these variables are considered simultaneously, the importance of any one control variable may be obscured because its influence overlaps with that of other control variables. This type of finding can be clarified by examining subsets of the control variables as an intermediary step between the individual three-variable models and the comprehensive model containing the entire set of control variables.

ANALYSIS JOURNAL: Complex Spuriousness for Numeric Outcomes

To illustrate the use of several potential control variables, we return to the example of simple spuriousness presented earlier in this chapter. An additional source of spuriousness may be family structure, because it is almost certainly associated with family income, the focal independent variable, and because family types are likely to differ in family interactions in ways that are consequential to the development of mastery, the focal dependent variable. For example, single-parent families tend to exercise somewhat less control and supervision over their sons and daughters, which may place adolescents in situations in which they develop competence, or, conversely, in which they feel overwhelmed. In these data, intact nuclear families ($36,000) and parent and step-parent families ($32,900) have substantially higher incomes than single parent families ($22,500) ($p < .001$). However, the association between family structure and mastery is not statistically significant ($p > .40$). Consequently, the addition of family structure cannot generate spuriousness and its addition to the previous regression model does not change the coefficient for income (not shown).

Although males generally tend to have a greater sense of mastery than do females, the gender difference is not statistically significant for this sample of adolescents. Furthermore, there is no reason to expect that gender is associated with family income. Thus, gender is not a good candidate for spuriousness, and its addition to the previous regression model does not change the coefficient for income (not shown).

Finally, it is reasonable to expect that mastery increases from early to late adolescence because of autonomy-related experiences. However, in these data, age is not significantly associated with mastery ($p > .90$). In addition, there is no apparent reason for age of the adolescent to be associated with family income, and, indeed, these two variables are not significantly associated with one another ($p > .40$). Thus, age does not contribute to the explanation of either the focal relationship or the dependent variable (not shown).

As discussed earlier, covariation among control variables can alter results when multiple control variables are simultaneously included in the regression model. This possibility is evaluated in the table. The results from this comprehensive model are generally consistent with those of the preliminary models discussed above. Specifically, the coefficient for income is virtually unchanged from the bivariate analysis

Regression of Mastery on Income and Control Variables

Independent variables	Regression coefficients[a]
Family income	.003**
(thousands of $)[b]	(.001)
Ethnicity[c]	
African American	.052
	(.090)
Latino	−.076
	(.043)
Asian American/Other	−.132*
	(.058)
Male	.066*
	(.028)
Family structure[d]	
Parent and stepparent	−.012
	(.037)
Single-parent family	−.033
	(.036)
Age (years)	.001
	(.013)
Constant	2.757***
	(0.190)
R^2	.047***

[a]Numbers in parentheses are robust standard errors.
[b]Focal relationship is in italics.
[c]Omitted reference category is white.
[d]Omitted reference category is intact nuclear family.
*$p \le .05$. **$p \le .01$. ***$p \le .001$.

(b_f = .003), indicating that this association does not appear to be spurious. As in the earlier analysis, adolescents who are Asian American/Other tend to have lower levels of mastery than do comparable white teens. When the other variables in the model are controlled, the coefficient for being male is statistically significant, a change from the bivariate analysis reported above, with males, on average, having higher levels of mastery than do females. Family structure and age, in contrast, appear to be irrelevant to both the focal relationship and the dependent variable.

(An example of spuriousness for dichotomous dependent variables appears in Chapter 6.)

Complex Spuriousness for Dichotomous Outcomes

The analysis of complex spuriousness for dichotomous dependent variables entails a similar extension of the three-variable logistic regression model (Equation 5.4) to incorporate multiple control variables:

$$\log \hat{o}^{Y+} = b_0 + b_f X_f + b_{c1} X_{c1} + b_{c2} X_{c2} + \cdots + b X_{c+} X_{c+}, \qquad (5.8)$$

where b_0 is the log odds of being positive on the dependent variable when the focal independent variable and all of the control variables equal 0. Again, note the similarity between the multiple linear regression model (Equation 5.7) on the right-hand side of the equation and the differences in the form of the dependent variable on the left-hand side. The coefficient b_f represents the partial association between Y and X_f net of the entire set of control variables, as distinct from the total association given in the simple regression equation (Equation 5.3). The other coefficients $(b_{c1}, b_{c2}, \ldots, b_{c+})$ estimate the influence of each control variable net of all other control variables and the focal independent variable. These coefficients are usually of substantive importance, aside from any influence on the focal relationship, because they help to explain the occurrence of the dependent variable. The contribution of the entire set of control variables to the simple regression model is assessed with the likelihood ratio test, which is analogous to the F test for the increment in R^2 in multiple linear regression.[8]

Our main interest, however, is with changes in the focal relationship between Equation 5.3 and Equation 5.8. If the addition of the set of control variables does not alter b_f to a noticeable degree, then none of the focal relationship can be attributed to spuriousness with any of the control variables. If instead b_f decreases toward 0, the value indicative of no relationship, then the bivariate association between the focal independent and dependent variables is due, at least in part, to the spurious influence of one or more of the control variables. This spuriousness is complete if the null hypothesis, $H_0: b_f = 0$, cannot be rejected. This test occurs in two steps: the regression equation, which simultaneously tests all regression coefficients with the model χ^2, followed by the individual coefficient tests with the Wald's χ^2.

We usually wish to know which control variables generate any change observed in b_f. It may be due to a single control variable, several variables, or all of them. The multiple variable model may obscure the impact of individual control variables if some of these variables capture a common source of shared covariation. As just discussed for the multiple linear regression model, this situation is best diagnosed by examining models for subsets of independent variables.

R_L^2 is an indicator of the total explanatory efficacy of the logistic model. Although this is useful information, our emphasis on the focal relationship calls for an assessment of the separate influence of X_f over and above the influence of the set of control variables. This determination entails the comparison of two logistic regression equations: the comprehensive model (Equation 5.8) containing the focal independent variable and the entire set of control variables and a similar model containing all of the control variables but not the focal independent variable. As before, this is a reversal of the model-building strategy because the focal independent variable is removed from the comprehensive model. The difference between the R_L^2 values gives the incremental explanatory efficacy exclusively due to X_f. This approach is analogous to the test of the change in R^2 between steps in the multiple linear regression. In logistic regression, the likelihood ratio test evaluates whether the addition of X_f is statistically significant.[8]

Taking the exponent of the preceding equation converts it to a multiplicative expression:

$$\hat{o}^{Y+} = e^{b_0} e^{b_f X_f} e^{b_{c1} X_{c1}} e^{b_{c2} X_{c2}}, \dots, e^{b_c + X_{c+}}, \tag{5.9}$$

where e^{b_0} gives the odds of being positive on Y when all of the control variables and the focal independent variable equal 0. We are once again concerned with changes in b_f or, more precisely, e^{b_f}. However, in the multiplicative model these changes are evaluated as movement toward 1.00 (as distinct from movement toward 0 in the additive model). If spuriousness is present, e^{b_f} should move toward 1.00. If some or all of the focal relationship is not spurious, e^{b_f} should deviate from 1.00.

Death Looms on the Horizon: An Example of Partial Spuriousness

An explicit example of the use of control variables to rule out spuriousness is provided by Mirowsky (1997) for two focal relationships, one between age and sense of control, and the other between sense

Figure 5.6

Impact of Control Variables on the Focal Relationship: Aging and the Sense of Control

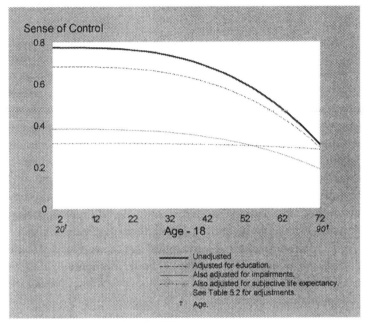

Source: Adapted from Mirowsky (1997).

of control and subjective life expectancy. Sense of control is very similar to the concept of mastery, described earlier, and refers to the belief that you shape your own life. Like mastery, this belief has pervasive beneficial effects on health on the one hand and appears to reflect objective conditions on the other hand, insofar as it increases with social status. However, sense of control declines at an accelerating rate as age increases, as illustrated in Figure 5.6. The so-called young-old (60–70) feel less control than middle-aged adults (40–60), a difference that is more pronounced for the old (70–85) compared to the young-old, and intensified for the next comparison, the old and the oldest old (over 85).

Mirowsky (1997) contends that a sense of control is shaped by the individual's expectations about how long he or she will continue to live: the fewer the years left, the less one can expect to accomplish or enjoy, referred to as the horizon hypothesis. Without thinking, people figure out their personal life expectancy, starting with the average for their age and then adjusting for what they know about others who are like themselves in terms of gender, ethnicity, socioeconomic status, family history, lifestyle, physical fitness, health impairments, and so forth. According to Mirowsky (1997), this subjective life expectancy constrains a person's sense of control because the belief that one can influence what happens to oneself necessarily presupposes an imagined future for oneself, a continued personal existence. He contends that subjective life expectancy should explain some or all of the association between sense of control and age.

More importantly for our purposes, Mirowsky points out that the association between sense of control and subjective life expectancy is likely to result, at least in part, from their joint dependency on common antecedents. In other words, the association may be spurious. For example, education is negatively related to morbidity and mortality, but positively related to sense of control, and older Americans have less education, on average, than younger cohorts. This pattern of covariation means that education may contribute to the negative association between sense of control and subjective life expectancy. Alternately, the association may be due to poor health, which becomes more likely with age and which, in turn, increases mortality while eroding self-efficacy. In this instance, the association between sense of control and subjective life expectancy may be explained by declining health.

The data used to test the horizon hypothesis are from a telephone survey of a national sample of adults over the age of 18 ($N = 2,593$). Subjective life expectancy was calculated by subtracting current age from the individual's response to being asked, "To what age do you expect to live?" For the association between sense of control and age, two control variables are included: education and physical impairment. For sense of control and subjective life expectancy, three potential sources of spuriousness are considered: *ascribed status*—being female and being a member of a racial/ethnic minority group; *socioeconomic status*—education and income; and, *health or life course status*—being widowed, being unable to work, having an impairment (e.g., having some difficulty with daily activities such as climbing stairs), and being fit (e.g., frequency of feeling physically fit).

The focal relationship between age and sense of control is described by the following cubic function:

$$\widehat{Y} = b_0 + b_f[\text{age} - 18]^3, \qquad (5.10)$$

where b_0 is the expected value of sense of control at age 18 and $b_f < 0$. The youngest age (18) for this sample of adults is subtracted from age to force the intercept through zero. The value of b_f in Equation 5.10 estimates the total association between sense of control and the term $[age - 18]^3$. This quantity is raised to the third power to operationalize the nonlinear functional form of the association between age and control as a linear function of $[age - 18]^3$. Specifically, the association between age and control is flat at age 18 and becomes increasingly negative at progressively older ages, as shown in Figure 5.6. This curve departs from linearity (constant slope) not because of variation in b_f across age, but because sense of control is plotted as a function of $[age - 18]$. If b_f were instead plotted against $[age - 18]^3$, the curve in Figure 5.6 would be a straight line with a slope of b_f and intercept b_o of zero. As a result, this term can be modeled as a linear function using multiple linear regression. This example serves as a reminder that it is imperative to operationalize the focal relationship according to its theory-based functional form and not to automatically use an unmodified linear form.

To test the horizon hypothesis, Mirowsky (1997) progressively expands the simple regression of sense of control on age to take into consideration education and impairment and then expands it further to include subjective life expectancy. Results of this analysis appear in Table 5.1. Model 1 shows the total association between

Table 5.1

Regression of Sense of Control on Age

	Model 1	Model 2	Model 3	Model 4
$[Age - 18]^3 \ 10^{-6}$	−1.252***	−1.044***	−0.529***	−.087
Education		.054***	.046***	.046***
Impairment			−.345***	−.332***
Subjective life expectancy ÷ 10				.027***
Intercept	.773	.033	.175	.067
R^2	.034	.106	.141	.146
b_f explained				
Increment %		16.6	41.1	35.4
Cumulative %		16.6	57.7	93.1
$\Delta b_f / SF_b$		1.396	3.456	2.966

Source: Mirowsky (1997).
***$p < .001$.

sense of control and age, operationalized as $[age - 18]^3$. We are interested in whether the coefficient for $[age - 18]^3$ changes when control variables are added to the regression. The addition of education in Model 2 and impairment in Model 3 reduces substantially the coefficient for $[age - 18]^3$, meaning that at least some of the original association can be attributed to age differences in education and impairment. These adjustments are shown in Figure 5.4 by the flattening of the curve. The adjustment for education in Model 2 decreases the coefficient for the focal relationship by 16.6%, which lowers the curve at the origin more than at the maximum, meaning that the curve becomes less steep at older ages than in Model 1. The addition of impairment in Model 3 provides a substantial decline from Model 2 (49.3%), which is reflected in the lower and flatter curve shown in Figure 5.4. However, there remains statistically significant covariation between sense of control and the age term after the addition of these two variables (Model 3). These two variables also substantially increase the amount of explained variance in the dependent variable from the model containing only the age term.

The addition of subjective life expectancy in Model 4 is of particular interest because it operationalizes a key aspect of the horizon hypothesis, specifically that expectations about how long one will live account for the covariation between $[age - 18]^3$ and sense of control that remains after education and impairment are taken into consideration. In Model 4, we see that the addition of subjective life expectancy substantially reduces the coefficient for $[age - 18]^3$, which becomes statistically nonsignificant. As shown in Figure 5.6, the curve for the adjusted focal relationship is now flat because its coefficient does not differ significantly from 0. The three explanatory variables collectively account for all of the relationship between sense of control and the age term. Model 4 does not substantially increase the amount of explained variance in the dependent variable relative to Model 3, but the addition of subjective life expectancy does substantially reduce the association between sense of control and the age term. In other words, perceived longevity explains the focal relationship to a greater extent than it independently explains the dependent variable.

Mirowsky (1997) also considers a second focal relationship, the impact of subjective life expectancy on sense of control. In particular, he asks whether the association between these two variables is merely an artifact of the joint dependency of these two variables on the control variables enumerated above. Results appear in Table 5.2.

Table 5.2

Regression of Sense of Control on Subjective Life Expectancy

	Model 1	Model 2
Subjective life expectancy ÷ 10	.057***	.030***
Minority		−.081***
Female		−.047*
Education		.042***
Income ($10K)		.005*
Widowed		−.094*
Unable to work		−.228**
Impairment		−.187***
Fitness		.021***
Intercept	.513	.006
R^2	.042	.170

Source: Mirowsky (1997).
*$p < .05$. **$p < .01$. ***$p < .001$.

Model 1 is the simple regression of sense of control on subjective life expectancy, which gives the total association between the two focal variables. Model 2 shows the addition of ascribed status, socioeconomic status, and health or life course status. Adding these variables accounts for about half of the total association between subjective life expectancy and sense of control but leaves significant covariation unexplained. The set of control variables collectively explains a substantial amount of the variation in the dependent variable (shown by the increase in R^2), and each of the control variables is significantly associated with sense of control as is subjective life expectancy. Based on these results, Mirowsky (1997) concludes that the apparent effect of subjective life expectancy on sense of control cannot be attributed solely to its association with membership in a racial/ethnic minority group, female sex, low education, low income, widowhood, inability to work, physical impairment, or lack of physical fitness.

Summary

From the perspective developed in this volume, the key question in the analysis of spuriousness is whether control variables, singly or in combination with one another, account for the association between the focal independent and dependent variables. This question can be answered by testing the null hypothesis, H_0: $b_f = 0$, in a comprehensive model containing the entire set of control variables (Equation 5.7 or Equation 5.8). If this hypothesis cannot be rejected, we conclude that the association is spurious. Otherwise, we can conclude that there is nonspurious covariation between the focal independent and dependent variables. This conclusion, as should be familiar by now, necessarily remains tentative because it is not possible to rule out all potential sources of spuriousness.

Our interest in spuriousness comes in a roundabout fashion: We wish to eliminate spuriousness as an alternative explanation for an empirical association that we would like to interpret as a relationship. From this perspective, the analysis of spuriousness can be seen as establishing the internal validity of the focal relationship by default: The relatedness component of the total association is the covariation remaining after the spurious component is removed. The more strenuous the test of spuriousness, the greater our confidence in the inference of relatedness. Thus, we diligently seek out potential sources of spuriousness but hope to fail in this task, leaving most if not all of the association intact.

Although spuriousness is a pervasive problem, many variables that seem likely to play this role can be discarded upon closer inspection because they do not meet the requirements for spuriousness. In particular, potential control variables often are associated with only the independent variable or only the dependent variable. Furthermore, covariation among control variables frequently means that some control variables are superfluous. Thus, the total impact of a set of control variables usually is considerably less than the sum of the individual impact of its component variables.

Although our interest in control variables primarily centers on their impact on the focal relationship, their relationship to the dependent variable usually emerges as an important finding. After all, our interest in the focal relationship has usually arisen within the broader context of explaining the occurrence of the dependent variable. Control variables serve this more fundamental purpose. However, it is easy to become sidetracked by the lure of maximizing the explanation of the dependent variable and to drift away from the focal relationship. Accordingly, this text continues to emphasize the explication of the focal relationship as a prime analytic objective.

Various other multivariate techniques can be used to apply this general strategy, for example, latent variable causal models or multinomial logistic regression. Readers should adapt the general strategy described above to the statistical technique that is most appropriate to their theories and data. The analytic procedure follows the same format. First, bivariate analysis is used to estimate the total association between the independent and dependent variables. Second, bivariate analysis is used to ascertain whether the criteria for an effectual exclusionary variable have been met, specifically that the test factor is associated with both the focal independent and dependent variables. Third, multivariate analysis is used to estimate the partial association between the focal independent and dependent variables that remains when control variables are included in the model. Demonstrating that an association remains when potential spuriousness is taken into consideration lends credence to the supposition that the association indeed represents a relationship.

Notes

1. Zero is a true 0 (the absolute absence of X) only for ratio variables. Many variables have computer codes of 0 that should not be confused with a true value for 0.

2. The assumption of linearity can and should be tested. Transformations of the independent variables (e.g., quadratic terms) can be used to accommodate some nonlinear associations.

3. The comparison of regression coefficients across regression equations assumes that the models are "nested" (one model is a subset of the other). It also assumes that the models being compared have been estimated with the same sample, which means that N is constant across models. N should be monitored closely, because it often varies across models because of missing values on added independent variables. A formal test for the difference between the simple and partial regression coefficients is given by Clogg, Petkova, and Haritou (1995).

4. As with multiple linear regression, the comparison of coefficients across models is predicated on the models being nested and estimated on the same N.

5. This interpretation pertains to natural dichotomies, to categorical variables expressed as a set of dichotomous dummy variables, and to continuous variables reduced to a set of dichotomous dummy variables, although this last approach is undesirable (unless it is used to represent a nonlinear form) because it sacrifices information for ease of presentation.

6.
$$F = \frac{\Delta R^2/m}{(1 - R^2_{\text{total}})/(n - k - 1)}$$

with degrees of freedom of $m, n - k - 1$, where m is the number of variables in the subset differentiating the two equations and k is the total number of independent variables. Note that this equation requires that the sample be identical in the two regression equations, i.e., n is invariant.

7. Increases in the magnitude of the focal relationship usually reflect suppression, as discussed earlier in this chapter.

8. Likelihood ratio test $= -2(\log L_{X_c+X_f} - \log L_{X_c})$,

which is distributed as χ^2 with degrees of freedom m, where m is the number of variables in the subset differentiating the two equations.

6 Ruling Out Alternative Theoretical Explanations: Additional Independent Variables

Exclusionary strategies for establishing relatedness are based on the premise that an association can be interpreted as a relationship to the extent that alternative explanations for the association are eliminated. The preceding chapter considered one alternative to relatedness, spuriousness, and described an analytic strategy for estimating the nonspurious component of an association. If control variables account for all of the covariation between the independent and dependent variables, there is no need for further analysis because the association is deemed completely spurious. Covariation remaining after control variables are taken into consideration, however, requires additional analysis to rule out a second source of coincident associations, redundancy.

Redundancy is relatedness that the focal independent variable shares with other independent variables. It occurs when other independent variables supply the same information about the dependent variable that is supplied by the focal independent variable. Redundancy is produced by covariation between the focal independent variable and other independent variables. These other independent variables typically represent competing theories for the occurrence of the same dependent variable.

This second exclusionary strategy examines changes in the impact of the focal independent variable when the effects of other independent variables are removed. The goal is to ascertain whether the theory being tested is separate and distinct from other theoretical explanations. This objective entails evaluating whether the focal independent variable remains associated with the dependent variable when other independent variables are taken into consideration. This remaining covariation can be attributed to the unique influence of the focal independent variable because it is not accounted for by redundancy or by spuriousness.

The analytic strategy used to eliminate redundancy, then, parallels the strategy used to eliminate spuriousness. The analysis of redundancy follows the analysis of spuriousness because it addresses the nonspurious component of the association, that is, the association remaining after the spurious component of the association has been eliminated.

The unique contribution of the focal independent variable, therefore, is the association between this variable and the dependent variable that remains when control variables and other independent variables are taken into consideration. This remainder will approach 0 if there is no unique connection between the focal independent variable and the dependent variable; it will approximate the total association if most of this connection is relational and unique. This is an exclusionary strategy in the sense that the unique component is estimated as the component remaining after the influence of other independent variables is ruled out.

Procedurally, this analysis entails estimating the covariation between the focal independent variable and the dependent variable remaining when other independent variables are added to a multivariate model that also contains control variables. As was the case for the analysis of control variables, this technique emphasizes changes in the estimate of the focal relationship that accompany the addition of other variables into the analytic model. Demonstrating that some portion of the nonspurious association with the dependent variable uniquely pertains to the focal independent variable supports the inference of relatedness.

Redundancy: Alternative Theories

Observation of a phenomenon typically generates more than one plausible theory to account for its occurrence. The presentation of one theory to account for a phenomenon typically carries within it the seeds of alternative explanations. The specification of a model lays bare its assumptions, definitions, reasoning, and leaps of faith. Once these aspects of a theory become explicit, they invite challenge; each point spawns its counterpoint. The development of a powerful and coherent theory, therefore, encourages the development of alternative theories.

Competing theories share the observed phenomenon, but differ in their explanation of this phenomenon. In most instances, competing theories pertain to the same outcome or dependent variable, but differ with regard to their independent variables. Each model typically contains independent variables not included in the other model, although some variables may be shared in common.

Of particular interest are theories that do *not* contain the focal relationship. These models can be tested and compared to a more comprehensive model that additionally contains the focal relationship. An increment in explanatory efficacy between these two models is evidence that the focal independent variable exerts a unique influence on the dependent variable. This result indicates that the focal independent variable contributes something to our understanding of the dependent variable that is over and above the contribution of other independent variables. This strategy sets a stringent criterion for relatedness: The focal independent variable must exert a unique influence on the dependent variable. It is a proof-by-elimination strategy because the focal relationship is estimated by excluding the influence of other independent variables.

From this perspective, our interest in alternative theory concerns its impact upon the focal relationship. This is a rather narrow focus, considering the many ways in which theoretical models might intersect. This orientation is useful, however, because it keeps the objective of the analysis in the forefront: establishing the focal relationship as a relationship. Nevertheless, our interest in the focal relationship typically exists together with a more encompassing interest in the theoretical origins of the dependent variable. As we have seen before, then, the explanation of the dependent variable remains a vital goal along with the explanation of the focal relationship.

Covariation as Artifact

Redundancy means that the focal relationship does not represent the unique influence of one variable on another, but rather a coincident association. In this sense, redundancy is similar to spuriousness: Both generate an illusory relationship between the focal independent and dependent variables. The distinction between redundancy and spuriousness concerns the nature of the association between the focal independent variable and the "third variable."

Figure 6.1

The Focal Relationship and Redundancy

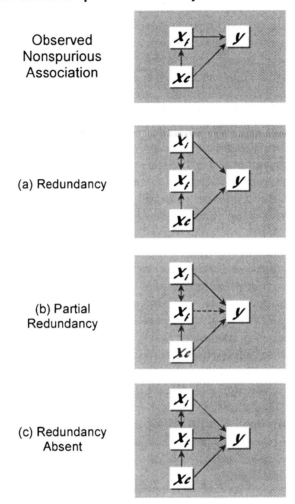

Observed
Nonspurious
Association

(a) Redundancy

(b) Partial
Redundancy

(c) Redundancy
Absent

The concept of redundancy is illustrated in Figure 6.1. The top panel shows the final step from the analysis of spuriousness, which is the first step in the analysis of redundancy. It shows a focal independent variable and dependent variable that continue to be associated with one another net of any spuriousness generated by control variables. In other words, there is covariation left over to analyze for redundancy. This covariation may represent a cause-and-effect type of relationship, the inference we would eventually like to make.

The alternative of redundancy is shown in Figure 6.1a. The focal relationship is replaced by the relationship between the dependent variable and another independent variable, X_i, that, in effect, substitutes for X_f. This displacement occurs because X_f and X_i are associated with one another. The association between the independent variables is shown as a two-headed arrow to call attention to the fact that this connection need not be relational, the result of one variable influencing another; instead, these variables may simply happen to covary with one another.

Redundancy occurs because X_f and X_i overlap in their relationships with Y. This overlap occurs because the independent variables are associated with one another and associated with Y. When there is no association between X_f and X_i, X_f cannot be redundant with X_i. In other words, covariation among the independent variables is a requirement of redundancy. Thus, redundancy should be considered as a possibility when independent variables are associated with one another.

Furthermore, it should be apparent that redundancy requires that the dependent variable be associated with both the focal independent variable and the alternative independent variable. If one connection with the dependent variable substitutes for the other, then each connection must be present. Thus, there are three empirical prerequisites to redundancy: The focal independent variable must be associated with the dependent variable net of control variables, the alternative independent variable must be associated with the dependent variable, and the alternative independent variable must be associated with the focal independent variable. In other words, all three variables must be associated with one another (see Table 4.2, criteria for an effective exclusionary variable).

The empirical test of whether these conditions indeed generate redundancy entails the comparison of results from two multivariate analyses. The base model contains the focal independent variable and any relevant control variables. The second analysis adds the alternate independent variable. The most important aspect of this analysis is the extent to which the addition of this independent variable alters the magnitude of the association between the focal independent variable and the dependent variable.

This mutable quality is evident only when the two models are compared to one another. Redundancy is not evident in the more comprehensive model by itself because only the final value of the coefficient is known, not how it has been changed by the addition of the other independent variable. The comprehensive model is informative, however, about whether there is a unique contribution from the focal independent variable.

The possible results from the analysis of redundancy are isomorphic to the results of the analysis of spuriousness. First, the association between the focal independent variable and the dependent variable may be eliminated. This result means that the nonspurious association between these variables is completely redundant with the effects of the other independent variable on the dependent variable (Figure 6.1a).

The second possibility is *partial redundancy*. In this instance, the alternate independent variable accounts for some, but not all, of the nonspurious focal association. The introduction of X_i reduces the magnitude of the association between X_f and Y, but some covariation remains, a possibility illustrated by the dashed line in Figure 6.1b. Although some of the nonspurious focal association can be attributed to covariation between X_f and X_i, some of it appears to be due to the unique influence of X_f on Y.

Third, the association between the focal independent and dependent variable may remain unchanged when the other independent variable is added to the analysis, as suggested in Figure 6.1c. Here we see that the prerequisites for redundancy have been satisfied insofar as all three variables are associated with one another. However, adding the alternate independent variable to the model does not alter the magnitude of the association between the focal independent variable and the dependent variable. Y depends upon X_i, which is also associated with X_f, but X_f continues to influence Y. The independent variables are associated with one another, but none of the association between X_f and Y can be attributed to redundancy with the other independent variable.

Fourth, the analysis of redundancy may reveal instead suppression. In this instance, the addition of a second independent variable *increases* the magnitude of the association between the focal independent variable and the dependent variable. The bold line in Figure 6.2 signifies that X_i magnifies the association between X_f and Y. The concealed association is revealed only when the other independent variable is taken into consideration. When this variable is not part of the model, X_f and Y appear to be unrelated to one another. In other instances, a weak association is strengthened when the suppressor variable is introduced into the analysis.

Figure 6.2

The Focal Relationship and Suppression

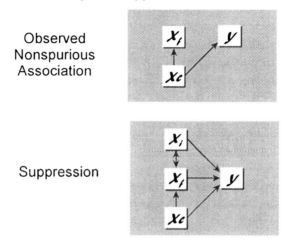

Observed
Nonspurious
Association

Suppression

In sum, there are four possible outcomes of the analysis of redundancy (Figures 6.1 and 6.2), but only two of these results are indicative of redundancy. Redundancy is present when there is a complete (Figure 6.1a) or partial (Figure 6.1b) reduction in the magnitude of the association between the focal independent variable and the dependent variable with the addition of another independent variable. If instead this association is intensified (Figure 6.2), then an association that was suppressed is revealed. Finally, if the association remains unchanged (Figure 6.1c), then redundancy can be ruled out as the source of the nonspurious association between the focal independent and dependent variables.

Our analytic goal continues to be establishing the focal relationship as a relationship. This interpretation gains credence when the addition of other independent variables does not account for the association between X_f and Y. In this context, we hope the test for redundancy fails.

Mate Availability: An Example of Redundancy

The role of other independent variables in elucidating a focal relationship is illustrated by a recent analysis of racial differences in marriage (Lichter, McLaughlin, Kephart, & Landry 1992). This analysis attempts to explain the substantially lower rate of marriage among African American than among white women. Thus, race and marriage are the independent and dependent variables, respectively. The alternative independent variable is the availability of marriageable males, operationalized as the ratio of males to females among unmarried persons of the same race. As shown in Figure 6.3, the analysis of this basic three-variable model—race, marriage, and mate availability—also takes into consideration several other variables that are known antecedents of marriage. Although these other independent variables contribute to the explanation of race differences in marriage, the emphasis of this research is on one particular independent variable, the availability of males in the local marriage market.

Lichter and colleagues (1992) contend that shortages of males in local marriage markets lower transitions to first marriages among women. They note that black women encounter especially marked shortages of marriageable men, a scarcity that accounts, at least in part, for the lower transitions to first marriages of black women compared to those of white women. The observed association between race and marriage, then, is seen as being due to an association between the two independent variables, race and mate availability.

Figure 6.3

Racial Differences in Marriage

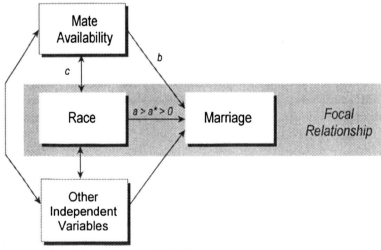

Source: Adapted from Lichter et al. (1992).

This idea is feasible insofar as the three variables are associated with one another in the expected manner. First, a, the focal relationship—race and marriage: Among never married women aged 18 to 28 years, black women are only about 43% as likely as white women to marry at any given age. Second, b, the sex ratio has a positive effect on the transition to first marriage: Areas with a high density of men tend to have high rates of marriage among women. Finally, c, the two independent variables are associated: The sex ratio is much lower on average for blacks than whites, especially for "economically attractive" men. For every three unmarried black women in their 20s, there is roughly one unmarried man with earnings above the poverty threshold; for whites, there are two such men for every three unmarried women.

Although consistent with redundancy, these associations alone are insufficient to demonstrate that racial differences in mate availability do indeed account for racial differences in marriage. To determine whether this effect occurs, the impact of race on marriage was compared across two models that differed only by whether the sex ratio was included. The addition of this variable reduced the average racial difference in marriage by 20% (a^*). However, it did not eliminate the race effect (i.e., $a^* \geq 0$). The researchers also report that the effects of mate availability are similar for unmarried women of both races.

Racial differences in mate availability, therefore, account for some but by no means all of the racial difference in marriage. Although a small effect, market composition nevertheless accounts for more of the observed racial difference in first marriage than the set of other independent variables, which includes family background, premarital childbearing, economic independence, and multigenerational living arrangements. Lichter and associates (1992) conclude that racial differences in marriage are located more in structural marriage market opportunities than in the individual-level factors typically considered in previous research.

The economic emphasis of this report may seem a bit cynical to those who view marriage more romantically, emphasizing love, passion, and enchantment. It appears, however, that women are not the only ones with a market orientation toward marriage. The researchers also report that women with the most economic resources are the most likely to marry. Alternatively, one could say that men seem to prefer women with economically attractive traits.

Multiple Sources of Redundancy

As just mentioned, we usually hope that the focal relationship will survive the test for redundancy. This result means that X_f continues to be associated with Y when X_i is included in the analysis. This association may be smaller than before, but it is still present. Although we would like to interpret the remaining covariation as the unique influence of X_f on Y, we must first consider the possibility that it is redundant with yet other independent variables. Stated differently, the focal relationship may be redundant with more than one other relationship. Each of several independent variables may overlap somewhat with the effects of the focal independent variable. Although none of these variables may fully account for the focal relationship by itself, the set as a whole may do so, a possibility illustrated in Figure 6.4a.

Instead of one additional independent variable, we now have a set of additional independent variables, X_{i1} to X_{i+}. Each of these independent variables is associated with the focal independent variable X_f. Each independent variable is also related to the dependent variable Y. In combination, the set of other independent variables fully accounts for the focal relationship, even though each individual independent variable by itself may leave some covariation between the focal independent variable and the dependent variable.

Most real data applications are not this tidy, however, and yield mixed results, as illustrated in Figure 6.4b. In this example, X_f and Y are each associated with three of the other independent variables. Only two independent variables, X_{i2} and X_{i4}, are associated with both X_f and Y; These are the only variables contributing to redundancy. Although X_{i1}, X_{i3} and X_{i6} are part of a set of variables that collectively produces redundancy, these particular variables are not contributing to that redundancy. Thus, the set as a whole may generate redundancy without every component variable contributing to this result. In this instance, redundancy can be attributed to only some of the variables in the set (in this example, X_{i2} and X_{i4}). However, the inclusion of several other independent variables does not necessarily account fully for the focal relationship. Covariation net of the other independent variables is indicated in Figure 6.4b by the dashed line.

Figure 6.4

Complex Redundancy

(a) Multiple Sources of Complete Redundancy

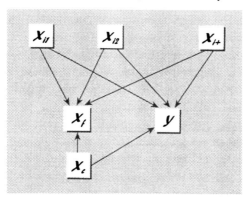

(b) Mixed Case of Partial Redundancy

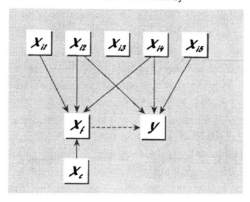

Considerations in the Selection of Independent Variables

The analytic value of differentiating redundancy from the unique influence of the focal independent variable hinges upon the worthiness of the other independent variables used in the analysis. This set should include all variables that are theoretically linked to the dependent variable and that covary with the focal independent variable. As just discussed, these are the only independent variables that can produce redundancy in the focal relationship.

These variables are identified in two ways. The first approach is a thorough review of the existing literature on the phenomenon under investigation. This review should encompass all meaningful perspectives on the phenomenon, including those with which the researcher disagrees. Variables identified in this manner are likely to be associated with the dependent variable because competing theories generally address the same phenomenon. The existing literature may be mute about their association with the focal independent variable, however, because the latter is ideally a novel addition to our understanding of the phenomenon. In these circumstances, one should err on the conservative side and include these other independent variables in the analysis.

The second approach is decidedly "nonscientific": intuition combined with common sense. This approach is likely to identify variables that are not specific elements in competing theories, but are generally understood to have a bearing on the phenomenon under investigation. We often lack specific evidence that these variables are empirically linked to the focal relationship simply because this research has not yet been conducted. In addition, we often have hunches about relationships that cannot be linked to a specific theoretical framework. This awareness flows from our absorption in the phenomenon we are investigating. Such contemplation often yields vague ideas about how to proceed. It is generally a good idea to listen to these whispers from the unconscious. Variables such as these are added to the model, then, with the supposition that they *may* produce redundancy.

It is also desirable to include variables that are connected to the dependent variable, but lack an association with the focal independent variable. These independent variables cannot produce redundancy and, therefore, are not helpful in distilling the uniqueness of the focal relationship. They are, however, empirically useful in accounting for the phenomenon under investigation. Since this phenomenon was the origin of our interest in the focal relationship, we remain interested in factors that account for it even if these factors do not advance our understanding of the focal relationship. In addition, the model is misspecified when such variables are omitted.

The preceding point does not apply to independent variables that are associated with the focal independent variable but not the dependent variable. The inclusion of these variables does not add anything to the analysis of the focal relationship or the phenomenon under investigation.

These comments do not mean, however, that any old variable should be added to the model. The hodgepodge approach more often clouds our understanding of the phenomenon than enlightens it. In addition, this approach unnecessarily uses up degrees of freedom, thereby detracting from the statistical power of the analysis. The selection of other independent variables, even when aided by intuition, should tap only those variables that are likely to advance our understanding of the phenomenon under investigation, especially the focal relationship.

The selection of the set of alternative independent variables is of obvious importance to the quality of the assessment of any unique effect of X_f. When no other explanatory factors are considered, we have little confidence that the focal relationship is unique. Our confidence increases as the number of relevant independent variables that are ruled out increases. However, we necessarily remain skeptical because we cannot rule out all possible sources of redundancy because these possibilities are endless.

Analytic Models for Redundancy

The analytic strategy for redundancy is similar to that described in the previous chapter for spuriousness, but starts where the analysis of spuriousness leaves off. In the analysis of spuriousness, we compared the total association from a bivariate model to the partial association from a multivariate model that controls for spuriousness. Covariation remaining at the end of this analysis was interpreted as a probable relationship between the independent and dependent variables.

The analysis of redundancy starts not with the total association between X_f and Y, but with the partial association remaining after spurious covariation has been removed. The nonspurious or relational component of the association between X_f and Y is then decomposed into two pieces: one reflecting the unique causal impact of X_f and the other reflecting the causal impact X_f shares in common with other independent variables.

This is an exclusionary strategy in that the uniqueness of the focal relationship is established by eliminating relatedness shared with other independent variables. Our interest lies with the covariation between the focal variables that remains when other independent variables are taken into consideration. Ideally, we would like to demonstrate that at least part of the focal relationship is separate and distinct from other influences on the dependent variable.

Redundancy for Numeric Outcomes

The multiple linear regression used in the analysis of spurious-ness is easily expanded to include additional independent vari-ables. In the analysis of redundancy, we compare the regression coefficient b_f across two equations: a base equation that contains the set of control variables and a comprehensive equation that addi-tionally contains a set of other independent variables, $X_{i1}, \ldots, X_{i+}$. A decrease in the regression coefficient b_f between these equations is interpreted as evidence of redundancy between the focal inde-pendent variable and one or more of the additional independent variables, whereas no change indicates the absence of redundancy. A nonzero b_f in the comprehensive equation is interpreted as a probable unique relationship between X_f and Y.

The analysis of redundancy starts with the partial association b_f from the regression equation that controls for spuriousness. The relevant equation is from the last step of the analysis of spurious-ness (Equation 5.7) and is reproduced here as the first step in the analysis of redundancy:

$$\widehat{Y} = b_0 + b_f X_f + b_{c1} X_{c1} + b_{c2} X_{c2} + \cdots + b_{c+} X_{c+}. \qquad (6.1)$$

This equation gives the total nonspurious association between the focal variables as b_f given that the model contains the control vari-ables $X_{c1}, X_{c2}, \ldots, X_c$.

We then estimate the unique component of the focal relationship by estimating the effects it shares in common with other indepen-dent variables and removing this redundant component from the estimate of the total focal relationship. This separation is accom-plished by adding other independent variables $X_{i1}, X_{i2}, \ldots, X_{i+}$ to Equation 6.1:

$$\widehat{Y} = b_0 + b_f X_f + b_{c1} X_{c1} + b_{c2} X_{c2} + \cdots + b_{c+} X_{c+}$$
$$+ b_{i1} X_{i1} + b_{i2} X_{i2} + \cdots + b_{i+} X_{i+}, \qquad (6.2)$$

where b_0 is the estimated value of Y when the focal independent vari-able and all of the control and other independent variables equal 0. $b_{i1} \cdots b_{i+}$ are the unstandardized regression coefficients for the other independent variables, and, as before, $b_{c1} \cdots b_{c+}$ are the coefficients for the control variables, and b_f is the coefficient for the focal inde-pendent variable. Each coefficient gives the change in Y for a one-unit increase in X with all other variables in the equation held constant.

The incremental contribution of $X_{i1}, X_{i2}, \ldots, X_{i+}$ is assessed as the difference in R^2 (see Chapter 5, note 6), which tests the null hypothesis $b_{i1} = \cdots = b_{i+} = 0$. If this test is not statistically significant, then the set of independent variables does not contribute to the explanation of Y. Otherwise, the individual coefficients are tested using the t test.

Again, our focus is on what happens to the regression coefficient for the focal relationship, b_f, when the set of other independent variables $(X_{i1}, \ldots, X_{i+})$ is added to the model. If b_f is reduced to 0 from Equation 6.1 to Equation 6.2, then all of the nonspurious focal relationship can be attributed to the redundancy of X_f with the set of other independent variables.

If, instead, b_f is unchanged by the addition of the set of other independent variables, then none of the nonspurious focal association can be considered redundant. From this perspective, it is immaterial whether any of the other variables are also related to Y. The concern is solely with any change in b_f that accompanies the addition of the set of independent variables. Finding an association between other variables and the dependent variable is insufficient to demonstrate redundancy; it is also necessary that the value for b_f be reduced in size.

In between these two extremes, redundancy accounts for some, but not all, of the nonspurious covariation between X_f and Y. In this instance, the addition of the set of other independent variables reduces b_f in size, but the coefficient continues to differ significantly from 0. The remaining nonzero component of b_f can be interpreted as the probable unique effect of the focal independent variable.

One other result merits attention: the possibility that b_f increases when other independent variables are added to the multivariate model. This increase means that one or more of the other independent variables act as a suppressor of the focal relationship. In this instance, controlling for the other independent variable reveals a previously concealed component of the focal relationship or shows it to be greater than originally estimated.

The unique contribution of X_f can also be ascertained by calculating the increment in R^2 achieved by the comprehensive model (Equation 6.2) relative to a reduced model that contains all of the same variables except the focal independent variable (see Chapter 5, note 6). This comparison provides a straightforward interpretation of the unique effect of the focal independent variable as the increment in explained variance over and above the variance accounted for by the combined influence of all other independent and control variables. This is the same as the test for b_f in the full equation.

ANALYSIS JOURNAL: Redundancy for Numeric Outcomes

We return to our continuing example of family income and mastery and ask whether this association is produced by redundancy between family income and some other independent variable. One possibility concerns the social environment, in particular the neighborhood in which the family lives. Research has linked characteristics of neighborhood to several adolescent outcomes including starting sex at an early age, early age at birth of first child, problem behavior, and symptoms of emotional distress (Aneshensel & Sucoff, 1996). Mastery is a nonspecific protective factor for these types of outcomes, raising the possibility that mastery may also be linked to characteristics of neighborhood. For example, living in a threatening environment may impede the development of mastery among teens because their perception of being subject to forces outside of their control is accurate. For income to be redundant with neighborhood, however, neighborhood has to be associated not only with mastery, but also with income. This connection is highly probable because families choose neighbors with matching incomes. An alternative perspective on neighborhood is that young people who live in one place for a long time may come to feel secure in that location, even if the location itself contains danger.

The measure of neighborhood used in this example is ambient hazards, which comprises 11 statements, such as, "violent crimes happen here," "there's tension between different ethnic groups," and "this is a safe place to live." Adolescents were asked how well these statements described their neighborhoods, with response categories ranging from (1) for "strongly disagree" through (4) for "strongly agree"; positively worded items were reversed so that a high score indicates a high level of threat. The summated scale was calibrated to these response categories by dividing by the number of items. It has very good reliability ($\alpha = .90$). The composite scale covers its full potential range, indicating that some of these teens live out of harm's way, whereas others live in extremely menacing neighborhoods. Residential stability is measured simply as whether the adolescent has lived in the same home for (1) 5 years or more versus (0) a shorter time.

A simple regression model shows that teens who perceive their neighborhoods as threatening tend to have lower levels of mastery ($b_i = -.137$; SE = .031; $p \leq .001$) than those living in more secure neighborhoods. The four-point difference between the extreme scores on the ambient hazards measures translates into a difference of slightly less than one-half point on the four-point mastery scale $[(-.137 \times 1) - (-.137 \times 4) = -.411]$. Residential stability is also associated with mastery $(b_i = .115; SE = .040; p \leq .01)$: Teens who have lived in their present home for at least 5 years score approximately one-tenth point $[(.115 \times 1) - (.115 \times 0) = .115]$ higher on the four-point mastery scale than those who have moved during this time. These variables need to be associated not only with mastery, but also with income, however, to generate redundancy. Both variables meet this criterion: Perceptions of the neighborhood as threatening are inversely correlated with

Regression of Mastery on Income and Other Independent Variables: The Impact of Neighborhood

Independent variables	Regression coefficients[a]
Family income	.002*
(thousands of $)[b]	(.001)
Ethnicity[c]	
African American	.095
	(.099)
Latino	−.053
	(.043)
Asian American/	−.118*
Other	(.058)
Male	.063*
	(.028)
Family Structure[d]	
Parent and Stepparent	.020
	(.038)
Single-Parent Family	−.010
	(.037)
Age (years)	.002
	(.012)
Ambient hazards	−.115***
	(.031)
Residentially stable	.085*
5 years or more/less	(.042)
Constant	2.963***
	(.184)
R^2	.072***

[a]Numbers in parentheses are robust standard errors.
[b]Focal relationship is in italics.
[c]Omitted reference category is white.
[d]Omitted reference category is intact nuclear family.
*$p \leq .05$. **$p \leq .01$. ***$p \leq .001$.

family income ($r = -.081$; $p \leq .001$), and family income is significantly lower among teens who have lived in their homes for less than 5 years ($27,788) than among those who have lived there for 5 or more years ($37,686; $p \leq .001$). Thus, these two variables are viable candidates for redundancy with income.

The impact of adding the two neighborhood variables to the regression equation containing all of the independent variables used in the analysis of spuriousness is shown in the table. Both variables are statistically significant, paralleling the bivariate results just reported. The inclusion of ambient hazards and residential tenure produces a substantial reduction in the magnitude of the coefficient for income from the spuriousness model. Despite this reduction, income continues to have a statistically significant association with mastery, although its probability level has become more uncertain. In other words, redundancy with neighborhood and residential stability accounts for some, but not all, of the association between income and mastery.

In addition to their impact on the focal relationship, ambient hazards and residential stability help to account for the dependent variable. This is demonstrated by their significant coefficients in the regression model, of course, but also by the increment in explanatory efficacy of this model compared to the model containing only income and the control variables that deal with spuriousness. The difference in R^2 values ($.073 - .048 = .025$; $p \leq .001$) is approximately half again the previous R^2 value.

Redundancy for Dichotomous Outcomes

The analysis of redundancy in the logistic regression model parallels the strategy just described for multiple linear regression. Despite computational differences, the logic of the analysis is identical for the two forms of regression. Our goal is to ascertain whether the focal independent variable X_f exerts a unique influence on the dependent variable Y net of the influence of all other independent variables (and net of the spurious influence of control variables).

To accomplish this goal, we test the null hypothesis that X_f does not influence Y when these other variables are included in the analysis. As usual, we hope to reject this null hypothesis.

Because we are interested only in the relatedness component of the covariation between the focal independent and dependent variables, we first remove any covariation that can be attributed to spuriousness with one or more control variables. In practice, this proviso means that the last step in the analysis of spuriousness is the first step in the analysis of redundancy. The final step in the logistic model for spuriousness (Equation 5.8) is reproduced here as the first step in the model for redundancy:

$$\log \hat{o}^{Y^+} = b_0 + b_f X_f + b_{c1} X_{c1} + b_{c2} X_{c2} + \cdots + b_{c+} X_{c+} \ . \qquad (6.3)$$

This equation gives the total nonspurious focal relationship as b_f.

To separate the unique and redundant components of the focal relationship, we add to the regression model the set of other independent variables:

$$\log \hat{o}^{Y^+} = b_0 + b_f X_f + b_{c1} X_{c1} + b_{c2} X_{c2} + \cdots + b_{c+} X_{c+}$$
$$+ b_{i1} X_{i1} + b_{i2} X_{i2} + \cdots + b_{i+} X_{i+}, \qquad (6.4)$$

where b_0 is the estimated log odds of being positive on Y when all of the X variables, including the focal independent variable, are 0. The unstandardized regression coefficients—b_f, $b_{c1} \cdots b_{c+}$, $b_{i1} \cdots b_{i+}$—give the increase in the log odds of being positive on Y for a one-unit increase in the corresponding variable, with all other X variables held constant. Redundancy is demonstrated by a decrease in b_f, this time from Equation 6.3 to Equation 6.4. The likelihood ratio test (see Chapter 5, note 8) is used to test the null hypothesis, H_0: $b_{i1} = \cdots = b_{i+} = 0$. If this hypothesis cannot be rejected, it means that the set of other independent variables does not contribute to the explanation of Y. If instead this overall test is rejected, the coefficients for individual variables are tested with Wald's χ^2.

If b_f decreases toward 0, the value indicative of no relationship, then the focal relationship is redundant with one or more of the other independent variables. This redundancy is complete if b_f approaches 0; it is partial if b_f differs significantly from zero. An increase in the regression coefficient, by contrast, is indicative of suppression. If the addition of the set of other independent variables does not alter b_f to a noticeable degree, then none of the nonspurious relationship can be attributed to redundancy between the focal independent variable and any of the other independent variables.

If redundancy is uncovered, we usually wish to know which independent variables produce this effect. Redundancy may be due to one other independent variable, several variables, or all of these variables. The model with multiple other independent variables gives the impact of each independent variable while simultaneously taking into consideration the impact of all of the other variables. This model may obscure the impact of individual variables if some of these variables are associated with one another and capture a common source of redundancy. As discussed earlier, this kind of situation is best diagnosed by examining models for subsets of other independent variables.

The unique contribution of X_f can also be ascertained by comparing the fit of the comprehensive model (Equation 6.4) to a reduced model that contains all of the same variables except the focal independent variable. The difference is tested with the likelihood ratio test (see Chapter 5, note 8), which tests the null hypothesis, H_0: $b_f = 0$, and is distributed as χ^2 with 1 degree of freedom. The difference in explanatory efficacy between these two models can be approximated by the difference in R_L^2 between models. These approaches assess the unique effect of the focal independent variable over and above that achieved by the combined influence of all other independent and control variables.

Although the additive expression of the logistic regression model demonstrates comparability in analytic strategy with the multiple linear regression model, it can be somewhat difficult to interpret substantively because coefficients are given in terms of log odds. As noted previously, the multiplicative expression is generally easier to interpret because effects are expressed in terms of odds, which have a more intuitive or familiar interpretation. The multiplicative expression for the logistic models for redundancy is obtained by taking the exponential of the previous models.

Specifically, the base comparison model—the final step in the analysis of suppression (see Equation 5.9)—is the exponential of the additive base model (Equation 6.3):

$$\hat{o}^{Y+} = e^{b_0} e^{b_f X_f} e^{b_{c1} X_{c1}} e^{b_{c2} X_{c2}} \cdots e^{b_{c+} X_{c+}} .$$
(6.5)

To assess redundancy, this base model is compared to a comprehensive model that also contains the influence of other independent variables. This model is obtained by taking the exponent of the additive comprehensive logistic model (Equation 6.4):

$$\hat{o}^{Y+} = e^{b_0} e^{b_f X_f} e^{b_{c1} X_{c1}} e^{b_{c2} X_{c2}} \cdots e^{b_{c+} X_{c+}} e^{b_{i1} X_{i1}} e^{b_{i2} X_{i2}} \cdots e^{b_{i+} X_{i+}} ,$$
(6.6)

where e^{b_0} is the estimated odds of being positive on Y when the focal independent variable, and all other independent variables and control variables are 0. The exponents of the regression coefficients give the multiplicative effect on the odds of being positive on Y for a one-unit change on the corresponding variable, holding all other variables constant. These exponential terms can be interpreted as odds ratios for dichotomous comparisons.

The unique contribution of X_f is given by e^{b_f}. Because this is a multiplicative model, a value of 1.00 indicates no association (rather than the value of 0 in the additive model). If redundancy is present, e^{b_f} should approach 1.00.

ANALYSIS JOURNAL: Redundancy for Dichotomous Outcomes

In the preceding analysis, we examined whether the association between income and mastery could be attributed to redundancy between income and the safety of the neighborhood in which the adolescent resides or how long he or she has lived in that neighborhood. We speculated that a threatening neighborhood might damage an adolescent's developing sense of mastery because the perceived lack of control over one's life is real. This would be the case if the menacing aspects of the neighborhood translated into personal experience, for example, if they led to being the victim of trauma.

To assess this possibility, we examine whether threatening conditions in the neighborhood are associated with whether the adolescent has experienced traumatic events. Exposure to trauma was assessed by asking three questions: Has anyone you know ever been hurt very badly or killed or been frightened that something terrible like this was really going to happen to them? Have you ever seen anyone being injured badly or killed or in real danger of having something horrible like this happen? Has anything like this ever happened to you? Additional information about the event and its circumstances, such as the type of event and its severity was obtained, but the present analysis focuses simply on whether the teen had been victimized and whether he or she knew someone or saw someone being victimized. Vicarious victimization is included because we learn not only from our own experiences, but also from observing what happens to the people around us. These are dichotomous dependent variables, which illustrate the use of logistic regression to analyze redundancy.

Overall, about a quarter of the sample had personally experienced a traumatic event, more than half had experienced trauma vicariously, and only a third had not had either experience. The simple logistic regressions show that ambient hazards are significantly associated with the log odds of having experienced a traumatic event, either personally ($b_f = .509$; SE = .177; $p \leq .005$; $e^{b_f} = 1.66$) or vicariously ($b_f = .657$; SE = .142; $p \leq .001$; $e^{b_f} = 1.93$). The exponents of the regression coefficients express these associations as odds ratios. For example, teens who are at the worst extreme of the ambient hazards measure (code 4), have 4.6 times ($1.66^4/1.66 = 1.66^3$) and 7.2 times ($1.93^4/1.93 = 1.93^3$) greater odds of having experienced trauma personally or vicariously, respectively, than those at the most benign extreme (code 1).

For each dependent variable, Model 1 adds the variables used in the analysis of the income-mastery association to control for spuriousness as shown in the table. Several of these demographic characteristics—income, ethnicity, and family structure—affect the options and constraints that families face in choosing a home and, thus, influence indirectly the exposure of their sons and daughters to traumatic events that occur within the neighborhood. These family characteristics may also be associated with parental behavior, especially the control that parents seek to exert over their children and, thus, their risk of victimization. Similarly, older teens and males generally are granted more independence and latitude to take risks and, therefore, are more likely to be in contact with threatening aspects of their neighborhoods and to be exposed to traumatic events.

As can be seen, however, only one coefficient is statistically significant for both dependent variables: Being older is associated with a slight increase in the odds of exposure to trauma net of the other variables in the model. In addition, Latino teens have about half the odds as white teens of personally experiencing a traumatic event and teens living with a parent and stepparent have substantially higher odds of vicarious exposure than do teens living in intact nuclear families. Relative to the bivariate regression, the inclusion of these control variables increases the coefficient for ambient hazards for personal victimization, but decreases it for vicarious victimization. In both equations, however, the coefficient for ambient hazards remains large and statistically significant.

Let us consider an alternative. Perhaps teens are not put at risk by their neighborhoods, but are instead jeopardized by their own actions. The presence in the neighborhood of conditions such as violent crime, property damage, gangs, and drug use and dealing—the conditions assessed in the ambient hazards measure—is likely to be associated with engaging in these kinds of behavior oneself, a contagion model of delinquent behavior. This alternative hypothesis is tested with a count of the number of problem behaviors the adolescent self-reports over the past year, including, for example, having a serious fight, damaging property, using a weapon, lying, and taking anger out on others. Almost 90% of these teens engaged in at least 1 of 23 possible behaviors, and the average is about 4. The simple logistic regression coefficients indicate that problem behaviors are associated with both personal (b_i = .175; SE = .032; $p \leq$ .001; e^{b_i} = 1.19) and vicarious (b_i = .201; SE = .028; $p \leq$ .001; e^{b_i} = 1.22) exposure to trauma.

Model 2 shows the impact of adding problem behaviors to the previous model containing ambient hazards and the sociodemographic control variables. The regression coefficient for ambient hazards is reduced by about a third for both personal and vicarious exposure to trauma. Both of these coefficients, however, remain statistically significant although with more uncertainty. Thus, the tendency for teens who engage in problem behaviors (the other independent variable) to experience trauma either personally or vicariously (the dependent variables) accounts for some, but not all of the association between these experiences and living in a hostile neighborhood (the focal independent variable). This reduction in the magnitude of the focal relationship is due to the association between neighborhood threat (X_f) and adolescent problem behavior (X_i).

In addition to reducing the impact of the focal independent variable, adolescent problem behaviors help to account for the occurrence of the dependent variables, as also shown in Model 2. Even teens who have an average score (4) on these behaviors have about twice the odds of experiencing personal (odds ratio [OR] = 1.84) or vicarious (OR = 2.19) traumatic events as teens with none of these behaviors, net of other variables in the model. Teens at the 90th percentile (7) for problem behaviors have 3 to 4 times greater odds of experiencing personal (OR = 2.92) or vicarious trauma (OR = 3.97), other things being equal. Thus, the behavior of teens contributes to their own experience of trauma and accounts for some of the risk associated with living in a hostile neighborhood, indicating redundancy, but some of the neighborhood risk remains even when behavior is taken into consideration.

Logistic Regression Coefficients for Personal and Vicarious Exposure to Traumatic Events: Problem Behaviors

Independent Variables	Personal Exposure[a]				Vicarious Exposure[a]			
	Model 1		Model 2		Model 1		Model 2	
	b	e[b]	b	e[b]	b	e[b]	b	e[b]
Ambient hazards[b]	.600***	1.822	.413*	1.511	.523***	1.687	.335*	1.398
	(.179)		(.178)		(.157)		(.160)	
Problem behaviors			.153***	1.165			.197***	1.212
			(.032)				(.034)	
Family income (thousands of $)	.002	1.000	-.001	0.999	.003	1.003	-.001	.999
	(.005)		(.005)		(.004)		(.004)	
Ethnicity[c]								
African American	-.350	0.704	-.194	0.823	.252	1.287	.431	1.538
	(.385)		(.364)		(.246)		(.253)	
Latino	-.686*	0.503	-.665*	0.514	.472	1.603	.549*	1.731
	(.298)		(.295)		(.250)		(.262)	
Asian American/Other	-.447	0.639	-.375	0.687	-.182	.833	-.084	.919
	(.301)		(.302)		(.277)		(.284)	

Male	*.424** (.192)	1.528	*.411** (.195)	1.509	*.134* (.155)	1.143	*.147* (.158)	1.158
Family structure[d]								
Parent and Stepparent	*.278* (.270)	1.321	*.216* (.279)	1.299	*.526** (.242)	1.692	*.553** (.245)	1.739
Single-parent family	*.385* (.212)	1.469	*.262* (.217)	1.299	*.181* (.194)	1.198	*.044* (.206)	1.045
Age (years)	*.126** (.058)	1.134	*.085* (.059)	1.089	*.120** (.053)	1.128	*.078* (.052)	1.082
Constant	*-4.411**** (1.072)		*-3.954**** (1.062)		*-3.214****** (.840)		*-2.853**** (.837)	
Model χ^2 (df)	*41.39 (9)****		*75.09 (10)****		*52.43 (9)****		*86.87 (10)****	
Pseudo-R^2	*.046*		*.077*		*.044*		*.091*	

[a]Numbers in parentheses are robust standard errors.
[b]Focal relationship is in italics.
[c]Omitted reference category is white.
[d]Omitted reference category is intact nuclear family.
*$p \leq .05$ **$p \leq .01$ ***$p \leq .001$.

Control Versus Independent Variable

Redundancy Versus Spuriousness

The requirements for redundancy are highly similar to the requirements for spuriousness (see Table 4.2, criteria for an effectual exclusionary variable). Indeed, these requirements are identical when viewed solely as patterns of associations among variables. Control variables and other independent variables also appear to be quite similar insofar as each plays an exclusionary role in the estimation of the focal relationship. The analytic technique is similar as well: estimating the impact of the focal independent variable that remains when the effects of these other variables are taken into consideration. Furthermore, multivariate analytic techniques do not require this differentiation and control variables are treated in the same manner as any other independent variable. Thus, the difference between spuriousness and redundancy is conceptual not empirical. It lies not in the covariation among the three variables, but in the meaning attributed to this covariation.

The difference between redundancy and spuriousness is illustrated in Figure 6.5. The two components of the focal relationship, X_f and Y, are the same in these two configurations. Each model also contains a third variable and this third variable influences the dependent variable. The difference lies in the placement of this third variable. The third variable is causally antecedent to the focal independent variable in spuriousness, whereas these two variables merely covary in redundancy.

The different label for the third variable—control variable versus other independent variable—calls attention to the different

Figure 6.5

Spuriousness and Redundancy

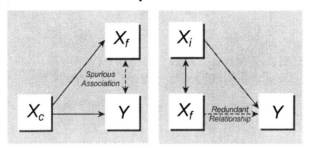

functions it performs in spuriousness and redundancy. In spuriousness, the control variable functions as an independent variable and the remaining two variables function as dependent variables. There are two relationships (X_c and Y and X_c and X_f) that account for one association (X_f and Y). In redundancy, there are two independent variables and only one dependent variable. There is one association (X_i and X_f) that makes two apparent relationships (X_i and Y and X_f and Y) empirically interchangeable with one another.

The distinction between these types of variables pertains to the nature of the covariation that is being removed from the estimate of the focal relationship. Control variables are used to remove spurious covariation, whereas other independent variables are used to remove redundant covariation. The analysis of redundancy logically follows the analysis of spuriousness. Whether an effect is unique or redundant matters only when it is reasonable to suppose that an effect is present, that is, when at least some of the empirical association is nonspurious. Whereas redundancy pertains to a causal process, spuriousness is noise.

The value of this differentiation lies in the distinctive conceptual meaning of spuriousness and redundancy relative to the focal relationship. In the case of spuriousness, X_f depends upon the third variable; in the case of redundancy, X_f merely happens to covary with the third variable. Thus, for spuriousness, the issue is whether covariation is indicative of a relationship. For redundancy, the issue is whether covariation that appears to be a relationship indicates a unique effect for the focal relationship. This conceptual distinction flows from the nature of the association between the third variable and the focal independent variable.

The distinction I draw between control and independent variables, therefore, is conceptual. Its value comes in the formulation of the theoretical model and in the interpretation of results. If the analysis is primarily concerned with the explanation of the dependent variable (as distinct from the explanation of a focal relationship), then the distinction between control and other independent variables is immaterial because the placement of independent variables relative to one another is extraneous. If instead, the analysis seeks to elaborate the focal relationship, the distinction between spuriousness and alternative theoretical processes adds considerable insight.

Summary

To recap, redundancy refers to that part of the focal relationship that overlaps with other causal processes, whereas the unique component pertains to the separate and distinct influence of the focal independent variable. In general, we hope to show that the contribution of the focal relationship to our understanding of the dependent variable is over and above the understanding provided by other theoretical explanations. In this case, the addition of the focal independent variable necessarily increases the total explanatory power of the model.

Despite the use of multiple control variables, the covariation between the focal variables may nevertheless be redundant with omitted variables. It is not possible to exclude all potential sources of redundancy because the list of other independent variables is infinite. In addition, we often lack measures of some important variables. Even when all reasonable independent variables are taken into consideration, therefore, there remains the possibility that the focal relationship is redundant with some other unknown causal factor.

However, we are now on far firmer ground than at the start of our analysis. The original bivariate association could have been a chance occurrence, but we used probability theory to determine that this is unlikely to be the case. It could also have been spurious, but we have used control variables to demonstrate that at least some of this association persists when spuriousness is controlled. The remaining covariation might also have been redundant, but we have now taken into consideration a reasonable set of other independent variables. The cumulative result of these exclusionary strategies enables us to assert with some confidence, which nevertheless falls short of certainty, that the focal relationship represents the unique influence of the focal independent variable on the dependent variable.

7 Elaborating an Explanation: Antecedent, Intervening, and Consequent Variables

We turn now to inclusive strategies for establishing the focal relationship as the relationship anticipated by theory. Exclusionary strategies, considered in the preceding two chapters, demonstrate that the observed association is neither spurious nor redundant, and, although essential, merely whet one's appetite for affirmative evidence. Ideally, the analyst also seeks to demonstrate that the focal relationship fits within a surrounding set of other relationships that collectively comprise the complete theoretical model.

This goal is accomplished by linking the focal relationship to other relationships. These linkages are forged with three types of variables: *antecedent*, *intervening*, and *consequent* variables. These variables correspond, respectively, to the origins of the focal relationship, the mechanics by which it operates, and its sequelae.

The explanatory function of these variables is most evident for the intervening variable, which delineates the causal mechanisms producing the observed relationship between the focal independent and dependent variables. The specification of intervening variables clarifies how the independent variable affects the dependent variable. The intervening variable is used to decompose the focal relationship into its component parts: An indirect relationship that is transmitted through the intervening variable, and a direct relationship, which is the relationship between the independent and dependent variables that remains after the indirect relationship is taken into account.

If one's theory is valid, then the inclusion of the intervening variable should account for some or all of the focal relationship. The analytic goal is to increase the indirect component, which necessarily decreases the direct component. When the intervening variable instead leaves the focal relationship intact, the underlying theory is discredited. In this instance, the observed association between the focal independent and dependent variables may indeed represent a relationship, but a relationship generated by mechanisms other than those specified by the theoretical model.

The focal relationship also is elaborated through the inclusion of antecedent variables and consequent variables. These variables are like bookends supporting the focal relationship: The antecedent variable conceptually precedes the primary independent variable, whereas the consequent variable extends the causal sequence beyond the primary dependent variable. In contrast to the intervening variable, the addition of antecedent and consequent variables is not expected to alter the focal relationship. These "third variables" help us to understand the focal relationship by examining it as an element within a lengthy sequence.

The theoretical framework guiding the research determines whether a variable occupies the role of an antecedent, intervening, or consequent variable. For example, Cooksey and Fondell (1996) call attention to the various ways in which the social role of father has been conceptualized with regard to child achievement. They summarize two perspectives that have been used in previous research. The first treats father-child relations, in particular, time spent with children, as the dependent variable when examining differences between various forms of family structure. This focal relationship is illustrated as pathway *a* in Figure 7.1. From this vantage, child achievement can be seen as a consequent variable. The analysis of child achievement as an additional dependent

Figure 7.1

Antecedents and Consequences of the Time Fathers Spend With Their Children

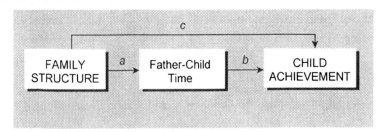

Source: Adapted from Cooksey and Fondell (1996).

variable does not alter the results from the analysis of father-child time because these are separate dependent variables.

The second approach treats time spent with children as an independent variable predicting child outcomes, in particular academic achievement. This focal relationship is illustrated as pathway b in Figure 7.1. From this perspective, family structure can be seen as an antecedent variable. As an antecedent variable, it may affect not only the independent variable, but also the dependent variable, indicated by pathway c. In this situation, the key distinguishing feature of family structure as an antecedent variable (versus a control variable) is that the inclusion of family structure is not expected to alter the relationship between father-child time and child achievement (pathway b).

Note the subtle distinction between the roles of family structure in these two perspectives. Family structure is the focal independent variable with regard to the dependent variable of father-child time, but it is an antecedent variable with regard to the focal relationship between father-child time and child achievement. A similar shift in viewpoint is evident for child achievement. Although it is a dependent variable in both perspectives, it is the focal dependent variable with regard to father-child time, but extends the causal sequence for the primary dependent variable of father-child time, functioning as a consequent variable.

Father-child time plays several roles in this example as well. In the first approach, it is a dependent variable, but in the second approach, it is an independent variable. When these two perspectives are integrated, father-child time functions as an intervening variable. The juxtaposition of these two approaches, therefore, changes the function of father-child time. More importantly, it integrates two relationships to form an extended causal sequence involving three variables. To the extent that this sequence fits theoretical expectations, the sequence supports the internal validity of both of its constituent relationships; that is, the connection between family structure and father-child time on the one hand and the connection between father-child time and child achievement on the other hand.

Cooksey and Fondell (1996) test the supposition that father-child time serves as an intervening variable, mediating the impact of family structure on child achievement. They analyze survey data from a nationally representative sample of families and households. The analytic subsample comprises 1,250 males residing in a household with a child between 5 and 18 years of age. They find that the type of family structure connecting fathers and children influences both the activities that fathers engage in with their children (pathway *a* in Figure 7.1) and their children's grades in school (pathway *c* in Figure 7.1). Compared with biological fathers with intact marriages, stepfathers spend less time with their children, but single fathers spend more time in activities with their children. Gender matters as well: Compared to fathers with only sons, fathers with daughters (only daughters or both sons and daughters) are less likely to take part in activities with their children. On average, children from intact nuclear families perform better in school than children from other types of families, especially children from single-father households and children living with stepfathers. In addition, father-child time, measured across a wide array of activities, is positively associated with academic achievement (pathway *b* in Figure 7.1). Father-child time, however, does little if anything to diminish the direct effects of family structure on achievement (pathway *c* in Figure 7.1). In other words, both family structure and father-child time are associated with children's academic achievement, but father-child time does not mediate the effects of family structure on achievement. The influence of family structure on child achievement is either direct, or it operates through mechanisms other than the time fathers spend with their children.

Intervening Variables: The Causal Mechanism

Mediation

The specification of an intervening variable means that the connection between the independent and dependent variables is thought to be indirect, transmitted by means of an intermediary. In this situation, the focal relationship exists because the independent variable influences the intervening variable, which, in turn, influences the dependent variable. The effect of the independent variable is transmitted through the intervening variable. Thus, intervening variables are often referred to as *mediating variables*.

The intervening variable elaborates the focal relationship by specifying its internal mechanisms. From this perspective, the focal independent variable and the dependent variable form the external boundaries of the focal relationship. Its interior is composed of intervening variables. An intervening variable is a bridge connecting the end points of the focal relationship. This connection, independent-intervening-dependent variable, illustrated in Figure 7.2, is explanatory insofar as it describes how the focal independent variable affects the dependent variable.

In the simplest case (Figure 7.2a), the focal relationship is produced by a single intervening variable (X_v).[1] This one mediator conveys the entire impact of the focal independent variable on the dependent variable. In other instances, several intervening variables may be arrayed in a chain-like sequence; the bridge between the independent variable and the dependent variable, formed by a series of indirect pathways (Figure 7.2b), resembles a viaduct. In still other instances, there are several bridges (Figure 7.2c), each of which conveys part of the influence of the focal independent variable on the dependent variable, alternate routes to the same destination. In addition, these patterns may be intermixed with one another (not shown).

The intervening variable *always* plays dual analytic roles. First, it is a dependent variable, affected by the focal independent variable. Second, it is an independent variable, affecting the dependent variable. Both of these connections are necessary components of the intervening variable. If a third variable is connected only to the focal independent variable or only to the focal dependent variable, it cannot serve a connective function and, therefore, is not an intervening variable.[2] This principle is analogous to contiguity in

Figure 7.2

The Focal Relationship and Intervening Variables

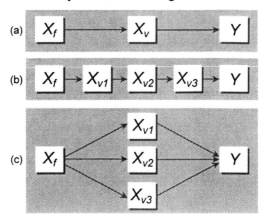

mechanical devices, in which components must be touching for an effect to be transmitted (Little, 1991).

In expanding the explanatory sequence, the intervening variable transforms the nature of the focal relationship. In the absence of an intervening variable, the focal relationship specifies a *direct link* between the independent and dependent variable: The impact of the independent variable is firsthand, immediate and proximal. The addition of an intervening variable modifies this connection so that the independent variable has an *indirect link* to the dependent variable. Its impact is secondhand, delayed, and distal. The effect of the independent variable becomes one step removed when an intervening variable intercedes.

A brief example illustrates how intervening variables are used to explicate a focal relationship. Broman (1993) dissects an empirical association between race and marital well-being to ascertain its sources. Using national survey data for a large sample ($N = 1,793$) of married persons, he finds that African Americans have lower levels of marital well-being than whites, with marital well-being assessed along two dimensions, harmony and satisfaction. Being older and male also contribute to marital well-being, whereas having a large number of children in the household detracts from it. Education, income, and employment status are included in the analysis, but do not have independent effects on marital well-being. The inclusion of these control variables means that the race difference in martial well-being cannot be attributed to corresponding differences between African American and whites in these demographic characteristics, illustrating the exclusionary strategy presented in the previous two chapters.

Broman (1993) considers three potential intervening variables to account for the racial difference in well-being: spousal emotional support, in-house work demands, and financial satisfaction. Previous research indicates that these dimensions are important to marital well-being, leading Broman to ask whether these factors intervene in its association with race and, therefore, account for some or all of the difference in marital well-being between African Americans and whites. In other words, these three variables are treated as mediators of the focal relationship between race and marital well-being. The results of his analysis are presented in Figure 7.3.

Two of the three potential intervening variables are independently associated with the focal dependent variable of marital

Figure 7.3

Mediators of the Relationship Between Race and Marital Well-Being

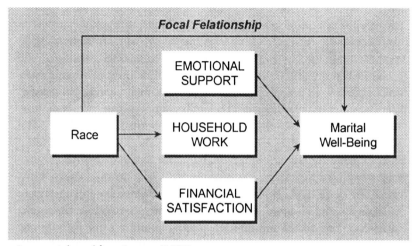

Source: Adapted from Broman (1993).

well-being: emotional support and financial satisfaction. The greater the support provided by one's husband or wife and the greater one's satisfaction with family finances, the greater one's sense of marital harmony and satisfaction. In addition, two of the potential intervening variables are independently associated with the focal independent variable of race: household work and financial satisfaction. African Americans are more likely than whites to perform large numbers of household chores and are less likely to be satisfied with finances. However, the inclusion of these potential mediators accounts for only a small portion of the total association between race and marital well-being. Compared to whites, African Americans report less harmony and satisfaction in their marriages even when some of the potential mechanisms for creating this differential are taken into account. This set of intervening variables, then, has only limited success in attaining the goal of explaining the focal relationship insofar as most of the relationship remains intact.

As shown in Figure 7.3, only one of these variables, financial satisfaction, actually functions as an intervening variable: It is affected by race and affects martial well-being. The other two variables play one of these roles, but not the other. Emotional support influences marital well-being, but does not differ between African Americans and whites. In contrast, household work differs by race, but does not independently contribute to marital well-being. For these two variables, any potential causal connection with the focal relationship is broken at one end of the sequence or the other. Consequently, neither emotional support nor household work serves as an intervening variable. Thus, the impact of race on marital well-being is mediated by only one variable, financial satisfaction.

This example illustrates several key analytic points. Most importantly, it shows how missing links in the causal sequence disconnect the flow of causal influence. The explanation of the focal relationship can be accomplished only by variables with continuous links to both the focal independent variable and the dependent variable. In this example, only financial satisfaction can perform this function; emotional support and household work cannot. Thus, only one of the three hypothesized linkages is validated by this analysis.

This example also demonstrates the distinction between explaining the focal relationship and explaining the dependent variable. For instance, emotional support contributes to our understanding of marital well-being, but does not advance our understanding of differences between African Americans and whites in martial well-being. In other words, this variable helps to account for the dependent variable, but not the focal relationship. Financial satisfaction, in contrast, helps to account for both the dependent variable and the focal relationship. This distinction is crucial. Variables that affect the outcome are not necessarily mediators. Contributing to the dependent variable is necessary for mediation but not sufficient; the mediator also needs to depend upon the focal independent variable.

Finally, this example illustrates not only an indirect link between race and marital well-being, but also the persistence of a direct link. This result means that the hypothesized causal mechanism explains some, but not all, of the impact of race on marital well-being. In other words, the pathway through financial strain is insufficient to carry the entire impact of race on marital well-being. Some other causal mechanisms presumably account for the left over covariation between the focal independent and dependent variables, mechanisms not examined in this particular research.

Explanation Through Elaboration

Whereas exclusionary strategies follow a negative proof procedure—what is neither spurious nor redundant supports theory—

elaboration with intervening variables follows a positive proof: that which can be explained in ways consistent with theory supports theory. Demonstrating that the focal independent variable affects the dependent variable in the manner specified by theory attests to the probable causal significance of the focal independent variable. This demonstration entails accounting for the unique focal relationship with intervening variables.

If we have been successful in deciphering the mechanisms generating the focal relationship, the inclusion of intervening variables into the statistical model will account for all of the effect of the focal independent variable on the dependent variable. This possibility is illustrated in Figure 7.4a: The absence of a pathway between X_f and Y indicates that there is no covariation remaining between the independent and dependent variables when the intervening variable

Figure 7.4

Elaboration of the Focal Relationship: Intervening Variables

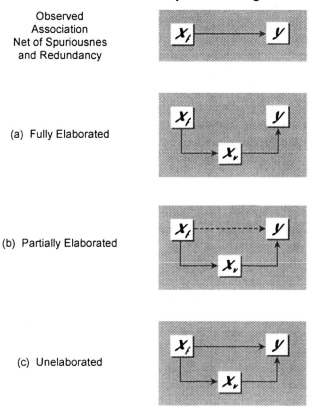

(X_v) is taken into account. This outcome is ideal in the sense that we have now fully explained how the independent variable affects the dependent variable. This elaboration of the focal relationship expands our understanding of the fundamental principles at work in generating the observed association between these variables.

At the end our analysis of spuriousness and redundancy, we hoped to have a large association remaining between the focal independent and dependent variables. With intervening variables, the goal is reversed: We hope to have little association left between the focal independent and dependent variables because it means that we have explained, in large part, how the relationship is generated. This explanation constitutes forceful evidence that the focal relationship is indeed not only a relationship, but also the specific relationship anticipated by theory. Thus, our goal is to fully specify the intervening linkages that form the focal relationship, which means that we hope to maximize the indirect effects and minimize any remaining direct effects.

The inclusion of intervening variables often substantially reduces the empirical association between the focal independent and dependent variables and may eliminate it entirely, as shown in Figure 7.4a. This pattern of results tends to occur because the dependent variable is more proximal to the intervening variable than the focal independent variable and because proximal effects tend to be stronger than distal effects. This full accounting is sometimes misinterpreted to mean that the focal independent variable is unimportant because it does not directly influence the dependent variable. This interpretation is simplistic because it equates the direct effect of a variable with its total effect, ignoring its indirect effect transmitted via intervening variables. Indirect effects have merely displaced the direct effect. Rather than showing the focal independent variable to be unimportant, this elaboration forcefully establishes its causal significance by showing how it operates. The focal relationship persists, but is now elaborated into its constituent elements. The specification of these constituents explicates rather than negates the focal relationship.

Detailing the means through which one variable influences another enhances the interpretation of the empirical association between these variables as a relationship rather than merely an association. It is ironic, then, that achieving this type of conceptual specification is sometimes misconstrued as demonstrating that the distal independent variable is irrelevant.

Incomplete Explanation

In many analyses, the specification of intervening variables accounts for some, but not all, of the focal relationship. This possibility is illustrated in Figure 7.4b. The dashed line between the independent and dependent variables signifies a direct relationship that remains over and above the indirect relationship operating through the intervening variable. This type of result is illustrated by the persistence of race differences in marital well-being when the potential intervening variable of financial satisfaction is taken into consideration (see Figure 7.3).

This pattern of results is quite common because our theories usually are incomplete accounts of the phenomenon under investigation. In this situation, theory explains some of the focal relationship but leaves some of this relationship unexplained. In other words, we have achieved explanation, but only partial explanation. The unexplained relationship, the persistence of a direct effect, suggests that other causal mechanisms are at work, a finding that is likely to redirect our attention to the further development of theory.

The specification of intervening variables may also leave the focal relationship unchanged, a possibility depicted in Figure 7.4c. The solid line between the independent and dependent variable signifies that the inclusion of the intervening variable has had little if any impact on the focal relationship. This pattern of results detracts a great deal from our theory because the focal relationship does not appear to be generated by the processes described in the theory being tested.

Note the following caveat. There is one particular instance in which we would like to observe the pattern of results illustrated in Figure 7.4c. This situation pertains to the "ruling out" function of intervening variables. Although intervening variables are usually used as an inclusive strategy, the technique may be applied as an exclusionary strategy as well. This would be the case, for example, when the intervening variable specifies an alternative theory that we hope to discount. This exclusionary use of intervening variables is strengthened when it is combined with other intervening variables used in an inclusive manner. Demonstrating that other internal mechanisms do not account for the focal relationship, does not, after all, demonstrate that the theorized mechanisms are indeed in operation. The ideal strategy, then, would be to demonstrate a lack of explanatory efficacy for alternative intervening variables while fully accounting for the focal relationship with the intervening variables specified by the theory being tested. This combined strategy provides exceedingly powerful support of one's theory. The successful application of this strategy obviously requires a well-developed theoretical framework complete with clearly articulated alternatives. This desirable state is elusive, however, because of underdeveloped theories.

Mediation, Spuriousness, and Redundancy

The successful elaboration of a focal relationship with intervening variables yields results that resemble those for spuriousness and redundancy: The addition of the third variable reduces or eliminates the empirical association between the focal independent and dependent variables. Indeed, the form of analysis is the same: A regression model is expanded to include a third variable, and we observe its impact on the regression coefficient for the focal independent variable. This coefficient diminishes or vanishes if the third variable uncovers spuriousness, redundancy, or indirect effects. The distinction between control variables, other independent variables, and intervening variables, then, must be sought on conceptual not empirical grounds.

The distinctions among these types of variables can be found in the structural arrangements thought to exist among the focal inde-

Figure 7.5

Spuriousness, Redundancy, and Indirect Effects

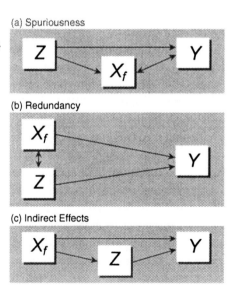

(a) Spuriousness

(b) Redundancy

(c) Indirect Effects

pendent and dependent variables and the third variable, as illustrated in Figure 7.5. For spuriousness (Figure 7.5a), there is one true independent variable (Z) and two dependent variables (X_f and Y); in this instance Z is the same as X_c. The pseudo-independent variable (X_f) might be mistaken for an intervening variable because Z influences it. Y does not depend upon X_f, however, which means that X_f cannot mediate the relationship between Z and Y. If X_f were an intervening variable, its inclusion would account for the association between Z and Y, which is not the case. Instead, the inclusion of Z accounts for the empirical association between X_f and Y, demonstrating spuriousness.

For redundancy (Figure 7.5b), there is one true independent variable (Z), a pseudo-independent variable (X_f), and one dependent variable (Y); here Z could also be labeled X_i. Again, X_f might be misconstrued as an intervening variable because it is connected to both Z and Y. However, the association between the true independent variable and the pseudo-independent variable is not causal in nature, meaning that X_f does not mediate the impact of Z on Y.

For the intervening variable model (Figure 7.5c), the connections between all three variables are assumed to reflect relationships, a characteristic that distinguishes this arrangement of variables from both spuriousness and redundancy (for which one of the connections is not causal in nature). The intervening variable (Z) plays a distinctive role in functioning first as a dependent variable, and then as an independent variable; here Z is the same as X_v.

In practice, it is easy to confuse mediation with redundancy and spuriousness although these models appear quite distinctive when viewed in graphic form. This confusion is understandable because the regression models are identical: Y regressed on X_f and Z. Although the intervening variable functions as an independent variable, its explanatory value comes from its simultaneous function as a dependent variable. This role distinguishes it from control and other independent variables.

The Analysis of Intervening Variables

Mediation for Numeric Outcomes

Regression techniques are well suited to the analysis of indirect effects because the equation is easily expanded to include intervening variables. Our analysis starts not with the total or bivariate association between X_f and Y, but with the partial association b_f remaining after spuriousness and redundancy are taken into consideration. Thus, the first step in the analysis of intervening variables is the last step of the analysis of redundancy (Equation 6.2), which is reproduced here:

$$\widehat{Y} = b_0 + b_f X_f + b_{c1} X_{c1} + b_{c2} X_{c2} + \cdots + b_{c+} X_{c+}$$
$$+ b_{i1} X_{i1} + b_{i2} X_{i2} + \cdots + b_{i+} X_{i+} \tag{7.1}$$

where b_f gives the total focal relationship when the effects of control variables, $X_{c1}, X_{c2}, \ldots, X_{c+}$, and other independent variables, $X_{i1}, X_{i2}, \ldots, X_{i+}$, have been taken into consideration.

The direct effect of the focal independent variable is obtained by adding one or more intervening variables, $X_{v1}, X_{v2}, \ldots, X_{v+}$, to the regression equation:

$$\widehat{Y} = b_0 + b_f X_f + b_{c1} X_{c1} + b_{c2} X_{c2} + \cdots + b_{c+} X_{c+}$$
$$+ b_{i1} X_{i1} + b_{i2} X_{i2} + \cdots + b_{i+} X_{i+}$$
$$+ b_{v1} X_{v1} + b_{v2} X_{v2} + \cdots + b_{v+} X_{v+}. \tag{7.2}$$

The contribution of the entire set of intervening variables to the explanation of Y is assessed with the F test for the increment in R^2 (see Chapter 5, note 6), and, if significant, the t test is used for each of the individual variables.

Again, our focus is on what happens to the regression coefficient for the focal relationship (b_f) when an intervening variable or a set of intervening variables is added to the model. One or more of the intervening variables mediates the focal relationship when b_f is reduced. This mediation is complete if b_f is essentially 0; it is partial if b_f has a nonzero value. A nonzero b_f connotes a direct effect of the focal independent variable on the dependent variable.

In contrast, the focal relationship is not mediated by any of the intervening variables if b_f is essentially unchanged by the addition of the set of intervening variables.[3] In this instance, one or more of the intervening variables may have a nonzero coefficient. This coefficient is not indicative of an indirect effect, however, because it does not alter the impact of the focal independent variable. This variable helps to explain Y, a very important function, but does not advance our understanding of the relationship between Y and X_f.

ANALYSIS JOURNAL: Intervening Variables

Let us consider another possibility—that the impact of income on mastery does not represent so much the opportunities that affluence makes available or the hardships that poverty imposes, but rather a connection between socioeconomic status and parenting behavior, with parenting behavior being the instrument that shapes mastery among adolescents. To test this hypothesis, we use three measures of parental behavior as reported by the adolescent: a five-item measure of parental control, e.g., "my parents ask me too many questions about where I've been or what I've been doing" ($\alpha = .75$); a four-item measure of parental trust, e.g., "my parents trust me to make the right choices" ($\alpha = .75$); and a four-item measure of parental demands, e.g., "my parents expect too much of me" ($\alpha = .68$). Response categories were (1) strongly disagree, (2) disagree, (3) agree, and (4) strongly agree, and were reversed for some items so that a high score is consistent with the variable name. Scores were summed and divided by the number of items to maintain the metric of the response categories. Means for these variables indicate that, on average, these adolescents find their parents to be somewhat controlling (2.62; SD = .57) and demanding (2.63; SD = .60), but also fairly trusting (3.14; S.D. = .50). However, scores on each of these measures span almost their full potential, indicating that some teens are subject to intense parental control, demands, and distrust, whereas other teens report few if any negative evaluations of their parents.

Simple regression analyses demonstrate that each of these would-be intervening variables is significantly associated with mastery, the dependent variable: High levels of parental control ($b = -.239$; SE = 030; $p \leq .001$) and demands ($b = -.309$; SE = .026; $p \leq .001$) correspond to low levels of adolescent mastery, whereas high levels of parental trust ($b = .362$; SE = .028; $p \leq .001$) go with high levels of adolescent mastery. However, only one of these variables is significantly associated with income, the focal independent variable: Adolescents living in families with low incomes tend to see their parents as more demanding than do adolescents living in more well-to-do families ($b = -8.280$; SE = 1.380; $p \leq .001$). Parental trust and control do not meet the criteria for an intervening variable with respect to the focal relationship, therefore, because they are only associated with mastery and not income.

The base model used in this analysis is the final model from the analysis of spuriousness and redundancy expanded by the addition of problem behaviors based on the analysis of neighborhood and trauma (see Chapter 6). Problem behaviors are negatively associated with mastery net of other variables in the model, as shown in Model 1 of the accompanying table. The coefficient for income, however, is not appreciably changed from its previous value.

The results of adding parental demands are shown in Model 2. The coefficient for income has been reduced by 42% and is no longer statistically significant. In addition, the parental demands measure is significantly associated with mastery. For example, compared to teens who view their parents as most demanding (code 4), those who view their parents as least demanding (code 1) score, on average, almost a point (.84) higher on the four-point mastery scale net of other variables in the model. Parental control makes a substantial contribution to the explanation of mastery as indicated by the increment in R^2 from Model 1 ($\Delta R^2 = 12.4\%$; $p \leq .001$). Thus, parental demands seem to mediate entirely the impact of family income on adolescent mastery and to contribute substantially to the explanation of this outcome.

The presence of ambient hazards in the neighborhood was considered to be a control variable for income in earlier analysis. As can be seen in Model 2, this variable remains significantly associated with mastery, although its coefficient has been reduced by a third with the addition of parental demands and problem behaviors (see Chapter 6). Parents may try to protect their children in dangerous neighborhoods by restricting their autonomy and by closely monitoring their activities. If so, parental control and trust, which were not candidates for mediating the effects of income, may instead mediate the effects of ambient hazards on adolescent mastery. We have already seen that these dimensions of parental behavior are associated with mastery at the bivariate level. Simple regression analysis indicates that these variables are associated with ambient hazards as well: Adolescents who perceive their neighborhoods as threatening also perceive their parents as controlling ($b = .107$; SE $= .039$; $p \leq .01$) and lacking in trust ($b = -.191$; SE $= .049$; $p \leq .001$).

As can be seen in Model 3, the addition of these two variables to the previous model reduces the coefficient for ambient hazards by about a third, but it remains statistically significant, although with more uncertainty. Two of the three parental behavior variables are statistically significant in the multivariate model; although significant in the bivariate model, control does not independently contribute to the explanation of mastery. Parental trust and demands are measured in the same response codes, so we can compare the size of their unstandardized regression

Regression of Mastery on Income and Intervening Variables: The Impact of Parenting

Independent variables	Regression coefficients[a]		
	Model 1	Model 2	Model 3
Family income	.0026**	.0015	.0017
(thousands of $)[b]	(.0009)	(.0009)	(.0009)
Ambient hazards	−.086**	−.077**	−.048*
	(.027)	(.023)	(.022)
Parental demands		−.280***	−.200***
		(.025)	(.034)
Parental control			.054
			(.037)
Parental trust			.239***
			(.028)
Residentially stable	.090*	.077*	.061
5 or more years	(.041)	(.036)	(.032)
Problem behaviors	−.025***	−.015**	−.007
	(.006)	(.006)	(.006)
Ethnicity[c]			
African American	.070	.117	.067
	(.103)	(.095)	(.088)
Latino	−.061	.023	.022
	(.043)	(.037)	(.036)
Asian American/Other	−.131*	−.054	−.051
	(.055)	(.052)	(.052)
Male	.066*	.086**	.056
	(.027)	(.028)	(.029)
Family structure[d]			
Parent and Stepparent	.025	.019	.024
	(.037)	(.040)	(.037)
Single parent	.012	−.010	−.023
	(.035)	(.029)	(.029)
Age	.009	.009	.015
	(.012)	(.011)	(.011)
Constant	2.881***	3.532***	
	2.556***		
	(.176)	(.180)	(.223)
R^2	.097***	.221***	.280***

[a] Robust standard error.
[b] Focal relationship is in italics.
[c] Omitted reference category is white.
[d] Omitted reference category is intact nuclear family.
*$p \le .05$. **$p \le .01$. ***$p \le .001$.

coefficients, which are approximately equal, but opposite in sign. The decrease in adolescent mastery with a one-unit change in parental demands is about the same as the increase in mastery with a one-unit change in trust.

The mediation of ambient hazards appears to be due to parental trust rather than demands. Parental demands were included in Model 2. The coefficient for ambient hazards in Model 2 is almost 90% of its value in Model 1. In other words, the association between ambient hazards and mastery does not change much when parental demands are taken into consideration, suggesting that this variable does not mediate much of the impact of ambient hazards on mastery. However, it seems to perform this function for family income, as described above.

Notice too that the addition of parental demands and trust mediates entirely the association between problem behavior and mastery. In Model 1, this variable is significantly associated with mastery net of other variables in the model. It remains significant when parental demands are added in Model 2, but is substantially reduced in size. It is reduced further and is not statistically significant when parental trust is added in Model 3. Thus, parental trust seems to function as an intervening variable with regard to two independent variables: problem behaviors and ambient hazards. Similarly, the parental demands variable seems to function as an intervening variable with regard to two independent variables: problem behaviors and family income.

Finally, we consider the possibility that the residual adverse impact of living in a threatening neighborhood on mastery occurs through the adolescent's experience of trauma, either personal or vicarious. We have already seen that ambient hazards are strongly associated with the odds of experiencing a traumatic event (see Chapter 6), meaning that these variables meet the criteria of association with the independent variable. However, bivariate analysis indicates that mastery is not significantly associated with personal exposure to trauma ($b = -.060$; SE $= .050$; $p > .200$) and is only marginally associated with vicarious exposure to trauma ($b = -.055$; SE $= .028$; $p \leq .06$). When added to Model 3, neither of these variables is statistically significant, indicating that these trauma variables do not play a mediating role.

In sum, the intervening variables considered in this analysis mediate some of the effects of the independent variables considered in earlier analyses. The focal independent variable, income, is completely mediated by parental demands. The perception that one's neighborhood is threatening is partially mediated by parental trust. Problem behaviors are completely mediated by parental demands and trust. In contrast, parental control, and personal and vicarious exposure to traumatic events do not function as intervening variables.

Let us recap the series of analyses that led up to this final analysis. In the first step of the analysis (see Chapter 5), the focal relationship was estimated, revealing an inverse association between adolescent mastery and family income. We also saw that this association is not due to income differences among ethnic groups, although mastery is lower among Asian American and other ethnicities and among Latino adolescents (compared to white adolescents). The difference between Latinos and whites appears to be entirely due to lower family incomes, on average, among Latinos.

In the second step (see Chapter 5), control variables were added to rule out spuriousness as an explanation for the association between income and mastery. These control variables—gender, age, and family structure—do not appreciably change the association between mastery and income, meaning that the focal relationship is not a consequence of spuriousness with this set of variables. The low levels of mastery for Asian American and other teens compared to those of white teens also remain intact. Only one of the control variables is statistically significant in the multivariate model: males score, on average, somewhat higher in mastery than females, net of other variables in the model.

In Step 3 (see Chapter 6), we tested a competing explanation for the focal relationship: Family income only appears to be associated with mastery because income is associated with neighborhood: The social environment, rather than income, shapes mastery. To assess redundancy, two other independent variables were added to the model: the adolescent's perception of ambient hazards in his or her neighborhood and residential stability, an indicator of social cohesion. These two variables are significantly associated with mastery in the multivariate analysis, but account for only a small portion of the association between mastery and income. The inclusion of these variables also does not alter the coefficients for being male or for being of Asian American or other ethnic background.

The focal relationship, then, survives the tests for spuriousness and redundancy. In the analysis of intervening variables just reported, however, it is fully accounted for by parental demands. In other words, the impact of family income on adolescent mastery is mediated by income-related differences in parenting behavior. The addition of parental control also explains the difference in mastery between teens of Asian American or other ethnic backgrounds and whites. Furthermore, the addition of parental trust accounts for the gender difference. In the final analysis, living in safe neighborhoods enhances adolescent mastery, as does having parents who are trusting and not overly demanding.

Mediation for Dichotomous Outcomes

As with the other analyses we have considered, the analysis of mediation in the logistic regression model parallels the strategy used for multiple linear regression. The analytic strategy is identical even though the two forms of regression are statistically and computationally distinct.

As above, we begin with the final step in the logistic model for redundancy (Equation 6.4), which is reproduced here as the first step in the model for mediation:

$$\log \hat{o}^{Y^+} = b_0 + b_f X_f + b_{c1} X_{c1} + b_{c2} X_{c2} + \cdots + b_{c+} X_{c+}$$
$$+ b_{i1} X_{i1} + b_{i2} X_{i2} + \cdots + b X_{i+} X_{i+}. \qquad (7.3)$$

This equation gives the total relationship between the focal independent and dependent variables as b_f, which we now seek to divide into its direct and indirect components. This subdivision is accomplished by adding one or more intervening variables to the logistic regression equation:

$$\log \hat{o}^{Y^+} = b_o + b_f X_f + b_{c1} X_{c1} + b_{c2} X_{c2} + \cdots + b_{c+} X_{c+}$$
$$+ b_{i1} X_{i1} + b_{i2} X_{i2} + \cdots + b_{i+} X_{i+}$$
$$+ b_{v1} X_{v1} + b_{v2} X_{v2} + \cdots + b_{v+} X_{v+}. \qquad (7.4)$$

Once again, the addition of a set of variables, in this case intervening variables, is tested with the likelihood ratio test (see Chapter 5, note 8). If this test is significant, each variable is individually tested with Wald's χ^2.

Mediation is once again demonstrated by a decrease in b_f, this time from Equation 7.3 to Equation 7.4. If b_f is unchanged by the inclusion of the intervening variables, then none of the focal relationship operates through any of these intervening variables.[4] These variables may influence the dependent variable, but they are not transmitting the influence of the focal independent variable. In contrast, if b_f decreases toward 0, the value indicative of no relationship, then the focal relationship is explained, at least in part, by one or more of the intervening variables. This mediation is complete if b_f does not differ from 0; it is partial if b_f differs from zero.[5]

As we have seen before, the additive version of the logistic regression model illustrates comparability of analytic strategy with the multiple linear regression model, but is somewhat more difficult to interpret substantively than the multiplicative version. The multiplicative versions of the two relevant equations, one without and the other with intervening variables, are obtained taking the exponents of additive equations (Equation 7.3 and Equation 7.4), as should be familiar by now:

$$\hat{o}^{Y+} = e^{b_0} e^{b_f X_f} e^{b_{c1} X_{c1}} e^{b_{c2} X_{c2}} \cdots e^{b_c+ X_c+} e^{b_{i1} X_{i1}} e^{b_{i2} X_{i2}} \cdots e^{b_i+ X_i+} , \qquad (7.5)$$

and

$$\hat{o}^{Y+} = e^{b_0} e^{b_f X_f} e^{b_{c1} X_{c1}} e^{b_{c2} X_{c2}} \cdots e^{b_c+ X_c+} e^{b_{i1} X_{i1}} e^{b_{i2} X_{i2}} \cdots e^{b_i+ X_i+}$$
$$\times e^{b_{v1} X_{v1}} e^{b_{v2} X_{v2}} \cdots e^{b_v+ X_v+} . \qquad (7.6)$$

The change in e^{b_f} between these equations gives the extent to which the focal relationship is mediated by the set of intervening variables. e^{b_f} in the comprehensive model (Equation 7.6) gives the direct influence of X_f on Y—that portion of the relationship that is not mediated by any of the intervening variables. As usual, a value of 1.00 indicates no association (rather than the value of 0 in the additive model). If mediation is present, e^{b_f} should approach 1.00.

Countervailing Forces

Our treatment of intervening variables would be incomplete without consideration of the direction of the effects that are being transmitted via these variables. The simplest case is where all effects operate in the same direction. That is, all of the regression coefficients are of the same sign. For example, an increase in the focal independent variable generates an increase in all of the intervening variables, which, in turn, all produce increases in the dependent variable. Most theoretical models are not so tidy, however, and empirical results tend to mix positive and negative influences. As a result, some mediated effects may offset others. This situation is illustrated in Figure 7.6.

Figure 7.6

Countervailing Indirect Effects

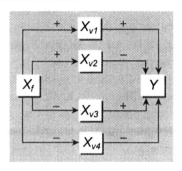

In this illustration, the focal independent variable is positively related to two of the intervening variables (X_{v1} and X_{v2}), but these variables are related to the dependent variable in opposite directions. An increase in X_f produces an increase in X_{v1}, which then increases Y. However, the same increase in X_f also produces a decrease in Y because it increases X_{v2}, which then decreases Y. In other words, the indirect effect via X_{v1} is positive (because: $+ \times + = +$), but the indirect effect via X_{v2} is negative (because: $+ \times - = -$). These influences act to offset one another. In addition, the focal independent variable in this illustration is negatively related to two of the intervening variables (X_{v3} and X_{v4}): As X_f increases, both X_{v3} and X_{v4} decrease. However, X_{v3} is positively related to Y, whereas X_{v4} is negatively related to Y. These opposite signs mean that an increase in X_f generates a decrease in Y via X_{v3}, but an increase in Y via X_{v4}. These influences are offsetting. Thus, the dynamics set in motion by a change in this focal independent variable produce forces that push the dependent variable in one direction and pull it in the opposite direction.

Although this example might appear extreme, real life systems more often than not encompass conflicting processes that work to offset one another. For example, emigrating may be emotionally distressing because émigrés face many challenges bereft of social support from family and friends who have remained in their home country, but emigrating may also enhance emotional well-being because it leads to freedom from political or religious persecution. If both processes are present, then the adverse emotional effects of migration may be offset so completely by its advantageous effects that the net effect is positive.

This type of situation emerges frequently because the processes we research are usually complex. Indeed, alternative theories often make contradictory predictions about relationships. These alternatives may be mutually exclusive, in which case support of one alternative disconfirms the other, or these alternatives may each contain elements of truth. Tracing the flow of indirect effects through intervening variables represents a powerful strategy for disentangling such complex processes.

Mediation Illustrated: Explaining the Intergenerational Transmission of Divorce

Let us consider a detailed example of how intervening variables can be used to clarify the processes that generate a relationship. The association in question is the increased risk of divorce among persons whose parents have been divorced. Although this association is well documented in the empirical research literature, the factors that account for it are less well understood. To help complete this picture, Amato (1996) tests an explanatory model that delineates some of the pathways connecting the marital experiences of parents with those of their sons and daughters.

According to Amato (1996), parental divorce sets in motion a series of events and processes that affect the likelihood of divorce by diminishing the rewards derived from the marriage, weakening the barriers to leaving the marriage, and/or increasing alternatives to the marriage. These general determinants are operationalized as three sets of mediating variables: life course and socioeconomic status (SES) variables, attitudes toward divorce, and interpersonal behavior problems. The conceptual model is shown in Figure 7.7.

Life course and SES factors are thought to transmit part of the impact of parental divorce. Early age at marriage, for example, is one of the best predictors of marital dissolution and having divorced parents is associated with marrying early, perhaps because marriage is seen as an escape from an unsatisfactory home life. Amato (1996) argues that young couples are prone to unrewarding marriages and divorce because they did not spend sufficient time searching for an appropriate partner, they are poorly prepared for marital roles, and they lack economic resources. He also contends that young couples are inclined to divorce because they have better opportunities in the remarriage market than older couples.

Figure 7.7

Potential Mediators of the Effect of Parental Divorce

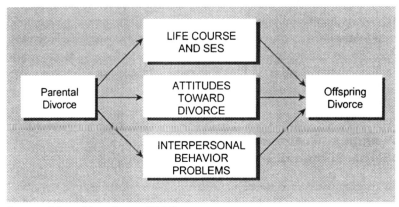

Source: Adapted from Amato (1996).

Attitudes toward divorce are seen as weakening barriers to divorce. According to Amato (1996), persons who grew up in divorced families are pessimistic about life-long marriages and are not as negative about divorce as those from intact nuclear families. They have learned firsthand that divorce can be a solution to an unsatisfactory marriage.

Problematic interpersonal behavior is the third potential mediator of parental divorce considered in this research. Amato (1996) argues that children whose parents divorce are socialized into personality traits (e.g., lack of trust or jealousy) and interaction styles (e.g., impaired communication skills) that interfere with rewarding, intimate relationships during adulthood. These dispositions arise from the disturbed family relationships that often precede and accompany divorce. He also contends that divorce promotes problematic interpersonal behavior because it limits firsthand exposure to models of successful dyadic behavior. The resultant inability to form mutually satisfying, long-term ties with others lessens the rewards associated with marriage and thereby increases the risk for divorce.

Amato (1996) examines the extent to which these factors— life course and SES factors, divorce attitudes, and interpersonal behavior problems—account for the empirical association between parental and offspring divorce. He uses data from a national sample of married persons 55 years of age and younger in 1980, the time of the baseline interview. Survey data were collected at

Table 7.1

Percentage Change in the Odds of Divorce

	Model[a]				
	1	2	3	4	5
Parental divorce[b]					
Husband's parents divorced	26	18	20	18	9
Wife's parents divorced	59*	44	55*	36	25
Both spouses' parents divorced	189**	154**	173**	85*	61
Couple's average age at marriage		−7*			−6*
Cohabitation before marriage		59*			30
Couple's average education		−5		−4	
Husband's income		−1			−1
Wife's income		3		2	
Wife employed part time		−26		−27	
Wife employed full time		2			2
Prodivorce attitudes			91***		57*
Interpersonal problems				19***	16***
χ^2	14.5*	39.0***	26.2***	40.6***	74.5***

Source: Amato (1996).
[a]Table values are based on logistic regression coefficients ($[e^{\beta} - 1] \times 100$). All equations control for the education of both the husband's and the wife's parents, the couple's race, and the individual's gender (not shown).
[b]Omitted reference category is neither spouse's parents divorced.
* $p < .05.$ ** $p < .01.$ *** $p < .001.$

several subsequent points in time, spanning the period through 1992. The analytic sample is limited to individuals in first marriages in 1980 (i.e., neither spouse had been married previously) for whom information on marital status existed at two points in time ($N = 1,387$). This longitudinal design permits a prospective assessment of the impact of mediators on the subsequent risk of divorce. The method of analysis is a discrete-time hazard model estimated with logistic regression (Allison, 1984).

During the 12 years of the study, 172 persons or 12% of the sample divorced from their spouses. The rate of divorce was lowest when neither spouse's parents had divorced (11%), was somewhat higher when either the husband's (14%) or the wife's (16%) parents had divorced, and was highest when both spouses' parents had divorced (28%). These data are presented in Table 7.1 Model 1 as percentage changes in the odds of divorce relative to the omitted reference category of neither spouse's parents divorced.[6] This re-expression of the logistic regression coefficients focuses attention on changes in the focal relationship as a result of adding the intervening variables. As shown in Model 1, two states differ significantly from the omitted reference category: wife's parents divorced and both spouses' parents divorced.

The impact of the intervening variables on the focal relationship is assessed in Models 2 through 5. In Model 2, seven indicators of life course and SES are added to Model 1. These variables reduce by 25% the estimated effect of divorce for the wife's parents [(59 − 44)/59], which is no longer statistically significant. The effect of dual parental divorce is similarly reduced by 19%, but this effect remains statistically significant. Amato (1996) concludes that life course and SES variables, in particular age at marriage and cohabitation before marriage, explain some but not all of the effect of parental divorce on offspring divorce.

In Model 3, attitudes toward divorce are added to Model 1. These attitudes do not appreciably alter the estimated effect of parental divorce on offspring divorce, although these attitudes themselves are related to divorce. That is, people who are accepting of divorce are more likely to divorce, but this association does not account for the elevated risk of divorce that occurs when the wife's parents have been divorced or when the husband's parents are also divorced.

The effects of interpersonal problems are taken into consideration in Model 4. These behaviors have a substantial impact on the focal relationship. Compared to Model 1, the effect of divorce of the wife's parents is reduced by 39% and is no longer statistically significant. Similarly, the estimated effect of divorce of both spouses' parents is reduced by 55%, although it remains statistically significant. In addition, parental divorce is associated with problematic interpersonal-behavior. Based on these findings, Amato (1996) concludes that a substantial portion of the effects of parental divorce is mediated through problematic interpersonal behavior.

Model 5 simultaneously takes into consideration all of the potential mediators considered in this study. The association between parental divorce and offspring divorce is not statistically significant in this model, suggesting that the model provides an adequate explanation for the intergenerational transmission of divorce. Three variables have independent effects on divorce in this expanded model: early age at marriage, prodivorce attitudes, and interpersonal problems. On the strength of these findings, Amato

(1996) concludes that parental divorce elevates the risk of offspring divorce because these children act in ways that interfere with the maintenance of mutually rewarding intimate relationships.

For our purposes, the value of this study lies in its strategic use of intervening variables to specify how the focal independent variable influences the focal dependent variable. Before testing the conceptual model, Amato (1996) establishes two necessary theoretical connections for each potential mediator: its dependency on the focal independent variable, parental divorce, and, its effect on the focal dependent variable, offspring divorce. The existing research literature suggests that each of the intervening variables considered in this study meets this standard for the role of mediator. However, only some of these potential pathways are substantiated in the multivariate analysis: age at marriage, prodivorce attitudes, and interpersonal behavior problems. Some of the variables that are not statistically significant in the multivariate models may have significant bivariate associations, but, if so, these associations appear to overlap with the three variables that do exert statistically significant independent effects on divorce in the final model. For example, cohabitation before marriage is statistically significant in Model 2, but is not significant when prodivorce attitudes and interpersonal behavior problems are also taken into consideration (Model 5). This result suggests that the effect of cohabitation is redundant with attitudes or behavior or is itself mediated by attitudes or behavior.

The most important aspect of these results, at least from our analytic perspective, is that the specification of mediators helps to establish the validity of interpreting the empirical association between parental and offspring divorce as a relationship. The feasibility of a causal interpretation of this relationship is enhanced by the description of at least some of the mechanisms that generate this empirical association. The three variables that attain statistical significance in the final model—early age at marriage, prodivorce attitudes, and interpersonal behavior problems—account fully for the empirical association between the focal independent and dependent variables, meaning that the mechanisms embodied in these variables provide a viable account of how parental divorce leads to offspring divorce. These pathways are not necessarily (or even probably) the only such pathways, but they do constitute one feasible set of linkages. The presence of these linkages attests to the legitimacy of inferring that parental divorce elevates the subsequent risk of divorce among adult children.

Antecedent and Consequent Variables

Placement in Connection to the Focal Relationship

Whereas intervening variables form the interior of the focal relationship, antecedent and consequent variables elaborate the relationship by giving it external moorings. An antecedent variable precedes the focal independent variable and helps to explain its origins. In comparison, the consequent variable follows the focal dependent variable and helps to explain its aftermath. In this fashion, antecedent and consequent variables extend the focal relationship beyond its original boundaries.

Like the intervening variable, antecedent and consequent variables are used to trace out a causal sequence. They are unlike the intervening variable insofar as their inclusion in the analysis is *not* expected to alter the focal relationship. However, the use of antecedent and consequent variables does change the analytic role of the focal variables: The focal independent variable becomes a dependent variable, and the focal dependent variable becomes an independent variable. This repositioning is illustrated in Figure 7.8.

The focal relationship remains intact in the center of the figure: X_f affects Y, now labeled Y_f to emphasize its role in the focal relationship. With regard to one another, then, these two variables retain their analytic roles of independent and dependent variables, respectively. With regard to the antecedent variable X_a, however, the focal independent variable plays the role of dependent variable. The X-variable notation for the focal independent variable is not changed to a Y-variable notation, even though it now functions as a dependent variable, to emphasize that the antecedent variable helps to explicate the role of X_f as a cause of Y_f.

With regard to the consequent variable Y_c, the focal dependent variable plays the role of independent variable. It now has a sub-

Figure 7.8

Antecedent and Consequent Variables

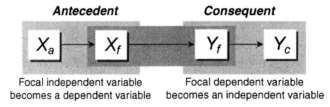

Antecedent	Consequent

Focal independent variable   Focal dependent variable
becomes a dependent variable   becomes an independent variable

script, which was not necessary in previous analyses because it was the only variable whose sole role was that of outcome. The consequent variable now occupies that role as well, necessitating the addition of the subscript. To emphasize this continuity in the focal relationship, the Y-variable notation for the focal dependent variable is not changed to an X-variable notation, indicating that the consequent variable helps to explicate the role of Y as an outcome of X_f.

Transformation Into Intervening Variables

The analysis of antecedent and consequent variables is an extension of the analysis of intervening variables, as also shown in Figure 7.8. The addition of an antecedent variable transforms the focal independent variable into an intervening variable insofar as it affects the focal dependent variable (Y_f) and is affected by the antecedent variable (X_a). In this manner, the focal independent variable transmits the effect of the antecedent variable to the focal dependent variable.

Similarly, the addition of a consequent variable (Y_c) transforms the focal dependent variable (Y_f) into an intervening variable. As before, it is affected by the focal independent variable (X_f). However, it now also affects the consequent variable (Y_c). The focal dependent variable has become the means through which the focal independent variable influences the consequent variable.

Thus, the original focal relationship can be seen as one of the links connecting the antecedent variable (X_a) to the consequent variable (Y_c). From this perspective, the addition of antecedent and consequent variables elongates the causal process that was the original focus of investigation. This lengthening of the causal sequence can be extended still further by the addition of precursors of the antecedent variable or repercussions of the consequent variable— an iterative process that could be interminable.

This hypothetical extension of the causal sequence into the distant past or faraway future reveals the arbitrary quality of the designation of one relationship as the focal relationship. It achieves this distinction by virtue of its centrality in the theoretical model guiding the research. This importance is not intrinsic to the variables, but is attributed to them based on theoretical concerns.

Other Independent and Control Variables

The antecedent variable bears some resemblance to other independent and control variables, but it is qualitatively distinct, as illustrated in Figure 7.9. Within the framework of the focal relationship, both the antecedent variable (X_a) and the other independent variable (X_i) function as independent variables, but do so with regard to different dependent variables. When the other independent variable is used to eliminate redundancy with the focal independent variable (X_f), the outcome is the focal dependent variable (Y). The outcome of interest for the antecedent variable, in contrast, is the focal independent variable (X_f), which, in this arrangement of variables, functions as a dependent variable. Thus, the distinction between antecedent and other independent variables concerns the selection of the dependent variable.

The impact of these variables on the focal relationship also differs. This relationship should be accounted for by the other independent variable to the extent that redundancy is present. The antecedent variable, in contrast, should leave the focal relationship intact because we are explaining the occurrence of X_f, not the relationship between X_f and Y_f.

Turning to the distinction between the antecedent (X_a) and the control variable (X_c), we see in Figure 7.9 that both variables influence the focal independent variable (X_f). In other words, they share the same dependent variable. However, the control variable has a necessary second outcome, the focal dependent variable (Y), which

Figure 7.9

Antecedent, Other Independent, and Control Variables

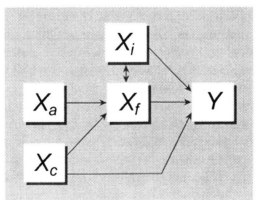

is not the case for the antecedent variable. The joint dependency of the focal independent and dependent variables on the control variable is the source of potential spuriousness. Controlling for this spuriousness should account for some or all of the focal relationship. In contrast, the addition of the antecedent variable is not expected to change the focal relationship. As above, we use the antecedent variable to explain the occurrence of X_f, not the relationship between X_f and Y_f. Thus, we expect no change in the focal relationship when it is elaborated by the antecedent variable.

Although the addition of an antecedent variable does not alter the estimate of the focal relationship, this qualification does not imply that antecedents are unrelated to the focal dependent variable. Indeed, the notion that an antecedent variable extends a causal sequence implies the opposite, that the antecedent variable is connected to the focal dependent variable given that these variables are part of a single causal sequence. This connection is indirect, however, transmitted via the focal independent variable. The addition of an antecedent variable does not alter the estimate of the focal relationship, then, because the focal relationship is the means though which the antecedent affects the focal dependent variable. In addition to this indirect effect, the antecedent may also have a direct effect on the focal dependent variable. However, this direct effect should leave the estimate of the focal relationship intact precisely because it is separate and distinct from the indirect effect transmitted by the focal independent variable.

If a presumed antecedent variable alters substantially the estimate of the focal relationship, the configuration of the entire set of interconnected variables should be reexamined empirically and conceptually to determine whether the presumed antecedent variable is instead another independent variable or perhaps a control variable. In other words, a third variable that alters the focal relationship is not likely to be simply an antecedent to X_f, but may represent instead an alternative explanation for Y or a source of spurious covariation between X_f and Y.

Figure 7.9 demonstrates quite forcefully the idea that variables are designated as "independent" or "dependent" not in absolute terms, but relative to a particular theoretical context. The same is true for independent variables that are labeled "focal," "other," "control," or "antecedent." It is the conceptual arrangement of these variables with regard to one another that determines their designation as a particular type of independent variable.

Antecedent and Consequent Variables Illustrated: Divorce and Intergenerational Family Relations

To illustrate the use of a consequent variable, we return to an example presented earlier in this chapter—the impact of parents' divorce on the odds that their children will also divorce (see Table 7.1 and Figure 7.7). Recall that the main thrust of Amato's (1996) analysis concerns the means through which divorce is transferred from one generation to the next, specifically three sets of intervening variables—life course and SES factors, attitudes toward divorce, and problematic interpersonal behavior. This causal sequence can be extended forward in time by another recent study that examines the impact of adult children's divorce on their subsequent relationships with their parents (Spitze, Logan, Deane, & Zerger, 1994). This reorientation is illustrated in Figure 7.10.

Here we see that the focus has changed from explaining divorce among adult children to explaining its impact on intergenerational family ties. Spitze and colleagues (1994) summarize several perspectives on how divorce alters interactions with one's parents. The predominant view is the resource perspective: Divorced children, especially daughters, are expected to need more help from parents (financial, household and child care, and emotional support) and to be less able to provide help parents may need. This connection arises because divorced persons have less time and energy

Figure 7.10

Intergenerational Family Relations as Consequences of Parental and Adult Children's Divorce

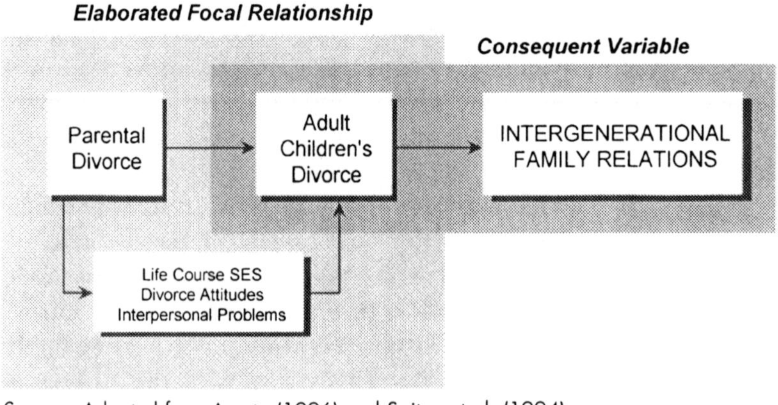

Source: Adapted from Amato (1996) and Spitze et al. (1994).

because of financial constraints, employment demands, and single parenthood. In contrast, the continuity perspective predicts no discernible overall effect of divorce. This view emphasizes the lengthy history of the parent-child tie, which may be temporarily jolted by divorce, but is unlikely to be permanently altered in its essential features. Finally, divorce may strengthen intergenerational ties, such as when it leads to co-residence with parents, which may result in increased contact and mutual help, although this living arrangement may also be fraught with conflict over an adult child's return to a dependent status. The empirical research literature on this connection is as mixed as these theoretical orientations, with some studies showing weakened intergenerational family ties following divorce, others showing strengthened ties, and still others showing no difference (Spitze et al., 1994).

To recap, the focal relationship in the Amato (1996) study concerns the impact of parents' divorce on the risk of divorce among their sons and daughters, whereas the focal relationship in the Spitze study (Spitze et al., 1994) concerns the impact of sons' and daughters' divorce on their ties with their parents. Juxtaposing these two studies permits us to treat the quality of intergenerational family ties as a consequent variable to the original focal relationship between parental and offspring divorce, as illustrated in Figure 7.10.

To address the impact of divorce on intergenerational family ties, Spitze and associates (1994) analyze survey data from a probability sample of 905 parents (aged 40 and older) from upstate New York studied in 1988 to 1989. For sons and daughters, current marital status and history are coded into the following categories: first marriage, remarried following divorce, divorced/separated with custody of a child, divorced/separated without custody of any child, widowed, and never married. The quality of intergenerational ties was assessed from the parent's point of view along three dimensions: amount of contact, help received and help given with everyday tasks, and closeness. Other independent variables include potential competing demands, such as employment and number of children in the household, and possible obstacles, such as geographic distance. Control variables include background characteristics, such as gender and age. Thus, the relationship between divorce and relations with one's parents is assessed net of relevant third variables, employing the by-now familiar exclusionary approach to internal validity.

The impact of divorce varies across the dimensions of the relationship and generally differs for sons and daughters. For closeness to parents, there are no differences according to the sons' or daughters' marital status, indicating no overall effect of divorce, child custody, or remarriage. However, parents' own earlier lack of custody (a proxy for parental divorce) for their now adult children matters importantly: Compared to parents with continuous childhood custody, noncustodial parents report less closeness to their adult sons and daughters. This finding suggests that a pathway should be added to the model, a direct connection between parental divorce and subsequent intergenerational ties as shown in Figure 7.11.

In the Spitze model, the focal relationship is between offspring divorce and subsequent intergenerational family ties. From this perspective, having been a noncustodial parent during the childhood of one's now adult son or daughter occupies the role of antecedent variable. The Amato (1996) findings link parental divorce to adult childrens divorce (as summarized above). Thus, even though Spitze and colleagues (1994) do not explicitly report effects of parental divorce on intergenerational family ties, the probable presence of this connection is revealed by bringing together results from these two studies.

Divorce affects contact with parents among daughters, but not among sons. Specifically, divorced daughters with custody of children visit and talk to parents on the telephone more often than married daughters; remarried daughters talk to parents on the telephone slightly less often than married daughters. In contrast,

Figure 7.11

Parental Divorce as an Antecedent to Intergenerational Family Relations

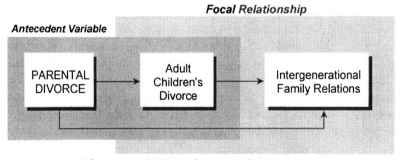

Source: Adapted from Amato (1996) and Spitze et al. (1994).

divorced, remarried, and married sons have approximately the same amount of contact with their parents.

With regard to help, divorced daughters receive significantly more help than married daughters, whereas remarried daughters get less help; divorced daughters with custody receive the most help with babysitting. Results differ for sons. Remarried sons get less help than married sons, but there are no differences between married and divorced sons. Finally, we shift to help from children to parents. For daughters, there are no differences between married and divorced or remarried daughters, but never-married daughters provide more help than married daughters. Never-married sons also provide more help than married sons, but divorced sons provide less help than married sons.

From our analytic perspective, these results are important because they illustrate how consideration of antecedent and consequent variables can illuminate the focal relationship. In the Amato model, parental divorce shapes the quality of parent-child relations in ways that are consequential to the child's subsequent experience of marriage, including, importantly, the likelihood of divorce. In the Spitze model, offspring divorce exerts comparable effects on the quality of ties with one's parents. In conjunction these two segments form a continuous trajectory of family marital transitions and relations that link generations. This point is most evident for the effect that having been a noncustodial parent has on parents' subsequent lack of closeness to their adult children. The continuation of the causal sequence with antecedent and consequent variables strengthens the internal validity of both of its components by showing the dynamic interplay between parents and children with regard to marital transitions and family relations over the life course. The coherence of this sequence of events and states strengthens the supposition that each segment is part of a single, integrated system of causal influence.

Summary

In sum, the antecedent variable represents a true relationship between the focal independent variable and its causes, and the consequent variable represents a true relationship between the focal dependent variable and its results. These two types of variables do not explain away the relationship between the focal independent and dependent variables, but clarify the influences that precede and follow this relationship. In contrast, the intervening variable helps to explain how the focal relationship works and should account for some or all of this relationship. The extension of the analysis to include antecedent, intervening, and consequent variables adds depth to one's understanding of the entire system.

Notes

1. Even though an intervening variable functions as both an independent variable and a dependent variable, the X-variable notation rather than the Y-variable notation is used to maintain our emphasis on explaining the focal dependent variable.

2. The connection of an intervening variable to the focal independent and dependent variables may itself be indirect through other intervening variables, e.g., X_{v2} in Figure 7.2b. In this instance, the entire series of intervening variables forms a continuous chain.

3. In some instances, the focal relationship may increase with the addition of intervening variables. As before, this result indicates that one or more of the added variables acts to suppress the focal relationship.

4. As with most rules, there is an exception. It is conceivable that there are countervailing mediational forces that completely offset one another and leave b_f intact. See below.

5. An increase in the regression coefficient, by contrast, is indicative of suppression.

6. The proportions given by Amato (1996) can be converted to odds using the equation $o^+ = p^+/(1 - p^+)$. These values are as follows: .12 for intact nuclear families; .16 for husband's parents divorced; .19 for wife's parents divorced; .39 for both spouses' parents divorced; and .14 for the total sample. The values in Table 7.1 are the difference from the reference category divided by the overall odds of divorce. For example, for both parents divorced the value is $(.39 - .12)/.14 = 193$. The slight differences from the values in the table are due to rounding error.

8 Specifying Conditions of Influence: Effect Modification and Subgroup Variation

We have traversed considerable terrain since first asking whether an empirical association can be interpreted as a relationship. Our journey has followed an exclusionary path to rule out alternative explanations and an inclusive set of bridges that connect the focal relationship to a network of causal relationships. We stand now at a vantage point from which we can see the empirical association as a relationship. We must now concern ourselves with two last questions: Does the focal relationship operate in all circumstances or only some and for all persons or only some? Thus far, our analytic strategy has assumed an answer to both of these questions: "Yes." This point may not be immediately apparent because these assumptions have been implicit. They are now made manifest to highlight the alternative: The focal relationship is a *conditional relationship*, which means that the effect of the focal independent variable on the dependent variable varies over the values of the "third variable" known as an *effect modifier*. Having satisfied ourselves that we can think about the focal relationship in a causal manner, we turn now to specifying the circumstances under which this cause-and-effect type of relationship operates.

Conditional Relationships

In the absence of conditionality, the focal relationship is assumed to operate under all circumstances. The circumstances of interest are usually captured by the other variables comprising the theoretical model. Unless otherwise specified, the focal relationship is assumed to be invariant across all values of these other variables. This assumption, however, may not be warranted.

Conditional, in contrast, means that the relationship between the focal independent and dependent variables is contingent upon the value of some third variable. For example, the focal relationship may be present for boys but absent for girls or be positive in sign for girls but negative in sign for boys. The key point is that the focal relationship differs across the various values of the third variable, in this instance, between boys and girls.

Types of Conditional Relationships

The circumstances that modify the focal relationship are usually embodied in the other variables that comprise the causal system under investigation. These variables operationalize two distinct types of contingencies. One is static: The modifying variable signifies a fixed or quasi-fixed characteristic, such as gender or socioeconomic status (SES). The other is dynamic: The modifying variable describes a state that changes over time or between situations, such as self-confidence.

Static modifiers frequently connote membership in more or less clearly defined subgroups of the population, often delineating the individual's location within a stratified social system (e.g., gender, ethnicity, or social class). Thus, static modifiers tend to also play the role of control variable.

The stress literature provides a provocative example of this type of contingency: Can the higher level of depression among women than among men be attributed to parallel gender differences in the effect of exposure to stress? This possibility is sometimes referred to as the differential vulnerability hypothesis and is illustrated in Figure 8.1a. According to this theory, the effect of stress (the focal independent variable) on depression (the dependent variable) is conditional upon gender (the effect modifier). Each unit increase in exposure to stress results in an increment in symptoms of depression for both genders, but this increment is greater for women than for men, as shown by the difference in slopes between the two lines. An alternative is shown in Figure 8.1b: stress is equally distressing to men and women. The parallel slopes of the two lines show this similarity.

The analysis of static modifiers often uses control variables, but it is distinctly different from the analysis of spuriousness. The issue

Figure 8.1

Gender as a Modifier of the Effect of Stress on Depression

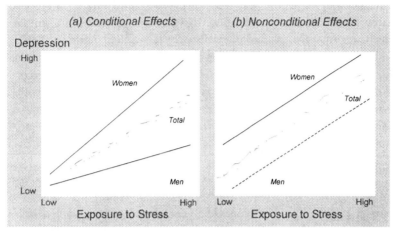

with spuriousness is whether the inclusion of the control variable alters the size of the focal relationship. In static conditionality, the issue is whether the focal relationship changes size across the values of the control variable.

To continue our example, the assessment of effect modification asks whether the relationship between stress and depression is contingent upon whether the person is a man or a woman. This question is distinct from whether women tend to have higher levels of depression than men. It is distinct as well from the question of whether stress accounts for the association between gender and depression (i.e., the possibility that men are less depressed than women because men, on average, encounter less stress than women). If gender differences in depression were due to gender differences in exposure to stress, then the two lines in Figure 8.1b would be superimposed on one another because there would be no residual gender difference when stress is controlled (as it is in this plot). This possibility is referred to as differential exposure (in contrast to differential vulnerability as shown in Figure 8.1a).

Kessler and McCleod (1984) contend that women are more distressed than men because women are more affected by exposure to a particular type of stressor—hardships encountered by persons in their social networks. However, the apparent female disadvantage is specific to emotional distress, and males and females are similarly responsive to stress when outcomes include a more comprehensive range of impairments, including substance abuse and dependence, which are more common among men (Aneshensel, Rutter, & Lachenbruch, 1991). Although differential vulnerability has been attributed to group differences in coping, this interpretation has not been directly tested (Aneshensel, 1992).

In contrast to static modifiers, dynamic modifiers are variables that can change. Often these variables are influenced by other components of the theoretical system being investigated. As a result, dynamic modifiers often also play the role of intervening variable. Thus, an intervening variable may not only mediate the effect of the focal independent variable on the dependent variable, it may additionally modify this effect.

The stress literature also provides a good example of this type of contingency, the stress-buffering model of social support shown here as Figure 8.2a. This model is germane to the present discussion because it does not assume that the effects of stress and social support are separate and distinct from one another. On the contrary, the buffering model posits that the distressing impact of stress is contingent upon whether social support is present or absent. In statistical jargon, there is an *interaction* between these two variables.

For the purposes of this illustration, the most important aspect of social support is its changeable nature. It is influenced by many of the same social, demographic, and economic processes that

Figure 8.2

Social Support as a Modifier of the Effect of Stress on Depression

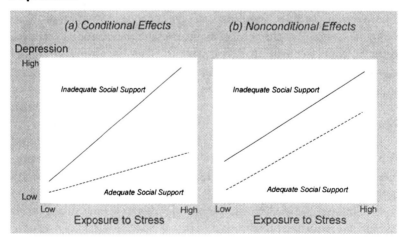

generate stress and that result in depression. Most germane is the fact that support may be affected by exposure to stress. For example, the appearance of a hardship or threat may mobilize social support networks, as friends and family rally around and extend a helping hand, suggest coping strategies, or console and encourage. Alternately, the persistence of problems over time can deplete support as people become fatigued, bored, or occupied with other problems. Whereas the stress-related activation of support mediates the impact of stress, offsetting some or all of its deleterious emotional consequences, stress-related depletion of support is the means through which stress damages emotional well-being (Ensel and Lin, 1991; Wheaton, 1985).

The stress-buffering model of social support, however, is concerned with the role of support as an effect modifier. According to this model (Figure 8.2a), the impact of stress varies according to whether the person has ties to others or must face hard times alone. Stress generates the most symptoms of depression when social support is absent. This contingency is reflected in the different slopes of the two lines.

The issue with regard to a dynamic modifier is not whether the intervening variable accounts for the focal relationship: Does stress seem to increase depression because people who are exposed to numerous stressors also tend to have limited social resources and because social isolation causes depression? In dynamic conditionality, the issue is whether the focal relationship varies across the various values of the intervening variable, specifically, is the relationship between stress (the focal independent variable) and depression (the dependent variable) stronger among those lacking social ties than among those with social support (the effect modifier)? In contrast, the alternative model assumes that the effects of stress and social support are autonomous, as shown in Figure 8.2b. Stress is equally depressing at all levels of social support, illustrated here as parallel lines. In reviewing the contradictory literature in this area, Kessler and McLeod (1985) conclude that the mental health impact of stress is buffered by emotional and perceived social support, but not by membership in social networks.

Note that Figure 8.2 is quite similar to Figure 8.1. In each figure, the panel to the left illustrates a conditional relationship between exposure to stress and depression, whereas the panel to the right illustrates a relationship that is not conditional. The difference between these two examples concerns the nature of the effect modifier. In the stress-buffering model, the effect modifier of social support is dynamic, potentially influenced by other variables in the model. In the differential vulnerability model, the effect modifier of gender is static.

The analytic strategies we have considered in previous chapters have been "main effects" models. This term indicates that only the separate effects of variables are modeled, not their synergistic effects. In particular, we have assumed that the magnitude of the focal relationship remains the same when the values of other variables change. The statistical methods we have been using, multiple linear regression and logistic regression, make this assumption, although it often goes unrecognized. In the following sections, we take up the alternative that the impact of one variable hinges upon the values taken by another variable and see how these effects are operationalized in regression models.

Social Support Among Caregivers: An Example of Conditional Relationships

A recent study of caregiving to elderly family members illustrates both static and dynamic modifiers. Li, Seltzer, and Greenberg (1997) examine the stress-buffering effects of social support among wives caring for an impaired elderly husband ($N = 103$) and daughters caring for an impaired elderly parent ($N = 149$). Wives and daughters are analyzed separately because there are fundamental differences in the social role of wife versus daughter. In addition, wives usually are at the same stage of life as their elderly husbands, whereas daughters are a generation younger and often face competing family and work demands. On this basis, the researchers hypothesize that the effects of social support are contingent upon family role. This variable is a static modifier because the social status connecting caregiver with care recipient (i.e., wife or daughter) is constant over time.

Li and associates (1997) find that social participation—the frequency of activities such as spending social time with friends and relatives—has differential effects on depressive symptoms for wives compared to daughters. This effect is estimated with a multiple linear regression that also includes indicators of caregiving stress and several characteristics of the caregiver that function as control variables (age, education, employment status, health status, and duration of care). The regression coefficient for social participation is

Figure 8.3

Family Relationship as a Static Modifier of the Effect of Social Participation on Caregiver Depression

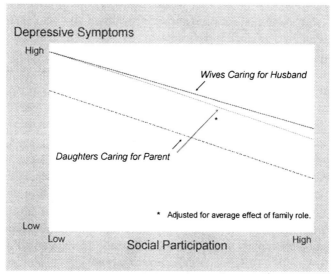

Source: Adapted from Li et al. (1997).

negative and statistically significant ($b_f = -.514$; $p \leq .05$) for daughters; it is negative ($b_f = -.449$) but not statistically significant for wives. This conditional relationship is graphed in Figure 8.3.

As can be seen, this effect modification is not as dramatic as the hypothetical examples in the previous figures. Indeed, to the naked eye the regression line for wives appears to be virtually parallel to the line for daughters. The lines appear quasi-parallel because the coefficient for wives, although not statistically significant, is almost 90% ($-.449/-.514$) as great as the coefficient for daughters.[1]

The distance between lines is the effect of being a wife versus a daughter. Note that this distance varies slightly according to the level of social participation, another manifestation of effect modification. In other words, the impact of family role is conditional upon the extent to which wives and daughters engage in social activities. The role effect is taken into consideration in the second plot for daughters (marked with an asterisk) to more clearly show the difference in slopes. As can be seen, the lines are not parallel, nor do they substantially diverge, an indication of statistically significant but relatively weak effect modification.

Li and associates (1997) also examine a dynamic modifier, the amount of stress encountered in the caregiving role. Stress exposure is considered dynamic because it ebbs and flows over time, varying, at least in part, as a function of other components of the system, for example, according to the health of the care recipient. The researchers ask whether exposure to care-related stress alters the impact of social support. Results are illustrated in Figure 8.4.

With regard to stress buffering, emotional support (rather than social participation) is the relevant dimension of support. The impact of emotional support on depression is conditional upon stress exposure for both wives (Figure 8.4a) and daughters (Figure 8.4b). For wives, depression is most strongly associated with emotional support when stress exposure is high, that is, when husbands frequently engage in problem behaviors, such as hiding things or using foul language. This inverse association is also present when stress exposure is medium, although its magnitude is somewhat smaller. However, when husbands do few of these sorts of things, their wives tend to have consistently low levels of symptoms irrespective of how much emotional support is received by the wives. For daughters, depression is negatively associated with emotional support only when parents exhibit numerous behavioral problems. When parents exhibit few behavioral problems, depression is not associated with emotional support. Although the precise pattern of results differs somewhat for wives and daughters, both patterns are consistent with the stress-buffering hypothesis.[2]

The Mechanics of Conditional Relationships

The unconditional relationship can be thought of as the overall or average effect in the sense that it is influenced by all observations and, hence, represents some hypothetical set of typical characteristics. In this manner, the heterogeneity inherent in a set of observations is simplified into a description of the overall association, much as the distribution of a variable is summarized by its mean.

From this perspective, conditional relationships can be thought of as *deviations* from the average relationship. Whereas the unconditional relationship is implicitly constrained to be the same across all values of the modifying variable, the conditional relationship is free to have different sizes across these values. The conditional focal relationship is essentially estimated separately for each of the various values of the modifying variable. This idea,

Figure 8.4

Stress as a Dynamic Modifier of the Effect of Social Support on Caregiver Depression

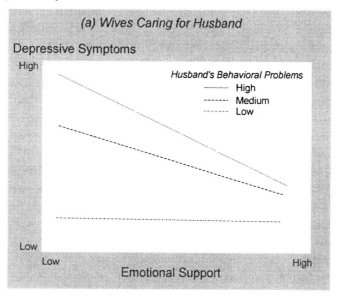

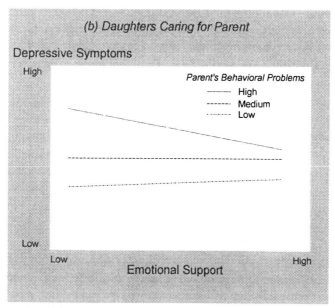

Source: Adapted from Li et al. (1997).

to extend the analogy to the mean used above, is equivalent to expressing between-group mean differences as deviations from the grand mean. When the discrete estimates of the focal relationship are combined, they reproduce the estimate of the average or overall association.

The simplest case is the dichotomous effect modifier, previously illustrated in Figure 8.1 for the example of gender differences in the effect of stress on depression. If the relationship between stress and depression is stronger for women than men, as hypothesized, then the conditional relationship among women is necessarily stronger than the relationship for the total population, whereas the conditional relationship among men is necessarily weaker than the total. Thus, the slope for the female line is steeper than the slope for the male line. If there are approximately equal numbers of men and women, then the total relationship will be about midway between the relationships observed separately for men and women, as suggested in Figure 8.1.

This simple case is easily extended to variables that signify more than two subgroups, for example, ethnicity, region of the country, or family structure. When there are multiple subgroups, conditional means that the focal relationship within one or more of the subgroups differs from the overall relationship estimated across all subgroups. The analogy to mean differences is once again useful: In analysis of variance the null hypothesis that each subgroup mean is equal—to each other and to the grand mean—is rejected if at least one mean differs. Correspondingly, an association is conditional if its size within at least one subgroup differs.

Although the arithmetic differs, the logic of conditional relationships is the same when the modifying variable is numeric rather than categorical. The focal relationship is estimated, in effect, separately across all of these numerous values. The relationship is conditional when its magnitude distinctly differs for at least some range of values of the modifying variable.

The analysis of conditional relationships reintroduces some of the complexity of the data that is lost in the analysis of average effects. The relationship that is not conditional treats all people and circumstances alike. The conditional relationship, in contrast, allows some people or circumstances to differ from others. It acknowledges that the real world is more complex than our linear models imply and seeks to specify some of this complexity.

SPECIFYING CONDITIONS OF INFLUENCE • 201

Strategies for the Assessment of Conditionality

There are two basic strategies for the analysis of conditional relationships: subgroup analysis and the analysis of interaction terms.
Subgroup analysis tends to be used when the values of the modifying variable delineate relatively distinct subgroups of the population. These subgroups may be natural groups, such as males
or females, or artificially constructed groups, such as families with
earnings below the median family income versus those with earnings at or above this income. Estimating the relationship separately
within each group and comparing these estimates across groups
addresses the possibility that the focal relationship is conditional.

An interaction term is a composite of the focal independent
variable and the modifying variable that operationalizes the sus-
pected contingency between these two variables.[3] This term is
added to the analytic model to determine whether it enhances the
fit of the model to the data over a base model that contains only
the main effects of the focal independent and modifying variables.
If not, the base model is preferable on the basis of parsimony.
Otherwise, the focal relationship is conditional, and the expanded
model is preferable because it more accurately reflects the data. In
this instance, the coefficient for the interaction term is examined to
determine the nature of the contingency.

Each approach has strengths and shortcomings. In practice,
many researchers conduct both types of analyses because each
alternative tends to illuminate the limitations of the other alternative. This issue is taken up again after these techniques have been
described.

Conditional Relationships as Interactions

To simplify the equations in this section, we limit our attention to
the two variables comprising the conditional relationship—the focal
independent variable and its modifier (X_m); control and other independent variables are indicated with ellipses (...). The subscript
m is used here to distinguish the modifier, omitting any additional
subscript that would indicate whether it also has another function,
such as control variable.[4]

Dichotomous Modifiers

Let us start with the simplest case: a numeric focal independent variable and a dichotomous modifying variable (X_m) treated as a dummy variable that is scored 1 for the presence of the characteristic and 0 for its absence. The conditional relationship is operationalized as a new variable that specifies the nature of the conditional relationship between these two components. In most instances, the interaction term is the product of the focal independent variable multiplied by the modifying variable ($X_f \times X_m$). This term frees the focal relationship to vary between the two categories of the effect modifier. In this example, we assume that the focal relationship is linear overall and within each category of the modifying variable, although nonlinear forms can be modeled.

The base model is the familiar regression model containing the focal independent variable and the variable that is thought to modify its effect on the dependent variable. The right-hand side of the equation is the same for numeric and dichotomous outcomes, so only one equation is presented, with both expressions for the dependent variable given on the left-hand side of the equation:

$$\widehat{Y} \text{ or } \log \hat{o}^{Y^+} = \cdots + b_f X_f + b_m X_m, \tag{8.1}$$

where X_m is the modifying variable and b_m is the change in the outcome associated with a unit difference in X_m, that is, the difference between the presence and absence of this characteristic. The expansion of the base model to include the conditional relationship becomes:

$$\widehat{Y} \text{ or } \log \hat{o}^{Y^+} = \cdots + b_f X_f + b_m X_m + b_c(X_f \times X_m), \tag{8.2}$$

where $X_f \times X_m$ is the cross-product interaction between the focal independent variable and the modifying variable and b_c is the unstandardized regression coefficient for this interaction term.

Recall that there are only two values for X_m: 0 and 1. When the modifying variable equals 0, the preceding equation is reduced to:

$$\widehat{Y} \text{ or } \log \hat{o}^{Y^+} = \cdots + b_f X_f. \tag{8.2a}$$

The terms $b_m X_m$ and $b_c(X_f \times X_m)$ drop out of the equation because each entails multiplication by 0. When X_m equals 1, Equation 8.2 reduces to:

$$\widehat{Y} \text{ or } \log \hat{o}^{Y^+} = \cdots + b_f X_f + b_m + b_c X_f$$
$$= \cdots + (b_f + b_c) X_f + b_m. \tag{8.2b}$$

Figure 8.5

The Dichotomous Modifying Variable

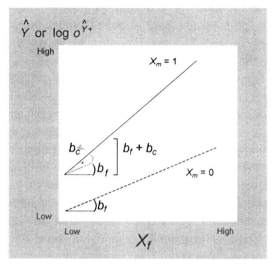

$b_m X_m$ becomes b_m because the value of X_m is fixed at 1. The term $(b_f X_f + b_c X_f)$ becomes $(b_f + b_c)X_f$ because the common term (X_f) is factored out.

When the focal relationship is linear and the modifier is dichotomous, conditionality is manifest as the difference in the slope of the regression lines between the two categories of the modifier, as illustrated in Figure 8.5.[5] In this illustration, the independent variable is related to the dependent variable in both categories, but this relationship is stronger in category 1 than in category 0. This differential is evident in the slope, which is steeper in category 1 than in category 0. Whereas the angle of ascent in category 0 is b_f (see Equation 8.2a), the angle of ascent in category 1 is $b_f + b_c$ (see Equation 8.2b). The difference in slopes is b_c, the coefficient for the interaction term.

When the focal relationship is positive, as shown here, a positive coefficient for the interaction term indicates that the slope is steeper in category 1, whereas a negative coefficient would indicate a slope that is steeper in category 0. In contrast, for a negative or inverse focal relationship, a negative sign for the interaction term yields a steeper slope for category 1, whereas a positive sign yields a steeper slope for category 0.

Is the difference in slopes statistically significant? The answer to this question can be ascertained in one of two ways. The first test is whether the addition of the interaction term $(X_f \times X_m)$ that operationalizes the conditional relationship enhances the explanatory power of the model beyond that attained by the base model that does not contain the interaction term. For a numeric dependent variable, the incremental R^2 test (Equation 8.1 versus Equation 8.2) is used to evaluate the null hypothesis, H_0: $b_c = 0$ (see Chapter 5, note 6). For logistic regression, the likelihood ratio test is used (see Chapter 5, note 8). We hope to reject this hypothesis when our theory posits a conditional relationship. The second test pertains to the slope differential, which is given by the regression coefficient for the interaction term in Equation 8.2. Specifically, is this coefficient different from 0? If not, the slopes of the two lines, although not identical, are indistinguishable from one another and the base model is preferable on the criterion of parsimony. Otherwise, the slopes of the two lines significantly differ from one another. The statistical test is the t test for the interaction term (b_c) for regression with a numeric outcome. The comparable test for the logistic model is Wald's χ^2. When only one interaction term is added, the first and second tests are equivalent.

One more facet of this analysis needs explanation, the interpretation of b_m. In the absence of conditionality (Equation 8.1), b_m is the effect of being in category 1 versus category 0 of X_m. In a conditional relationship (Equation 8.2), the effect of being in category 1 versus category 0 is not fixed, but varies over the values of the independent variable (X_f). Variability in the impact of the modifying variable is shown in Figure 8.5 by differences in the distance between the two lines across the values of X_f. As can be seen, this difference is smaller at low levels of X_f than at high levels. In the absence of conditionality, these lines would be equidistant from one another (see, for example, Figure 8.1b or Figure 8.2b).

The effect of the modifying variable, therefore, is conditional on the value of the focal independent variable (see, for example, Figure 8.1a or Figure 8.2a). When an interaction is present, b_m is the effect of being in category 1 (versus category 0) when X_f equals 0. If X_f has been mean deviated (see below), its mean is 0, i.e., b_m is the *impact* of X_m at the original mean of the focal independent variable. At other values of X_f, the impact of X_m is the sum of b_m and the regression coefficient for the interaction term (b_c) evaluated at the specific value (i) of X_f, that is, $b_c X_{fi}$. This derivation can be seen by comparing the estimated value of the dependent variable at several values of X_f for Equation 8.2a and Equation 8.2b, which represents the categories of 0 and 1 for the modifying variable.

This change in meaning for b_m (from the base model) flows from the fact that conditional relationships are symmetrical. If one variable is contingent upon a second variable, the reverse is also true: The second variable is contingent upon the first. This symmetry occurs because these two alternatives are operationalized with a single interaction term $(X_f \times X_m)$. Compare, for example, Figure 8.2 and Figure 8.4 for differing perspectives on the stress-buffering interaction with social support.

Although the interaction terms are identical, one interpretation usually is preferable to the other. In particular, viewing the focal relationship as contingent on another variable in the model is more consistent with our overall analytic strategy. The reverse, that some other variable is contingent upon the focal relationship, deflects attention away from the explication of the focal relationship. Nevertheless, the selection of an orientation for the interaction term is arbitrary in the sense that the statistical results are the same. This decision should flow from the theoretical model guiding the research.

A caveat concerning multicollinearity is needed. The variable that operationalizes the interaction term is an exact multiplicative function of the independent variable and the modifying variable. As a result, the correlation with the independent variable will ordinarily be very high and may produce problems of multicollinearity. In this case, the numeric variable is usually transformed before the creation of the interaction term. The transformation centers the distribution around zero by subtracting the variable's mean. This transformation diminishes the correlation between component variables and their cross-product interaction term. To avoid unnecessarily cumbersome equations, no additional notation has been added to the equations in this chapter to indicate that numeric variables have been mean deviated.

For the dichotomous dependent variable, it is useful to examine the exponentiated versions of the logistic regression model, given its ease of interpretation. The base model (see Equation 8.1) is:

$$\hat{o}^{Y^+} = \cdots e^{b_f X_f} e^{b_m X_m}. \tag{8.3}$$

Expanding the base model to include the interaction term yields (see Equation 8.2):

$$\hat{o}^{Y^+} = \cdots e^{b_f X_f} e^{b_m X_m} e^{b_c (X_f \times X_m)}. \tag{8.4}$$

When X_m is equal to 0, this equation reduces to:

$$\hat{o}^{Y^+} = \cdots e^{b_f X_f},\qquad(8.4a)$$

because multiplication by 0 reduces both $e^{b_m X_m}$ and $e^{b_c(X_f \times X_m)}$ to e^0 and $e^0 = 1.00$. When X_m is equal to 1, the equation becomes:

$$\hat{o}^{Y^+} = \cdots e^{(b_f + b_c) X_f} e^{b_m},\qquad(8.4b)$$

because $e^{b_1 X} \times e^{b_2 X} = e^{(b_1 + b_2)X}$ and because $e^{b_m X_m}$ becomes e^{b_m} as a result of multiplication by 1.

Because this model is multiplicative, effects are calibrated relative to 1.00, the value indicative of no effect. The effect of primary interest is for the conditional relationship and is given by e^{b_c}, which is the extent to which being in category 1 (versus category 0) of X_m alters the effect of X_f on the odds of being positive on Y. The direction of this effect modification depends upon the direction of the focal relationship. A positive focal relationship ($e^{b_f} > 1.00$) is intensified by a value greater than 1.00 for e^{b_c}, but diminished by a value between 0 and 1.00 (i.e., a fraction). In contrast, a negative or inverse focal relationship ($0 < e^{b_f} < 1.00$) is diminished when e^{b_c} is greater than 1.00, but is intensified by a fractional value.

As before, the inclusion of the interaction term also changes the interpretation of the term for the effect modifier, e^{b_m}. In the absence of conditionality, e^{b_m} is the odds ratio for being positive on the dependent variable given a value of 1 versus 0 on the modifier, and this odds ratio is invariant across all values of the focal independent variable.[6] When the interaction term is included in the regression equation, the effect of the modifying variable X_m differs across the values of X_f. The effect of X_m at a given value of X_f is obtained by multiplying the "main" effect of being in category 1 (e^{b_m}) with the specific effect ($e^{b_c X_{fi}}$) at the given value (i) of X_f, or $e^{b_m} e^{b_c X_{fi}}$, which can be seen by comparing Equation 8.4a to Equation 8.4b.[7]

The 2-by-2 Interaction: Backing the Winning Candidate

An example of this type of interaction can be found in a recent analysis of the so-called paradox of voter turnout (Kanazawa, 2000). The paradox pertains to the discrepancy between a prediction from the rational choice model that voters should take a free ride and abstain from voting and the actual participation of millions of voters in elections. According to Kanazawa, voting in large national elections is a collective action problem because a person's vote is almost certainly not decisive and because voters and nonvoters experience the same electoral outcome, which eliminates personal incentives to vote. (The subjective experience of the possibility of casting a decisive vote, however, may have changed following the 2000 presidential election because of the narrow margin of victory, especially in the key state of Florida.) These circumstances predict that rational actors will not invest time and energy in choosing a candidate and going to the polls to cast a ballot. Instead, they will opt for taking a free ride, depending on others to vote. If most potential voters are rational actors, very few people will vote, or so the theory goes.

Kanazawa (2000) presents an alternative model specifying circumstances that alter the likelihood that a person will vote. He starts with a calculus of voting model that asserts that a citizen will vote if the rewards of voting exceed the costs. The model contains two types of rewards: instrumental rewards, the benefits an individual personally receives only if his or her preferred candidate wins the election; and normative rewards, the fulfillment of one's sense of civic duty, that is, the intrinsic satisfaction of voting irrespective of who wins the election. Costs include time and energy invested in learning about candidates beforehand and going to the polls on election day, as well as the opportunity costs of what one could have done instead.

An additional consideration is the probability that a person's vote is decisive, that it makes or breaks a tie in favor of the favored candidate. In the calculation of benefits, instrumental rewards are weighted by this probability. This term approaches 0 in large national elections, which means that the personal incentive to vote approaches 0. The rewards of voting are, therefore, limited to the satisfaction of being a good citizen.

Kanazawa (2000) contends that voters perform a different calculus, one that is past-oriented rather than future-oriented and centered on having chosen the winning candidate rather than possibly casting a decisive vote. He criticizes the assumption that voters are subjective utility maximizers, who look forward, evaluate all options available to them within informational and structural constraints, assess their potential consequences, and choose a course of action. He argues instead that rational actors are backward looking and adaptive.

In the reformulated model, which applies a stochastic learning perspective, actors interpret the success and failure of collective action as a reinforcement or punishment from the environment that is associated with their own behavior. When someone contributes to a successful collective action, the contribution is reinforced and is likely to be repeated in the future, but unsuccessful contributions are punished and are not likely to be repeated. Successful collective action is also rewarding and reinforcing for those who do not contribute, leading to continued abstention, whereas unsuccessful collective action is punishing and leads to subsequent contribution. This reasoning leads Kanazawa (2000) to posit an interaction of voting behavior and election outcomes in the past with future voting behavior: Among those who voted, the probability of voting in the next election is greater for those who supported the winning rather than the losing candidate; among those who did not vote, the probability of future voting is greater among those who supported the losing candidate than among those who backed the winning candidate.

To test these hypotheses, Kanazawa (2000) analyzes data from the General Social Survey, which consists of personal interviews with a nationally representative sample of adults. This analysis uses seven surveys covering six consecutive presidential elections starting with the 1972 election; data are pooled across these years. Respondents were asked about the last two presidential elections: whether they voted and which candidate they supported. The independent variable concerns the earlier of the two elections: voted (no = 0, yes = 1). The modifying variable is whether the person backed the winning candidate (no = 0, yes = 1) in that election. The interaction term is the product of these two variables (voted for the winner = 1, other = 0). When these three variables are included in the regression equation, the omitted reference category is persons who scored 0 on all three variables: they did not vote and they backed the losing candidate. The dependent variable is whether the person voted (no = 0, yes = 1) in the second of the two elections. The analysis method is logistic regression.

The results of this analysis, which support some study hypotheses, are shown in Table 8.1. The first three coefficients test the interaction between voting and supporting a winner. The first column gives results for all elections and the second column limits analysis to elections without a major third-party candidate.

Table 8.1

Voting by Previous Voting Experience, Presidential Elections 1972 to 1992

	Logistic Regression Coefficients	
Independent Variables	All Elections	No Third Party Candidate
Previous voting experience[a]		
Voted in previous election (1 = yes)	2.564***	2.401***
	(.084)	(.094)
Supported the winner (1 = yes)	−.131	−.133
	(.087)	(.109)
Interaction (1 = voted & winner)	.219•	.368**
	(.115)	(.138)
Democrat	.432***	.455***
	(.069)	(.082)
Republican	.486***	.460***
	(.079)	(.097)
Age	.003	.004
	(.002)	(.002)
Race (not black = 1)	.130	.085
	(.080)	(.098)
Sex (male = 1)	−.139*	−.207**
	(.058)	(.068)
Education (years)	.060***	.069***
	(.010)	(.011)
Income	−.002	−.002
	(.002)	(.002)
Constant	−1.782	−1.850
	(.184)	(.218)
N	9,404	6,554

Source: Kanazawa (2000).
[a]Omitted reference category is not voting and not supporting a winner. Focal relationship is in italics. Standard errors in parentheses.
•$p < .06$. *$p < .05$. **$p < 01$. ***$p < .001$.

For all elections, only one voting variable is statistically significant, voted in previous election: Compared to nonvoters, those who voted in the previous election are more likely to vote in the next election. This difference applies irrespective of whether they backed the winner because the coefficient for whether the winner was supported is not statistically significant. However, the interaction term approaches statistical significance, meaning there is a tendency for those who voted in the previous election to be especially likely to vote in the next election if they voted for the candidate who won the election.

For elections without a third-party candidate, the interaction term is larger than for all elections and statistically significant. Persons who voted for the winner are more likely to vote in the next election than those who voted for the losing candidate. Alternately stated, the impact of voting in the previous election is greater among those who backed the winning candidate rather than the candidate who lost. Among those who did not vote, backing the winner or loser does not significantly influence the likelihood of voting in the next election.

The interpretation of the interaction of two dummy variables (e.g., voted and won) is an especially important case because it occurs quite frequently, perhaps because many characteristics of people are qualitative distinctions, such as gender or ethnicity. This example, then, merits close attention.

Figure 8.6 shows the cross-tabulation of the variables voted in the previous election (no/yes) by backed the winning candidate (no/yes) and their interaction (voted for the winner/other). Within the cells of this 2-by-2 table are the variables that are used to calculate the log odds of voting in the next election. The upper left cell contains nonvoters who backed the losing candidate, who are scored 0 on all three voting variables in the regression equation shown in Table 8.1, the defining characteristic of being the omitted reference category. In the lower right cell, voters for the winner are scored as 1 on all three variables; the contribution of this voting history to future voting, then, is the sum of the coefficients for these variables. Nonvoters who backed the winner are scored positive on only one variable (winner) and its coefficient signifies the contribution of this voting history to future voting. Similarly, those who voted for the loser are scored positive on only one variable, voted.

The interaction of the two voting history variables can also be operationalized as a conventional series of three dummy variables, scored 1 for one and only one of the four cells in Figure 8.6 and using the same reference of nonvoters backing the losing candidate. These dummy variables are labeled in the 2-by-2 table and their scoring is shown in the lower panel of Figure 8.6. Although the format of the original regression equation and the dummy variable approach do not have a one-to-one correspondence, these representations are equivalent. This equivalency applies to the sets of variables, however, not to any one variable in isolation from the others.

Figure 8.6

Interaction Terms: Voting and Backing a Winner

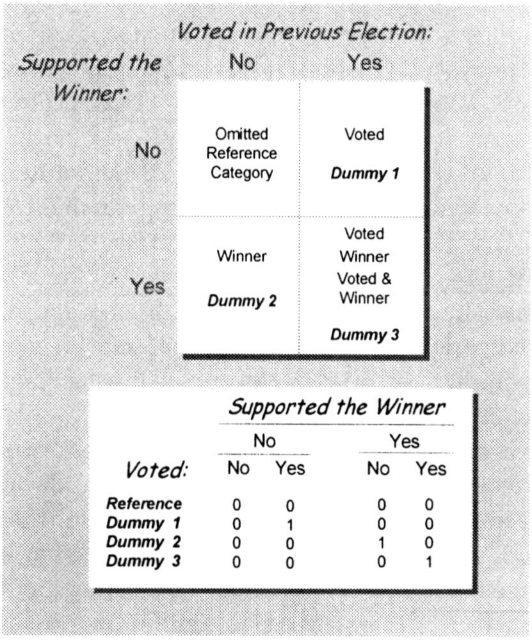

	Voted in Previous Election:	
Supported the Winner:	No	Yes
No	Omitted Reference Category	Voted Dummy 1
Yes	Winner Dummy 2	Voted Winner Voted & Winner Dummy 3

	Supported the Winner			
	No		Yes	
Voted:	No	Yes	No	Yes
Reference	0	0	0	0
Dummy 1	0	1	0	0
Dummy 2	0	0	1	0
Dummy 3	0	0	0	1

This correspondence is most apparent for the reference category, nonvoters backing the loser; this group is scored 0 on all three voting variables in the regression equation and on all three dummy variables. A similar equivalence is seen for the voted variable and dummy 1; both give the effect of voting for the losing candidate (relative to not voting and backing the loser). Likewise, the winner variable and dummy 2 identify nonvoters backing the winning candidate (relative to the same reference group).

The two representations differ, however, for voters for the winning candidate. In the regression equation, this group is scored as positive on all three voting variables and its difference from the reference group is the sum of these three coefficients (e.g., $2.401 - .133 + .368 = 2.636$ for the no third-party equation in Table 8.1). In the dummy variable approach, this group would be scored positive on only one dummy variable. It should be apparent that the coefficient in the dummy variable approach equals the sum of the three coefficients in the regression equation approach (i.e., 2.636).

The coefficients in Table 8.1 give the impact of the voting variables on the log odds of voting in the next election net of the other variables in the equation. The exponents of these coefficients can be interpreted as partial odds ratios because the voting variables are dichotomous. These are partial odds ratios, not odds ratios, because the effects of other variables in the regression equation are statistically controlled. These values are plotted in Figure 8.7 for the no third-party data of Table 8.1 that has a statistically significant interaction term.

These partial odds ratios are relative to the omitted reference category, nonvoters who backed the losing candidate in the last election. The partial odds ratio for this group is 1.00 that is, no effect on the odds of voting. Referring back to Table 8.1, we see that persons in this category are scored as 0 on the three variables that collectively define group membership, and the exponent of 0 is 1.00. The impact of being in the other three voting groups is expressed relative to this category.

As can be seen in Figure 8.7, one group has lower odds of voting than the reference group, nonvoters who backed the winner. The partial odds ratio for voting in the next election for this group is a fraction (.875), which indicates an inverse association because the odds ratio is a multiplicative measure of association. In the additive model (see Table 8.1) a negative sign signifies inverse associations. The translation between the two expression is given by $e^{-.133} = .875$ or $\ln(.875) = -.133$. The difference between nonvoters who backed

Figure 8.7

Voting by History of Voting: Winners and Losers

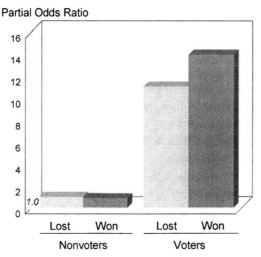

the winner and nonvoters who backed the loser, however, is not statistically significant, as reported in Table 8.1; this test applies as well to the exponentiated regression coefficient because these two expressions are mathematical transformations of one another.

The other two groups of voters have substantially higher odds of voting than the reference group as also shown in Figure 8.7. Voters who backed the losing candidate have about 11 times greater odds of voting in the next election than nonvoters who backed the losing candidate, other things being equal. Persons in this group are scored as 1 on one of the voting variables, voted in the previous election, and as 0 on the other two voting variables (because they did not support the winner). The partial odds ratio for this group, then, is $e^{2.401}e^0e^0 = e^{2.401} = 11.034$. As reported in Table 8.1, this difference is statistically significant. Notice that the coefficient for the voted variable does not give the effect of having voted for everyone, but only for those who backed the loser. This crucial distinction arises because the impact of having voted is modified by the interaction term.

Thus, voters who backed the winning candidate are even more likely to vote. Persons in this group are scored positive on all three of the voting variables. They voted in the previous election ($e^{2.401} = 11.034$), supported the winner ($e^{-.133} = .875$), and voted for the winner, the interaction term ($e^{.368} = 1.444$), meaning their odds of voting in the next election are about 14 times (13.950) greater than persons in the reference category. The significant interaction term indicates that persons in this group not only have higher odds of voting in the next election than those in the reference group, they also have substantially higher odds of voting than voters who backed the losing candidate ($13.950/11.034 = 1.264$). The impact of this interaction term is shown as the difference between the lost and won columns of *voters* in Figure 8.7.

Categorical Modifiers

The same type of effect modification can be assessed for categorical variables with more than two categories. The procedures for generating the appropriate interaction terms are outlined in Table 8.2. The first column lists the values $(a, \ldots, k)$ for the modifying variable X_m. Letters are used to emphasize the categorical nature of this variable. For inclusion in the regression equation, the modifying variable is transformed into a series of $k - 1$ dummy variables, as shown in the next set of columns. As always, one category is omitted as the reference category, in this instance category k.

As before, the conditional relationship is operationalized as a new variable, the product of the focal independent variable and the modifying variable, or $(X_f \times X_m)$. However, X_m is now represented by the $k - 1$ dummy variables listed in Table 8.2. The entire set of dummy variables is used to generate the interaction terms for representing the conditional effect. This multiplication produces $k - 1$ interaction terms, as also shown in Table 8.1. These interaction terms convert the linear base model to a linear model in which the slope of the focal relationship is free to vary across the categories of the modifier. This template can be used for analysis with either multiple linear regression or logistic regression.

The base regression model for the example given in Table 8.2 is:

$$\widehat{Y} \text{ or } \log \hat{o}^{Y^+} = \cdots + b_f X_f + b_{m1} X_{m1} + b_{m2} X_{m2}$$
$$+ \cdots + b_{m(k-1)} X_{m(k-1)}, \tag{8.5}$$

where $X_{m1}, X_{m2}, \ldots, X_{m(k-1)}$ is the set of dummy variables for the k categories of the modifying variable. The conditional focal relationship is operationalized as the product of the focal independent

Table 8.2

Interactions With a Categorical Modifier

Modifier code	Dummy variable				Interaction terms	Effect of X_f[a]	Differential effect of X_f within j[b]	Effect of being in condition[c]
	X_{m1}	X_{m2}	$\cdots$	$X_{m(k-1)}$				
a	1	0	$\cdots$	0	$X_f \times X_{m1}$	$b_f + b_{c1}$	b_{c1}	b_{m1}
b	0	1	$\cdots$	0	$X_f \times X_{m2}$	$b_f + b_{c2}$	b_{c2}	b_{m2}
$\cdots$								
$k - 1$	0	0	$\cdots$	1	$X_f \times X_{m(k-1)}$	$b_f + b_{c(k-1)}$	$b_{c(k-1)}$	$b_{m(k-1)}$
k[d]	0	0	$\cdots$	0	—	b_f	—	—

[a]Magnitude of the focal relationship within condition j of the modifier.
[b]Difference in the focal relationship between condition j of the modifier and the reference condition (k).
[c]Effect of being in condition j of the modifier (net of other variables in the equation) when X_f is O.
[d]Omitted reference category scored 0 on all dummy variables.

variable with each of these dummy variables. When these interaction terms are added to the base model, Equation 8.5 becomes:

$$\widehat{Y} \text{ or } \log \hat{o}^{Y^+} = \cdots + b_f X_f + b_{m1} X_{m1} + b_{m2} X_{m2}$$
$$+ \cdots + b_{m(k-1)} X_{m(k-1)} + b_{c1}(X_f \times X_{m1})$$
$$+ b_{c2}(X_f \times X_{m2}) + \cdots + b_{c(k-1)}(X_f \times X_{m(k-1)}). \quad (8.6)$$

Although this segment of the regression equation looks horrendous, it is simplified considerably by substituting values for the modifier because most of the terms drop out as a result of multiplication by 0. As shown in the bottom entry of Table 8.1, cases in the reference category k are scored as 0 on all dummy variables and, consequently, as 0 on all interaction terms involving these dummy variables. For the category k, then, Equation 8.6 reduces to:

$$\widehat{Y} \text{ or } \log \hat{o}^{Y^+} = \cdots + b_f X_f. \quad (8.6a)$$

The remaining categories $(a, \ldots, k - 1)$ of the modifying variable are scored as 1 on one and only one dummy variable and as 0 on all other dummy variables. As a result of multiplication by 0, each of these categories has a nonzero value for only one interaction term as well. Effect modification for each category, therefore, is operationalized as one interaction term, the product of X_f and the appropriate dummy variable. For example, the regression equation for being in category a of Table 8.1 is:

$$\widehat{Y} \text{ or } \log \hat{o}^{Y^+} = \cdots + b_f X_f + b_{m1} X_{m1} + b_{c1}(X_f \times X_{m1})$$
$$= \cdots (b_f + b_{c1})X_f + b_{m1}, \quad (8.6b)$$

where $b_f + b_{c1}$ is the effect of X_f given membership in category a, b_{c1} is the differential effect of X_f between category a and the omitted reference category k, and b_{m1} is the effect of membership in category a when X_f equals zero. The remaining categories of the modifying variable simplify in the same way.

The differential effect of the independent variable X_f within a specific category of the modifier is simply the regression coefficient for that interaction term, as shown in Table 8.2. This differential is b_{c1} for category a, for example, and b_{c2} for category b, as also shown in Table 8.2. It represents the deviation from the slope of the focal relationship within the reference category, that is, the deviation from b_f. These differentials are illustrated in Figure 8.8.

Figure 8.8

The Categorical Modifying Variable

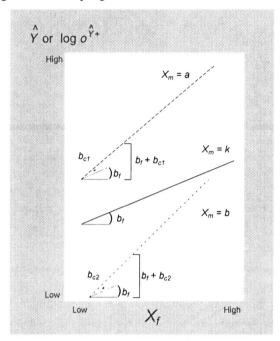

To emphasize the similarity between multiple linear regression and logistic regression, the Y-axis is given two labels, $\hat{Y}$ and $\log \hat{o}^{Y+}$.

The effect of being in a specific category of the modifying variable is the coefficient associated with its dummy variable, as listed in the last column of Table 8.2. The reference category continues to be k, and effects are expressed as deviations from this category. If the focal relationship is indeed conditional, the effect of being in other categories of the modifier is not fixed, but varies across the values of the focal independent variable. As before, these effects are expressed as deviations from the effect of group membership when the focal independent variable is 0 (net of other variables in the model). The impact of group membership at other values (x_i) of X_f is $b_{m_i} + b_{c_i} X_{f_i}$. This variability is shown in Figure 8.8 as the unequal distance between the regression line for the reference category k and the line for each of the other categories.

The statistical test for interactions with a modifier that has multiple categories is conducted in two parts. The first part is the increment in R^2 associated with the addition of the entire set of interaction terms $(X_f \times X_{m1}, X_f \times X_{m2}, \ldots, X_f \times X_{m(k-1)})$ to the base model for numeric outcomes (see Chapter 5, note 6). For dichotomous outcomes, the likelihood ratio test is used (see Chapter 5, note 8). This omnibus test (Equation 8.6 − Equation 8.5) takes into consideration the number of variables added to the model, reducing the probability of a Type I error. If this test is statistically significant, then the focal relationship is conditional upon the modifier. Each of the added interaction terms is then evaluated individually, specifically $H_0 : b_c = 0$. This part of the procedure uses the t test for the regression coefficient for each interaction term or, for logistic regression the Wald's χ^2 test. A statistically significant coefficient means that the slope of the focal relationship within that category differs from its slope within the reference category. If the overall test for the set of interaction terms does not attain conventional levels of statistical significance, then tests are not conducted for the individual interaction terms as usual.[8]

As before, the exponentiated version of the logistic model is useful because the interpretation is simplified. For the reference category k, the equation with interaction terms reduces to:

$$\hat{o}^{Y+} = \cdots e^{b_f X_f}. \tag{8.7a}$$

For category a the reduced equation is:

$$\hat{o}^{Y+} = \cdots e^{b_f X_f} e^{b_{m1} X_{m1}} e^{b_{c1}(X_f \times X_{m1})} = \cdots e^{(b_f + b_{c1})X_f} e^{b_{m1}}, \tag{8.7b}$$

and so on. $e^{b_{c1}}$ is the differential impact of X_f on the odds of being positive on Y that is associated with being in category a rather than the omitted reference category k of the modifier. $b_f + b_{c1}$ is the change in the odds of being positive on Y for a unit increase in the focal independent variable for persons in category a. $e^{b_{m1}}$ is the difference in the odds of being positive on Y given membership in category a rather than category k when X_f equals zero.

Two Categorical Variables

Suppose that the focal independent variable is categorical rather than numeric. In this instance, both variables are operationalized as a series of dummy variables, as illustrated in Table 8.3. As before, there are $k - 1$ dummy variables for the modifying variable with

Table 8.3

Interaction Terms for Two Categorical Variables

Focal independent dummy variables (X_f)	Modifying dummy variables (X_m)			
	X_{m1}	X_{m2}	$\cdots$ $X_{m(k-1)}$	X_{mk}[a]
X_{f1}	$X_{f1} \times X_{m1}$	$X_{f1} \times X_{m2}$	$\cdots$ $X_{f1} \times X_{m(k-1)}$	0
X_{f2}	$X_{f2} \times X_{m1}$	$X_{f2} \times X_{m2}$	$\cdots$ $X_{f2} \times X_{m(k-1)}$	0
$\cdots$	$\cdots$	$\cdots$	$\cdots$ $\cdots$	0
$X_{f(j-1)}$	$X_{f(j-1)} \times X_{m1}$	$X_{f(j-1)} \times X_{m2}$	$X_{f(j-1)} \times X_{m(k-1)}$	0
X_{fj}[a]	0	0	0 0	0

[a]Omitted reference category scored 0.

k categories, as arrayed across the top of Table 8.3. The independent variable with j categories, operationalized as $j - 1$ dummy variables, appears in the column to the far left.

The interactions between the modifying variable and the independent variable generate $[(k - 1) \times (j - 1)]$ dummy variables, as shown in the body of Table 8.2. Each unique combination of categories is represented by a dummy variable, which is coded 1 if both attributes are present; otherwise, it is coded 0. For example, someone who is positive on both X_{f1} and X_{m1} is also positive on $(X_{f1} \times X_{m1})$; this person is 0 on all other dummy variables and on all other dummy variable interaction terms. The exception to this pattern involves the reference categories of the focal independent variable (X_{fj}) and the modifying variable (X_{mk}), which are coded 0 on all dummy variables and, consequently, all interaction terms. The omitted reference category is coded 0 on both the focal independent variable and the modifying variable.

To determine whether the effect of the focal independent variable is contingent upon the modifying variable, two models are compared. The base model contains (in addition to any other explanatory variables) the dummy-coded focal independent variable $(X_f: X_{f1}, X_{f2}, \ldots, X_{f(j-1)})$ and the dummy-coded modifying variable $(X_m: X_{m1}, X_{m2}, \ldots, X_{m(k-1)})$. The expanded model adds the interactions between these two variables $(X_{f1} \times X_{m1}, \ldots, X_{f(j-1)} \times X_{m(k-1)})$.

The increment in explanatory efficacy between the base and conditional models is the overall test of whether the focal relationship is conditional upon the modifying variable as discussed above. If not, the base model suffices using the criterion of parsimony. Otherwise, the coefficients for the individual terms are examined from the expanded model. Statistically significant coefficients localize the categories under which the focal relationship differs from the effect of X_f within the omitted reference category.

Two Numeric Variables

In many instances both the independent variable and the modifying variable are numeric. In most applications, the interaction is modeled as the product of the two component variables: $(X_f \times X_m)$. Once again, two models are compared: one without the interaction term and the other with this term. The relevant equations are the same as Equation 8.1 and Equation 8.2 with the exception that X_m is now numeric not dichotomous. The overall statistical significance of the conditional relationship is given by the incremental R^2 test for multiple linear regression or the likelihood ratio test for logistic regression. The test of the regression coefficient (b_c) for the interaction term as estimated in the second model (t test or Wald's χ^2 test for multiple linear or logistic regression, respectively) provides the same test if only one term is added. If more than one interaction term is added, the individual test is conducted, as usual, only if the overall test for the entire set of added interaction terms is significant.

An illustration of a conditional relationship for two numeric variables is given in Figure 8.9a. As before, the Y-axis shows two alternative values, $\widehat{Y}$ and $\log \hat{o}^{Y^+}$, to emphasize that the principles here are the same for a numeric dependent variable as for a dichotomous dependent variable modeled with multiple linear and logistic regression, respectively. For this illustration, we assume that the regression coefficients are positive for the two component variables, the focal independent variable, and the modifying variable, and, further, that the regression coefficient is positive for their interaction. Under these conditions, the strength of the focal relationship increases as the values of the modifier increase and the lines disperse. The precise pattern of these lines will differ according to the signs and magnitudes of the coefficients for X_f, X_m, and $X_f \times X_m$. The key point to this illustration is the number of distinct regression lines, only some of which are shown here. In the earlier

Figure 8.9

Effect Modification for Two Numeric Variables

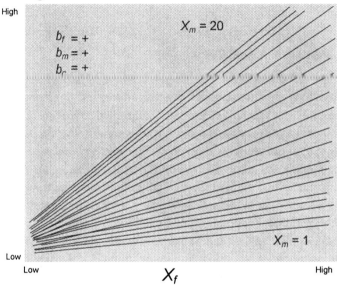

(a) X_m and X_f are numeric.

$b_f = +$
$b_m = +$
$b_c = +$

$X_m = 20$

$X_m = 1$

Low

Low X_f High

(b) X_m is collapsed into 3 categories.

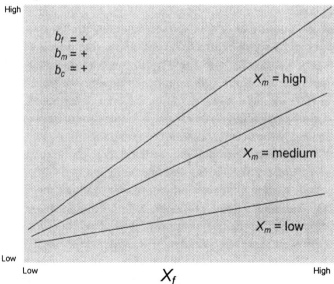

$b_f = +$
$b_m = +$
$b_c = +$

$X_m = \text{high}$

$X_m = \text{medium}$

$X_m = \text{low}$

Low

Low X_f High

examples of categorical variables, the number of lines was equal to the number of categories of the modifying variable. When both variables are numeric, the large number of values for the modifying variable generates a large number of regression lines. Plotting all of these lines is usually not informative, so it is customary to plot these lines for only a few select values as an aid to interpretation (e.g., high, medium, and low on the modifying variable), as shown in Figure 8.9b.

Recap

Table 8.4 lists the types of common interactions discussed in this chapter for multiple linear regression and logistic regression. The relevant coefficients are given for each regression format. In addition, the relevant expression of the dependent variable appears at the top of the column. This table demonstrates that the same logical approach is taken in each of these statistical procedures, although they differ in mathematical expression. The tests for statistical significance across these forms of regression shown in Table 8.4 are also isomorphic to each other. Two tests are performed. This strategy should be familiar by now: The first test is the increment in explanatory efficacy that tests the null hypothesis that the regression coefficients for all of the added interaction terms are 0. In other words, nothing is gained by adding these variables. The second test is of the individual coefficients. In multiple linear regression, these tests are (a) ΔR^2 (F test) and (b) H_0: $b_m = 0$ (t test). In logistic regression, these tests are (a) likelihood ratio test (χ^2 test) and (b) H_0: $b_m = 0$ (Wald's χ^2). The tests for the additive expression of the logistic model also apply to its multiplicative expression.

Subgroup Analysis of Conditional Relationships

The second method for determining whether the focal relationship is contingent upon the values of a modifying variable entails estimating the focal relationship separately within the subgroups defined by the values of the modifier. This technique is illustrated by the caregiver example for differences in the effect of social support between wives and daughters cited earlier in this chapter

Table 8.4

Summary of Common Interactions for Regression Models

Independent/ modifying variable	Multiple linear regression	Logistic regression	
		Additive	Multiplicative
(Dependent variable)	(Y: Y is numeric)	(lno^{Y+}: Y is dichotomous)	(o^{Y+}: Y is dichotomous)
Numeric/ dichotomous	$b_c(X_f \times X_m)$	$b_c(X_f \times X_m)$	$e^{b\ (X\ \times X\ )}$
Numeric/ categorical	$b_{c1}(X_f \times X_{m1})$ $b_{c2}(X_f \times X_{m2})$ ... $b_{c(k-1)}(X_f \times X_{m(k-1)})$	$b_{c1}(X_f \times X_{m1})$ $b_{c2}(X_f \times X_{m2})$ ... $b_{c(k-1)}(X_f \times X_{m(k-1)})$	$e^{b\ (X\ \times X\ )}$ $e^{b\ (X\ \times X\ )}$ ... $e^{b\ \ (X\ \times X\ \ )}$
Categorical/ categorical	$b_{c1}(X_{f1} \times X_{m1})$ $b_{c2}(X_{f1} \times X_{m2})$ ... $b_{c(k-1)}(X_{f1} \times X_{m(k-1)})$ $b_{c1}(X_{f2} \times X_{m1})$ $b_{c2}(X_{f2} \times X_{m2})$ ... $b_{c(k-1)}(X_{f2} \times X_{m(k-1)})$ ... $b_{c1}(X_{f(j-1)} \times X_{m1})$ $b_{c2}(X_{f(j-1)} \times X_{m2})$ ... $b_{c(k-1)}(X_{f(j-1)} \times X_{m(k-1)})$	$b_{c1}(X_f \times X_{m1})$ $b_{c2}(X_{f1} \times X_{m2})$ ... $b_{c(k-1)}(X_{f1} \times X_{m(k-1)})$ $b_{c1}(X_{f2} \times X_{m1})$ $b_{c2}(X_{f2} \times X_{m2})$ ... $b_{c(k-1)}(X_{f2} \times X_{m(k-1)})$ ... $b_{c1}(X_{f(j-1)} \times X_{m1})$ $b_{c2}(X_{f(j-1)} \times X_{m2})$ ... $b_{c(k-1)}(X_{f(j-1)} \times X_{m(k-1)})$	$e^{b\ (X\ \times X\ )}$ $e^{b\ (X\ \times X\ )}$ ... $e^{b\ \ (X\ \times X\ \ )}$ $e^{b\ (X\ \times X\ )}$ $e^{b\ (X\ \times X\ )}$ ... $e^{b\ \ (X\ \times X\ \ )}$ ... $e^{b\ (X\ \ \times X\ )}$ $e^{b\ (X\ \ \times X\ )}$ ... $e^{b\ \ (X\ \ \times X\ \ )}$
Numeric/ numeric	$b_c(X_f \times X_m)$	$b_c(X_f \times X_m)$	$e^{b\ (X\ \times X\ )}$

(see Figures 8.3 and 8.4). In brief, one regression equation is estimated for each value of the modifying variable, in this example, wives and daughters.

The subgroup approach is most appropriate when the subgroups are relatively distinct from one another (as in the socially constructed categories of gender), but the method can be adapted to subgroups that have fuzzy or arbitrary boundaries (e.g., categories of social support). This situation typically arises when a numeric modifier is collapsed into categories for the convenience of using subgroup analysis.

Although the regression equation that would be used to assess differences among subgroups is likely to include other variables, these variables are indicated in the following equations only by ellipses (...) to simplify the presentation, as in the previous discussion of interaction terms. The multiple linear regression and logistic regression models are shown together to emphasize the similarities between these approaches. The following discussion assumes that a linear focal relationship is conditional upon a categorical modifying variable (X_m) with k categories.

The model for the subgroup approach to conditionality is quite simple. The basic regression model containing the focal independent variable is estimated for each of the k categories:

$$\widehat{Y} \text{ or } \log \hat{o}^{Y_j^+} = \cdots + b_{f_j} X_f \qquad \text{for subgroup } j, \qquad (8.8)$$

where b_{f_j} is the estimate of the magnitude of the focal relationship within subgroup j. A separate estimate of b_{f_j} is obtained for each of the k subgroups. The exponentiated version of the logistic model should be evident:

$$\hat{o}^{Y_j^+} = \cdots e^{b_{f_j} X_f}. \qquad (8.8a)$$

In each method, the regression equation is estimated separately within each category of the modifying variable. Thus, there are as many regressions as there are values of X_m. The focal relationship is conditional if its regression coefficient (b_{f_j}) differs significantly across the subgroups defined by the modifying variable. This procedure is illustrated in Figure 8.10, where the coefficient for the focal relationship (b_f) takes on different values (b_{f_1}, b_{f_2}) in the two groups defined by the dichotomous modifying variable X_m.

It is not possible to ascertain whether the focal relationship is conditional upon group membership by examining the regression equation within a single subgroup (e.g., among males *or* among females). Instead, it is necessary to compare regression equations across the subgroups that comprise the modifying variable (e.g., between males and females). In particular, we are interested in whether the estimate of b_f differs across subgroups. For example, with regard to Figure 8.7 we would test the null null hypothesis, $H_0: b_{f_1} = b_{f_2}$. This test can be made by calculating the confidence interval for b_f within each subgroup to determine their overlap or by conducting a t test.[9]

Figure 8.10

The Conditional Focal Relationship by Subgroup Analysis

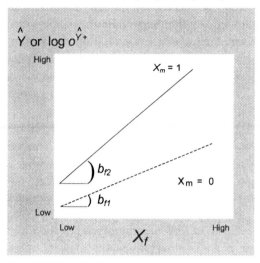

Subgroup analysis is illustrated by our continuing caregiver example (see Figure 8.3). In this instance, Li and associates (1997) estimate regression equations separately for wives caring for husbands and for daughters caring for parents. For the outcome of depressive symptoms, the regression coefficient for social participation is statistically significant for daughters but not for wives. In other words, the null hypothesis, H_0: $b_f = 0$, can be rejected ($p \leq$ .05) for daughters but not for wives. On this basis, the researchers conclude that the impact of social participation is conditional on family role (but see the earlier caveat concerning differential statistical power for these subgroups). This approach is not as precise as testing the hypothesis that b_f is the same for wives and daughters, however, because the coefficients may not differ significantly even though one is significantly different from 0 whereas the other is not.

When the confidence intervals for all subgroups overlap with one another, the focal relationship is not conditional upon group membership. Confidence intervals that do not overlap, in contrast, indicate a conditional focal relationship and identify the particular subgroups that differ from one another. If there are only two subgroups, the interpretation is clear: The effect of the independent variable on the dependent variable differs across these two groups.

If there are more than two subgroups, the comparison may reveal separation between some confidence intervals, but overlap among others. Such mixed results identify the specific groups that differ from other groups.

Note that the variable X_m does not appear in Equation 8.8. How can this variable modify the focal relationship if it does not appear in the regression equation? This variable drops out of the subgroup equation because it is a constant within each subgroup insofar as all members of the subgroup have the same value on the modifier—the value indicative of membership in that subgroup. For example, if groups are defined by gender, then gender is a constant among the subgroup of males and among the subgroup of females.

The absence of the modifying variable from the regression equation in the subgroup approach seems to eliminate the effect of group membership from the analysis. In the total sample, this effect would be given by the regression coefficients for the several dummy variables that operationalize X_m. These effects are still present, however; they are merely camouflaged in the intercept term.

In the total sample model, which contains both X_f and the set of dummy variables that operationalize X_m, the intercept is the estimated value of the dependent variable for the omitted reference category of X_m (when all other explanatory variables in the regression equation equal 0). The regression coefficients for the dummy variables that operationalize the other categories of X_m are deviations from the reference group value. In other words, within-group means are expressed as deviations from the intercept. In the subgroup model, the intercept for each subgroup is the estimate of Y when X_f equals 0 in that subgroup (again, with other explanatory variables set equal to 0). To ascertain whether these values differ, the confidence interval for the intercept can be calculated within each subgroup, and these intervals compared across subgroups.

Subgroup Versus Interaction Analysis

The interaction term approach is attractive because it preserves statistical power insofar as the sample is not divided into subgroups. In addition, it provides a direct statistical test of conditionality. The directness of this test and the precision of its p value are more aesthetically appealing than the more cumbersome calculation of confidence intervals at a preset p value in the subgroup approach.

In addition, the influence of other explanatory variables is held constant across values of the modifying variable. The only variables that are free to vary across values of the modifier are those that are explicitly modeled as interaction terms. This feature means that the identical model is estimated except for the interaction term or terms. In the subgroup approach, in contrast, the variables are the same within each subgroup, but the coefficients for these variables are free to take on different values across subgroups. If these variables are important within some subgroups but not others, a very real possibility, then conditionality is estimated taking into account different sets of other explanatory variables.

This point can be illustrated with the caregiver example (Li et al., 1997) described earlier. Recall that the coefficient for social participation is statistically significant for daughters, but not wives, for the outcome of depressive symptoms. Two other regression coefficients are statistically significant for both wives and daughters: health and behavior problems of the care recipient (not shown). For health, the coefficient is roughly twice as large for wives as that for daughters, whereas the reverse is found for behavioral problems. These are the only variables that are significant for wives. However, for daughters, age is also significant. Thus, the comparison of the coefficient for the focal independent variable, social participation, takes into consideration effects of other variables whose impact also differs for wives and daughters. This pattern obscures the interpretation of the coefficient for social participation across groups.

In addition, the subgroup approach obscures one very important variable, the modifier. This term drops out of the within-group analysis because all group members have the same value on the grouping variable by virtue of being group members. Although this information is preserved in the intercept, as discussed above, the absence of an explicit term and direct statistical test for the group membership variable deflects attention away from the modifying variable. The feature is especially troublesome when there is substantial between-group variation in the dependent variable.

There are however, some drawbacks to the interaction approach. In particular, its interpretation becomes complex when the modifier alters the effect of other variables in addition to the focal independent variable. This situation arises when the entire causal system or large portions of it functions differently within subgroups of the population. For example, gender might well have a pervasive impact on the numerous factors influencing depression beyond merely modifying the effect of stress. This type of situation requires the use of multiple interaction terms. These terms tend to be highly intercorrelated, however, because they share in common the modifying variable. Multicollinearity is the likely result. Interaction terms work best if limited to a few conditional relationships. If, instead, effect modification is widespread, then subgroup analysis is preferable.

A similar problem derives from complex conditional relationships. These interactions entail at least three variables: the focal independent variable and two (or more) modifying variables that specify the circumstances under which the focal relationship operates. Effect modification in this instance is modeled as a higher-order interaction term (e.g., $X_f \times X_{m1} \times X_{m2}$).[10] The interpretation of interaction terms becomes intricate as the number of interaction terms increase. For examples, see Ross and Wu (1996) and Umberson and Chen (1994).

To continue two of our running examples, suppose that both gender and social support modify the effect of stress on depression. If these modifiers are separate and distinct from one another, then the effect modification associated with gender is constant across the categories of social support, or, equivalently, the effect modification associated with social support is the same for men and women. Suppose instead that social support and gender jointly modify the focal relationship: The contingency associated with social support differs for men and women, or, equivalently, the contingency associated with gender differs by whether or not support is present. The third-order interaction term would be stress-by-social support-by-gender. For example, perhaps stress has an especially strong effect on depression for socially isolated men, more than would be expected from the individual contingencies of gender and social support. In this instance, the biggest effect modification for social support would be among men, or, equivalently, the biggest gender effect modification would be among persons lacking support.

The alternative approach to situations like this one is to simultaneously stratify on multiple variables. In the current example, analyses would be conducted within subgroups simultaneously defined by both gender and social support. The limitations of this approach are self-evident. Most importantly, the confidence intervals for regression coefficients grow wider as the number of subgroups increases because the within-group sample size decreases. Thus, it becomes increasingly difficult to detect true differences. At the same time, multiple comparisons are being made, increasing the possibility of making the opposite type of error, that is, finding an apparent contingency by chance. This possibility necessitates adjustments to the critical value of the test statistic to take into consideration the total number of comparisons (e.g., a Bonferroni-type adjustment).

Obviously, the interaction approach to conditional relationships becomes quite complex if the conditional relationship entails more than two variables or there are several conditional relationships. In such instances, subgroup analysis may be a desirable alternative, although complexity need not inhibit the use of the interaction approach. In any event, complex conditional relationships should be examined with subgroup analysis if only to ensure that multicollinearity has not produced misleading results. In addition, the interpretation of complex interactions is often facilitated by subgroup analysis.

The change in sample size with stratified analysis may have profound consequences for the results of conventional tests of statistical significance: Effects that are significant overall may not be significant in subgroup analysis even if the effect size remains about the same. This problem is especially pronounced when subgroups differ radically in size: A similarly sized effect may be statistically significant in the largest group, but nonsignificant in the smallest subgroup (e.g., Figure 8.3). Although the effect is about the same, the precision with which it is estimated decreases as the sample size decreases. Thus, one cannot rely solely on within-group tests of statistical significance when making between-group comparisons.

The selection of subgroup or interaction-term analysis entails balancing the strengths and limitations of each approach. For some theoretical questions, the interaction term is clearly superior; for example, the only conditional relationship involves the focal relationship and one effect modifier. In other cases, the subgroup analysis is clearly superior; for example, the impact of virtually all model variables is thought to differ among subgroups of the population. As I noted above, it usually is helpful to conduct both analyses and compare their results; this duplication counterbalances the weak points of each, permitting an assessment of which approach most accurately reflects the data. Finally, these two approaches serve the same purpose and should yield comparable results. If this is not the case, it is incumbent upon the analyst to determine the source of discrepancies.

Considerations in the Selection of Moderating Variables

In earlier chapters, we saw that empirical results can sometimes be anticipated based on the pattern of covariation among the independent, dependent, and third variables. The overall pattern of covariation, however, is not prescient with regard to conditional relationships. The association of the modifying variable with the other two variables is not informative about whether the focal association varies across the various values of this variable. Instead, it is necessary to examine the pattern of covariation between the independent and dependent variables within the values of the modifier.

This task can become quite tiresome if there are numerous potential modifiers. However, if no conditional relationships are examined, all relationships in the model are tacitly assumed to be invariant across all circumstances and for all subgroups. The basic form of most multivariate techniques makes just this assumption, although it often goes unnoticed. I emphasize the extreme nature of this assumption to call attention to the possibility that this assumption is erroneous for a particular research question.

Although it may seem desirable to test every conceivable conditional relationship, the "kitchen sink" approach creates the opposite type of problem, the mistaken identification of a conditional relationship that is merely the chance result of testing a large number of possibilities. As was the case with the selection of other types of variables, this approach also tends to be unwieldy.

The selection of moderating variables should flow from the theoretical model. Are there any interconnections in the theoretical model that are thought to be synergistic? Alternatively, is the joint effect of all independent variables merely the sum total of their individual effects? It is useful to frame these questions with reference to the focal relationship: Are there theoretical reasons to believe that some other component of the causal nexus intensifies the most central component of the model, or, in contrast, dilutes it? Alternately, are there theoretical reasons to expect that the focal relationship differs among some subgroups of the population?

In sum and to recap, the conceptual framework of the investigation should guide the selection of variables as effect modifiers. For static modifiers, we are especially interested in the relevance of group membership to the causal processes under investigation. For dynamic modifiers, we are especially interested in modifiers that are themselves outcomes of the causal processes under investigation. To reiterate a point made several times in this chapter: It is desirable to conduct parallel analyses using the subgroup approach and the interaction approach. The strengths and limitations of these two approaches counterbalance one another, at least to some extent. Results from these two approaches should be interchangeable. If not, resolving the discrepancies will lead to a more accurate set of results.

Summary

The focal relationship is assumed, often implicitly, to operate under all conditions and for all subgroups of the population unless it is explicitly treated as a conditional relationship. Conditional means that the focal relationship differs across the values of the modifying variable. The modifying variables of most interest are usually components of the theoretical model, specifically control variables signifying group membership, which tend to be static, and intervening variables specifying causal processes, which tend to be dynamic, that is, influenced by other elements of the model. Two basic strategies are used in the analysis of conditional relationships: subgroup analysis, which is generally used when the modifier delineates distinct subgroups of the population, and the analysis of interaction terms, which are composites of the focal independent variable and the modifying variable. These approaches should yield comparable results.

Notes

1. This comparison suggests that the difference in statistical significance may be an artifact of the larger sample of daughters than wives, especially given that the coefficient for daughters is significant only at the .05 level.

2. Figure 8.2 and Figure 8.4 both operationalize the stress-buffering hypothesis as an interaction between stress and social support, but this interaction is plotted differently in these two figures. In Figure 8.2, the impact of stress is conditional upon support, whereas in Figure 8.4 the impact of support is conditional upon stress. These are equivalent representations of the same stress-by-support interaction.

3. Higher order interaction terms are composites of more than two variables. For excellent examples, see Ross and Wu (1996) and Umberson and Chen (1994).

4. Interaction terms can involve any of the variables on the independent variable side of the equation. To maintain our emphasis on the focal relationship, however, this chapter is limited to conditional relationships that involve the focal independent variable. In addition, conditional relationships are not necessarily linear. In theory, any functional form of the focal relationship can be modified by any third variable. In practice, nonlinear conditional effects are rarely estimated because our theories are usually not developed to this level of precision. See Ross and Wu (1996) for an exception to this generalization.

5. Stated more precisely, it is the difference in the regression plane, but this subtlety is ignored in the text because we have set to the side other independent variables to simplify the presentation.

6. When $X_m = 0$, the term $e^{b_m X_m}$ becomes 1.00, the value indicative of no effect on the odds, because $e^0 = 1$. When $X_m = 1$, $e^{b_m X_m}$ simply becomes e^{b_m}.

7. When $X_m = 1$, $e^{b_c(X_f \times X_m)} = e^{b_c X_f}$ and $e^{b_m X_m} = e^{b_m}$.

8. On occasion, the overall test will not attain statistical significance but one or more of the individual coefficients will be statistically significant. Priority is given to the overall test because it adjusts for the number of added variables, whereas the tests for individual coefficients do not, increasing the probability of making a Type I error.

9. The confidence interval is given by: $b_f \pm z\ SE_{b_f}$. In logistic regression, this value can be expressed in multiplicative form by taking the exponents of the end points of the interval that is calculated for b_f (Hosmer & Lemeshow, 1989, p. 44). Alternately, Jaccard, Turrisi, and Wan (1990, p. 49) give the follow-

ing equation for testing the null hypothesis that the difference between the two coefficients equals zero:

$$t = \frac{b_j - b_k}{\{(SSE_j + SSE_k)/[(n_j + n_k) - 4](\sum X_{1j} + \sum X_{1k})/(\sum X_{1j} \sum X_{1k})\}1/2}},$$

where b_j is the unstandardized regression coefficient for group j, b_k is the unstandardized regression coefficient for group k, SSE_j is the sum of squares error for group j, SSE_k is the sum of squares error for group k, n_j is the number of individuals in group j, n_k is the number of individuals in group k, $\sum X_{1j}$ is the sum of the squared X_1 scores in group j, and $\sum X_{1k}$ is the sum of the squared X_1 scores in group k. The t statistic is distributed with $n_j + n_k - 4$ degrees of freedom.

10. The model for higher order interactions includes all implied lower order terms. For example, the model for the interaction $A \times B \times C$ would include as well $A, B, C, A \times B, B \times C$, and $A \times C$.

9 A Synthesis and Comment

In crafting this text, I have tried to articulate a rational analytic method that can be tailored to fit a wide range of research questions in the social and behavioral sciences. Although not applicable to every investigation, this approach can open the door to a productive line of analysis for many inquiries. In any case, the approach I have described is only a guide to informed critical thinking and not a road map to be followed in lock-step fashion.

This method is best suited to explanatory research with phenomena that are observed as they naturally occur, as distinct from experimentally manipulated situations, and to situations where coincident events may indicate a causal connection or be instead signs of some other set of circumstances, such as spuriousness. Establishing that the causal interpretation is viable requires that these alternative explanations be eliminated. It also entails demonstrating that the association fits the theoretical account of how the focal independent variable influences the dependent variable. I have labeled these strategies as exclusionary and inclusive, respectively, because they eliminate the effects of various "third variables" on the one hand, and incorporate the focal relationship within a system of different third variables on the other hand.

Two tools are necessary to implement the analytic strategies described in this text. The first is a theory that purports to explain how one construct affects another construct. The methods presented here are intended exclusively for explanatory research even though multivariate statistical techniques are also used in exploratory and descriptive research. This theory (at minimum) needs to explain how the focal independent variable exerts its influence upon the dependent variable. It does not suffice to simply hypothesize that "X_f influences Y" because this statement is uninformative about the nature of this influence and, consequently, the type of association that should be observed if the theory is indeed correct. An adequate theoretical model specifies the processes that generate the focal relationship. This requirement holds even when these processes have not been operationalized in a particular study. This specification is necessary because it provides vital information about the expected functional form of the focal relationship; in its absence, it simply is not possible to state meaningful null and alternative hypotheses.

This theoretical model is essential to both the exclusionary and inclusive strategies of analysis. This point is self-evident for the inclusive strategy, which explicitly entails elaborating the focal relationship with antecedent, intervening, and consequent variables. This information is equally important to the exclusionary strategy. It is necessary to identify the variables comprising the model being tested before one can identify the variables that are not part of this set and, consequently, should be ruled out as alternative explanations for covariation between the focal independent and dependent variables.

The second tool required to implement the analytic method developed here is a sound grasp of multivariate statistical techniques. The evolving technology of point-and-click computer software makes it possible for a novice to estimate sophisticated multivariate techniques. It does not, however, ensure that the results are correct, much less meaningful, nor will it suffice to hand this task off to a statistical consultant. As we have seen, theory-based statistical analysis requires more than one multivariate analysis because critical information is obtained from the comparison of parameter estimates across several versions of the analytic model. Determining which models should be compared is not a matter of statistical technique, but a matter of translating theory into a set of models that systematically establish internal validity. This is a task for a substantive researcher.

In sum, the strategies described in this text cannot be implemented in the absence of a well-developed theoretical model, and testing this theoretical model requires an understanding of the statistical techniques used to generate empirical results. Earlier I stated that the data analytic plan is the link between theory and statistics. It uses deductive logic to operationalize theory, that is, to translate ideas about general principles into hypotheses that are testable with empirical data. The data analysis plan also uses inductive logic to assess the fit between theory and observation, with inferential statistics being the technique used to evaluate fit. The data analysis strategies described in this text are not the only ones for performing these tasks, of course, but these ends cannot be realized without a well-reasoned data analysis strategy.

A Recap of Theory-Based Data Analysis

The theory-based data analytic method presented in this text entails the following steps: (1) assess whether the focal independent variable is associated with the dependent variable in the manner predicted by theory and at a level beyond chance; (2) eliminate alternative explanations for the observed associations through the use of control and other independent variables; (3) demonstrate that the focal relationship fits within an interlocking set of other relationships that are anticipated by the theory being tested, other relationships that are operationalized with antecedent, intervening, and consequent variables; and, (4) ascertain whether there are circumstances that modify the focal relationship and whether it applies uniformly to the entire population.

Step 1 entails estimating the bivariate association between the focal independent and dependent variables. As emphasized throughout this text, the choice of a statistical technique for this analysis is based on two equally important considerations: the level of measurement of the variables, which restricts the range of alternatives that are appropriate for the data; and the functional form of the hypothesized relationship, for example, whether it is expected to be linear, to follow a step-function or a quadratic function, and so on. Although the strength of this association can be gauged in various ways, the techniques developed in this text are based on the unstandardized regression coefficient (b_f) from the simple linear regression of Y on X_f, which gives the expected change in the dependent variable for a unit change in the focal independent variable. For numeric outcomes, the metric is change in units of Y per unit change in X_f for multiple linear regression; for logistic regression of dichotomous outcomes, the metric is change in the log odds of being positive on Y for each unit change in X_f.

The sample value of b_f is calculated precisely, but we are usually interested in the sample value as an estimate of the population parameter. To move from the known sample value to the hypothetical population value entails the application of inferential statistics.

In most applications, we are interested in the null hypothesis that $b_f = 0$ versus the alternative that $b_f \neq 0$. This null hypothesis is evaluated with a test statistic and its associated p value. We usually hope to reject the null hypothesis. If so, this step establishes the feasibility of the focal relationship by showing that the values on the dependent variable correspond to the values on the independent variable in the manner anticipated by theory *and* in a manner that is not likely to be just a chance occurrence. If not, our theory is discredited and should be critically revisited before proceeding with any analysis.

Step 2 in the analysis plan is to add exclusionary third variables to the simple regression of Step 1. Two types of variables are added: control variables to take spuriousness into consideration, and other independent variables that operationalize competing theoretical accounts for the occurrence of the dependent variable, especially those that are also likely to covary with the focal independent variable. Of primary interest is any change in b_f that accompanies the addition of control and other independent variables, especially decreases indicating that the focal relationship is explained, at least in part, by these additional variables. Of equal importance is whether b_f remains statistically significant, which indicates that some reliable covariation remains between the focal independent and dependent variables. The unique contribution of X_f, over and above the combined contributions of the exclusionary third variables, can be obtained by comparing the explanatory power of this model relative to a simpler model that contains *only* the exclusionary third variables; in other words, it drops the focal independent variable. This comparison (and its test of statistical significance) gives the unique contribution of the focal independent variable to the explanation of the dependent variable.

In addition, we are usually interested in the extent to which exclusionary third variables account for the occurrence of the dependent variable (as distinct from accounting for the focal relationship). Two standards are especially informative. The first is the increment in explanatory power (and its associated test of statistical significance) that is achieved by adding the exclusionary third variables to the simple regression of Y on X_f. This comparison gives the composite contribution of the entire set of added variables and shows whether these variables make a meaningful contribution beyond that achieved by the focal independent variable. The second standard is the set of regression coefficients for these variables. Here we are interested in the coefficient and significance test for each individual variable, which indicates its contribution to explaining the dependent variable when all other variables in the model are held constant.

Step 3 is the elaboration of the focal relationship. This elaboration entails connecting the focal relationship to a network of other relationships that are components of the theory being tested. This step involves three types of variables: those that are antecedent or consequent to the focal relationship and those that intervene between the focal independent variable and the dependent variable. The addition of antecedent and consequent variables explicates the focal relationship by extending the causal sequence in which it is embedded backward or forward in time, respectively. These connections help to establish the internal validity of the focal relationship by extending the string of theory-based cause-and-effect relationships. The addition of antecedent variables to the analysis should not alter the estimate of the focal relationship because antecedent variables account for the occurrence of the focal independent variable, not its association with the dependent variable. The focal relationship remains the same because the antecedent variable's effect typically is indirect, embedded within the focal independent variable. Consequent variables do not alter the estimate of the focal relationship because they are used only as dependent variables in separate analyses. The analysis of antecedent and consequent variables, therefore, should leave the estimate of b_f unchanged.

Intervening variables, in contrast, should account for some or all of the focal relationship that remains after Step 2. Intervening variables operationalize the causal mechanisms that theoretically produce the effect of the focal independent variable on the dependent variable. In other words, intervening variables specify how the independent variable affects the dependent variable. Specifying these processes should account, at least in part, for the impact of the focal independent variable. Thus, the introduction of intervening variables should reduce b_f. The internal validity of the focal relationship is compromised if instead b_f remains unchanged. Intervening variables are the most important components of the inclusive strategy because they directly test the theory-based causal mechanism linking the focal independent variable to the dependent variable. Aside from ruling out alternative explanations (Step 2), demonstrating the means by which an effect is produced is the strongest evidence in support of a causal interpretation (Little, 1991).

Step 4 assesses whether the focal relationship remains constant across an array of circumstances and for the entire population, or is instead conditional, limited to some particular situations or some specific subgroups. We are especially interested in two types of modifiers: static characteristics that define more or less homogeneous subgroups of the population, often corresponding to control variables; and, dynamic modifiers that connote moving states, often corresponding to intervening variables. Although effect modifiers can be classified along other dimensions, these labels emphasize the focal relationship and the types of modifiers that alter this one particular relationship.

The analysis of effect modification can be conducted using interaction terms that embody the expected contingency between the focal independent variable and the modifying variable, or by estimating the focal relationship separately within subgroups that are defined by this variable. As discussed in the previous chapter, there are advantages and disadvantages to each of these methods, but results conducted across these methods should converge. If not, the source of disagreement is usually extremely informative about the functioning of the entire set of variables.

To recap, the interpretation of the focal relationship as a relationship (as distinct from mere covariation) entails:

- Showing that this interpretation is feasible because the focal independent and dependent variables are associated in the manner predicted by theory and beyond what is expected by chance;

- Eliminating alternative explanations by adding control and other independent variables to remove spuriousness and redundancy, respectively;

- Establishing internal validity by elaborating the focal relationship with antecedent, intervening, and consequent variables; and,

- Identifying situations or subgroup characteristics that modify the focal relationship.

At this point, there are reasonable grounds for inferring a cause-and-effect type of relationship and describing the circumstances under which it operates and the subgroups of society who are affected by it.

This process ideally generates a comprehensive multivariate model that contains not only the focal independent and dependent variables but also control and other independent variables; antecedent, intervening, and control variables; and, interaction terms that operationalize contingencies among these variables. Most analyses, however, will contain some but not all of these types of variables. For example, many analytic models contain only control, other independent, and intervening variables, but lack antecedent and consequent variables. Thus, real-life analysis usually falls short of the ideal described in this text. Nevertheless, the complete model should be articulated if only to identify what is missing. This exercise not only identifies what needs to be included in subsequent research, but also aids in the interpretation of results.

The comprehensive multivariate model typically is superior to any of the simpler or partial models generated during the model-building process. This outcome is built into the process. The simple regression of the focal independent variable on the focal dependent variable is incrementally expanded to include variables that make substantively meaningful and statistically significant contributions to the explanation of the focal relationship and the dependent variable. The completeness of the full model is secured by the methods used to generate it: the systematic examination of variables that operationalize alternative explanations for the focal relationship, competing explanations for the occurrence of the dependent variable, causal mechanisms, and conditionally relevant effects. The comprehensive model is complete, then, in the sense that it cannot be meaningfully improved through the inclusion of additional variables, at least with the available data.

The comprehensive multivariate model, however, is likely to contain variables that do not have statistically significant unique effects on the dependent variable. For example, some variables that attained statistical significance early in the analysis may become nonsignificant when the model is subsequently expanded to include other variables. Indeed, this shift occurs more often than not. Should these variables be retained or dropped? If parsimony is the criterion, then the simplified model is preferable, but theoretical concerns may outweigh parsimony, leading to the retention of at least some statistically nonsignificant effects.

This issue is especially noteworthy for distal independent variables whose influence on the dependent variable is indirect, operating through variables that are more proximal. Distal independent variables may appear to be unimportant when their effects on the dependent variable are fully embodied by intervening variables. In other words, when the full model contains intervening variables that capture all of the causal mechanisms linking the focal independent variable to the dependent variable, the distal focal independent variable appears superfluous. This variable can be "trimmed" to produce a simpler model without sacrificing explanatory power. Alternately, it may be retained because of its relevance to the intervening and dependent variables. In this instance, theoretical significance is given priority over statistical significance.

This issue is vexing from a statistical perspective because only one of these models can be "true": either the complete model or the simpler model, not both. In practice, however, the models are functionally equivalent: One model contains variables whose regression coefficients are estimated to be no different from 0, whereas the other model constrains the regression coefficients for these variables to be 0 (because the variables are not part of the model). Decisions about deleting nonsignificant coefficients should be made on the basis of theory.

From beginning to end, then, the data analysis strategy described in this text is theory-driven. The selection of variables, the specification of their relationships with one another, and the articulation of contingently relevant effects all flow from the conceptualization of the research. Although statistical technique is essential to obtaining valid analytic results, the formulation of the analytic plan clearly is a theoretical not a statistical task.

Informative Comparisons

Analytic strategies for model building typically culminate in a single comprehensive regression equation that explains the occurrence of some outcome as a function of an extensive set of variables. This approach emphasizes the explanation of the outcome as its primary goal. In this text, an alternative has been developed, an emphasis on a single cause-and-effect type of relationship between the outcome and one independent variable, which I have referred to as the focal relationship. This approach also culminates in a comprehensive or "full" regression equation, but additionally entails its comparison to several restricted models. In this approach, the elaboration of the focal relationship is emphasized as much as the explanation of the outcome.

One important comparison is with the simple regression of the dependent variable on the focal independent variable. This equation estimates the total association between these variables as the unstandardized regression coefficient (b_f) for the focal independent variable. The change in the estimates of this coefficient between the restricted and the full models estimates the extent to which the total association is accounted for by the additional variables contained in the comprehensive model. This estimate is sometimes divided by the coefficient from the simple regression to yield a ratio, that is, the proportion of the original association explained by the additional variables.

A second crucial comparison is between the comprehensive model and the identical model except for the removal of the focal independent variable. This comparison gives the unique contribution of the focal independent variable to the explanation of the dependent variable. This contribution is unique in the sense that it is over and above the explanation collectively achieved by the other variables in the comprehensive model. This quantity is usually expressed as the increment in explanatory power attained by the addition of the focal independent variable. This comparison entails estimating an additional regression equation (the comprehensive model minus the focal independent variable) that is not routinely estimated as part of the model-building process, but is part of the evaluation of the model that results from this process.

It is also instructive to compare the full model to a restricted model that contains the focal independent variable and a particular subset of other independent variables. This subset contains all variables used in the exclusionary strategy, that is, the variables used to rule out alternative explanations for the focal relationship, specifically control variables to eliminate spuriousness and other independent variables to account for competing theoretical processes. This subset also includes antecedent variables, which are components of the inclusive strategy.[1] The difference between this partial model and the comprehensive model, then, is the subset of independent variables that function as intervening variables.[2]

Of particular interest is the difference in the unstandardized regression coefficient for the focal independent variable (b_f).[3] The coefficient in the partial model represents all of the covariation that is available for explanation by the intervening variables. The intervening variables specify the causal mechanisms that theoretically link the focal independent variable to the dependent variable. As a result, their inclusion in the comprehensive model should substantially reduce the association remaining between these two variables. In other words, the coefficient should decrease in the comprehensive model to the extent that the intervening variables do indeed capture the causal mechanisms articulated in the theoretical model.

So far, these comparisons comprise various main effects models, but, as we have seen, the best model for the data may additionally contain interaction terms that modify the focal relationship. The relevant comparison here is between the comprehensive main effects model and the same model with the addition of all theoretically relevant interaction terms. This comparison tests the importance of the entire set of interactions as a set. The incremental contribution of these interactions terms is evaluated relative to the number of added interaction terms. If this increment is statistically significant, then the individual interaction terms are examined to determine the precise nature of the contingency. The standard test for individual coefficients in the regression model is applied. If the overall increment in explanatory efficacy is not statistically significant, then the individual interaction terms are not examined separately; instead, they are considered not significant because the omnibus test encompasses all the individual tests. In this case, the main effects model is preferable based on parsimony. Otherwise, the conditional model is preferable because it more accurately represents the observed data.

Conditional relationships can also be assessed by conducting separate regressions within subgroups defined by the values of the variable. Contingency is evaluated by comparing regression coefficients for the focal independent variable across these separate regressions. Differences across subgroups can be evaluated statistically by calculating confidence intervals for the focal regression coefficient across regressions. To avoid capitalizing on chance as a result of comparing numerous confidence intervals, the confidence intervals should be adjusted for the number of comparisons.

In summary, the analytic approach described in this volume culminates in a comprehensive regression model for the dependent variable, but also entails the comparison of this comprehensive model to several restricted models.[4] The comprehensive model by itself is most informative about the occurrence of the dependent variable. For example, it yields the total amount of variance in the outcome that is accounted for by the entire set of independent variables and estimates the individual contribution of each of these variables. With regard to the focal relationship, however, the comprehensive model yields a single piece of information, the individual impact of the focal independent variable on the dependent variable when other variables are held constant. Although this information is important, additional information is needed to evaluate the extent to which the focal relationship can legitimately be interpreted as a relationship. This information is obtained from strategic comparisons among several restricted models as summarized in this section. In addition, the assessment of potential effect modification entails the comparison of the comprehensive model to a more complex one, a model that additionally includes variables that modify the impact of the focal relationship. The hallmark of the analytic strategy developed in this text, then, is the comparison of the focal relationship across models constructed by adding or deleting particular variables or sets of variables. These comparisons yield considerably more insight into the nature of the focal relationship than can be garnered from the final regression equation in isolation.

The selection of potential modifiers returns us to the theory guiding the entire analytic enterprise. The specification of the causal mechanism that generates the focal relationship is invaluable in identifying factors that may interfere with or promote this process. It also points toward subgroups of the population for whom the process may be uncertain. Thus, the potential sources of effect modification are usually found within the variables that comprise the conceptual model.

Imperfect Knowledge

Although science is only one source of knowledge, it has considerable credence in contemporary Western society because it works so well in solving so many problems of everyday life. The successes of science, from in vitro fertilization through exploration of deep space, create the illusion that scientific knowledge is absolute. This illusion is appealing because it implies that we can control important aspects of our lives, a reassuring prospect to those of us who believe in human agency. The practice of science, however, promotes an appreciation for the limits of the knowledge it produces. The closer one looks at a "fact," the more clearly one sees its provisional nature.

Our observations of the world, physical or social, are always incomplete and circumscribed by the very premises that enable observation to take place; that is, by the "mind's eye" (Keller, 1992). The recognition that science is inherently provisional is perhaps its most frustrating characteristic for those of us who are drawn to the practice of science by a need to know.

From the perspective of data analysis, the most vexing implication of this limitation is the inside-out strategy of proof-by-elimination. The double negative of not failing to reject the null hypothesis is inherently unsatisfying. As we have seen, the exclusionary strategy eliminates some alternative explanations for the focal relationship but cannot eliminate all possible alternatives because the list of possibilities is endless. These other possibilities also haunt the inclusive strategy. Finding that the focal relationship is connected to other constructs in the manner predicted by theory does not preclude the possibility that the data are truly generated by another process that has yet to be conceived. In the end, then, we usually conclude our analysis with new questions rather than definitive answers. The fruit of our labors, therefore, is reducing degrees of uncertainty rather than establishing unequivocal truth. The only good thing about this untidy state of affairs is that it creates the need to do more of what we do.

Multivariate models in the social and behavioral sciences typically account for less variance in the outcome under investigation than is left unexplained. Critics justifiably ask whether this record amounts to explanation in any meaningful sense: If we apply such findings to a new situation, are we not more likely to make an incorrect than correct choice?

On the contrary, expecting explanatory models to account for the preponderance of outcome variance reflects a misunderstanding about the kind of explanation produced by the social sciences. If we assume that people are capable of being instrumental agents in their own lives, then it is not possible to account fully for their behavior. Instead, the goal is to uncover general principles that operate, on average, for people in general, or for substantial segments of society. These general principles describe average tendencies, but ignore the idiosyncratic features that make each person unique. From this perspective, attaining even a modest amount of explanation is a remarkable achievement. In addition, the explanation achieved in this type of research is probabilistic, pertaining to aggregated outcomes, not to a particular situation or specific person. Over a large number of situations or persons, partial explanation will yield more accurate guesses about future outcomes than blind guesses. The alternative to partial explanation is not full explanation, but no explanation whatsoever, that is, blind guesses.

Notes

1. Consequent variables are not relevant to this comparison because they serve only as dependent variables, not as independent variables.

2. The inclusion of antecedent variables, which are part of the theory being tested, is desirable because it isolates the impact of the intervening variables. Conversely, it removes covariation is part of the theory being tested.

   The comprehensive model could be compared instead to a restricted model that contains only the exclusionary variables. This alternative is attractive because it removes only the effects of redundancy and spuriousness. In contrast, its comparison to the full model does not isolate the impact of the intervening variables, but also includes the antecedent variable. However, these two alternatives should yield roughly comparable results because the inclusion of antecedent variables should not alter the estimate of the focal relationship (see Chapter 7).

3. Note that the comparison is not to the simple regression of the dependent variable on the focal independent variable (as was the case in the first comparison), which estimates the total association between these two variables. Instead, the comparison is to a partial model that has the desirable feature of taking into consideration spuriousness and relatedness that can be attributed to other causal processes.

4. The comparisons described above are meaningful only because each of these restricted models is a subset of the independent variables contained in the full or unrestricted model. In other words, the restricted models are nested within the comprehensive model. In addition, as noted earlier, these comparisons are valid only when the sample is invariant across models. It should also be noted that the unrestricted and restricted model cannot both be true. One model is a superior representation of the data than all of the alternative models.

References

Afifi, A. A., & Clark, V. (1984). *Computer-aided multivariate analysis*. Belmont Lifetime Learning Publications.

Allison, P. D. (1984). *Event history analysis: Regression for longitudinal data*. Beverly Hills, CA: Sage.

Amato, P. R. (1996). Explaining the intergenerational transmission of divorce. *Journal of Marriage and the Family, 58*, 628–640.

Aneshensel, C. S. (1992). Social stress: Theory and research. In J. Blake & J. Hagan (Eds.), *Annual review of sociology* (pp. 15–38). Palo Alto, CA: Annual Reviews.

Aneshensel, C. S., Pearlin, L., Schuler, R., & Levy-Storms, L. (2000). The transition from home to nursing home mortality among people with dementia. *Journals of Gerontology: Social Sciences, 55B*, S152–S162.

Aneshensel, C. S., Rutter, C. M., & Lachenbruch, P. A. (1991). Social structure, stress, and mental health: Competing conceptual and analytic models. *American Sociological Review, 56*, 166–178.

Aneshensel, C. S., & Sucoff, C. A. (1996). The neighborhood context of adolescent mental health. *Journal of Health and Social Behavior, 37*, 293–310.

Barnes, B., Bloor, D., & Henry, J. (1996). *Scientific knowledge: A sociological analysis*. Chicago: University of Chicago Press.

Becker, J. (1974). *Depression: Theory and research*. Washington, DC: V. H. Winston.

Broman, C. L. (1993). Race differences in marital well-being. *Journal of Marriage and the Family, 55*, 724–732.

Carroll, L. (1910). *The hunting of the snark: An agony in eight fits*. London: Macmillan.

Clogg, C. C., Petkova, E., & Haritou, A. (1995). Statistical methods for comparing regression coefficients between models. *American Journal of Sociology, 100*, 1261–1293.

Cohen, J., & Cohen, P. (1975). *Applied multiple regression/correlation analysis for the behavioral sciences*. Hillsdale, NJ: Erlbaum.

Cooksey, E. C., & Fondell, M. M. (1996). Spending time with his kids: Effects of family structure on father's and children's lives. *Journal of Marriage and the Family, 58,* 693–707.

DeMaris, A. (1995). A tutorial in logistic regression. *Journal of Marriage and the Family, 57,* 956–968.

Derogatis, L. R., Lipman, R. S., Rickels, K., Uhlenhuth, E. H., & Covi, L. (1974). The Hopkins Symptom Checklist (HSCL): A self-report symptom inventory. *Behavioral Science, 19,* 1–15.

Dixon, W. J., & Massey, F. J., Jr. (1969). *Introduction to statistical analysis* (3rd ed.). New York: McGraw-Hill.

Ensel, W. M., & Lin, N. (1991). The life stress paradigm and psychological distress. *Journal of Health and Social Behavior, 32,* 321–341.

Gadow, K. D., & Sprafkin, J. (1987). *Stony Brook Child Psychiatric Checklist-3R.* Unpublished manuscript, Stony Brook, NY.

Gleick, J. (1992). *Genius: The life and science of Richard Feynman.* New York: Vintage Books.

Hiday, V. A. (1995). The social context of mental illness and violence. *Journal of Health and Social Behavior, 36,* 122–137.

Hosmer, D. W., & Lemeshow, S. (1989). *Applied logistic regression.* New York: Wiley.

Jaccard, J., Turrisi, R., & Wan, C. K. (1990). *Interaction effects in multiple regression.* Newbury Park, CA: Sage.

Judd, C. M., Smith, E. R., & Kidder, L. H. (1991). *Research methods in social relations* (6th ed.). Forth Worth: Harcourt Brace and Jovanovich.

Kanazawa, S. (2000). A new solution to the collective action problem: The paradox of voter turnout. *American Sociological Review, 65,* 443–442.

Keller, E. F. (1985). *Reflections on gender and science.* New Haven: Yale University Press.

Keller, E. F. (1992). *Secrets of life, secrets of death: Essays on language, gender, and science.* New York: Routledge, Chapman, and Hall.

Kemp, M. (2000). *Visualizations: The nature book of art and science.* Berkeley, CA: University of California Press.

Kessler, R. C., & McLeod, J. D. (1984). Sex difference in vulnerability to undesirable life events. *American Sociological Review, 49,* 620–631.

Kessler, R. C., & McLeod, J. D. (1985). Social support and mental health in community samples. In S. Cohen and S. L. Syme (Eds.), *Social support and health* (pp. 219–240). Orlando, FL: Academic Press.

Kovacs, M., & Beck, A. T. (1977). An empirical-clinical approach toward a definition of childhood depression. In J. G. Schulterbrandt & A. Raskin

(Eds.), *Depression in childhood: Diagnosis, treatment, and conceptual models* (pp. 1–25). New York: Raven.

Levine, S. S. (1994). *Monet, Narcissus, and self-reflection: The modernist myth of the self.* Chicago: University of Chicago Press.

Li, L. W., Seltzer, M. M., & Greenberg, J. S. (1997). Social support and depressive symptoms: Differential patterns in wife and daughter caregivers. *Journal of Gerontology: Social Sciences, 52B,* S200–S211.

Lichter, D. T., McLaughlin, D. K., Kephart, G., & Landry, D. J. (1992). Race and the retreat from marriage: A shortage of marriageable men? *American Sociological Review, 57,* 781–799.

Link, B. G., Monahan, J., Stueve, A., & Cullen, F. T. (1999). Real in their consequences: A sociological approach to understanding the association between psychotic symptoms and violence. *American Sociological Review, 64,* 316–332.

Liska, A. E., & Bellair, P. E. (1995). Violent-crime rates and racial composition: Convergence over time. *American Journal of Sociology, 101,* 578–610.

Little, D. (1991). *Varieties of social explanation: An introduction to the philosophy of social science.* Boulder, CO: Westview Press.

Lloyd, G. (1996). Reason, science, and the domination of matter. In E. F. Keller and H. E. Longino (Eds.), *Feminism and science* (pp. 41–53). Oxford, England: Oxford University Press.

Matsueda, R. L., Gartner, R., Piliavin, I., & Polakowski, M. (1992). The prestige of criminal and conventional occupations. *American Sociological Review, 57,* 752–770.

Mirowsky, J. (1985). Depression and marital power: An equity model. *American Journal of Sociology, 91,* 557–592.

Mirowsky, J. (1997). Age, subjective life expectancy, and the sense of control: The horizon hypothesis. *Journals of Gerontology: Social Sciences, 52B,* S125–S134.

Mirowsky, J., & Ross, C. E. (1984). Mexican culture and its emotional contradictions. *Journal of Health and Social Behavior, 25,* 2–13.

Mirowsky, J., & Ross, C. E. (1989). Explaining the social patterns of depression: Control and problem solving—or support and talking? *Journal of Health and Social Behavior, 30,* 206–219.

Nunnally, J. C. (1967). *Psychometric theory.* New York: McGraw-Hill.

Pearlin, L. I., & Radabaugh, C. W. (1976). Economic strains and the coping functions of alcohol. *American Journal of Sociology, 8,* 652–664.

Pearlin, L. I., & Schooler, C. (1978). The structure of coping. *Journal of Health and Social Behavior, 19,* 2–21.

Rathbone, E. E., Rothkopf, K., Brettell, R. R., & Moffett, C. S. (1996). *Impressionists on the Seine: A celebration of Renoir's Luncheon of the Boating Party.* Washington, DC: Phillips Collection.

Rosenberg, M. (1968). *The logic of survey analysis*. New York: Basic Books.

Rosow, I. (1994). Lessons from the museum: Claude Monet and social roles. *The Gerontologist, 34*, 292–298.

Ross, C. E., & Mirowsky, J. (1989). Explaining the social patterns of depression: Control and problem solving—or support and talking. *Journal of Health and Social Behavior, 30*, 206–219.

Ross, C. E., & Wu, C. L. (1996). Education, age, and cumulative advantage in health. *Journal of Health and Social Behavior, 37*, 104–120.

Siegel, J. M., Aneshensel, C. S., Taub, B., Cantwell, D. P., & Driscoll A. K. (1998). Adolescent depressed mood in a multiethnic sample. *Journal of Youth and Adolescence, 27*, 413–427.

Sobel, D. (1999). *Galileo's daughter: A historical memoir of science, faith, and love*. New York: Walker.

Spain, D., & Bianchi, S. M. (1996). *Balancing act: Motherhood, marriage, and employment among American women*. New York: Russell Sage Foundation.

Spitze, G., Logan, J. R., Deane, G., & Zerger, S. (1994). Adult children's divorce and intergenerational relationships. *Journal of Marriage and the Family, 56*, 279–293.

Turner, R. J., & Marino, F. (1994). Social support and social structure: A descriptive epidemiology. *Journal of Health and Social Behavior, 35*, 193–212.

Uggen, C. (2000). Work as a turning point in the life course of criminals: A duration model of age, employment, and recidivism. *American Sociological Review, 67*, 529–547.

Umberson, D., & Chen, M. D. (1994). Effects of a parent's death on adult children: Relationship salience and reaction to loss. *American Sociological Review, 59*, 152–168.

Wheaton, B. (1985). Models for the stress-buffering functions of coping resources. *Journal of Health and Social Behavior, 26*, 352–364.

White, B. E. (1996). *Impressionist side by side: Their friendships, rivalries, and artistic exchanges*. New York: Knopf.

Index